D1233743

3

Little Groups
of Neighbors

This book is the first in a series emanating from research sponsored in whole or in part by the Institute for Research on Poverty of the University of Wisconsin, pursuant to the provisions of the Economic Opportunity Act of 1964.

Little Groups of Neighbors:
The Selective Service System

JAMES W. DAVIS, JR.
KENNETH M. DOLBEARE

Markham Series in Public Policy Analysis

MARKHAM PUBLISHING COMPANY • CHICAGO

MARKHAM SERIES IN PUBLIC POLICY ANALYSIS

Julius Margolis and Aaron Wildavsky, Editors

Bogart, ed., *Social Research and the Desegregation of the U.S. Army*

Davis and Dolbeare, *Little Groups of Neighbors: The Selective Service System*

Feldstein, *Economic Analysis for Health Service Efficiency*

Hansen and Weisbrod, *Benefits and Costs of Higher Education*

Leites and Wolf, *Rebellion and Authority: An Analytic Essay on Insurgent Conflicts*

996 o/

"The . . . *functions* [*of Selective Service*] *are carried on in the local boards which are composed of little groups of neighbors on whom is placed the responsibility to determine who is to serve the nation in the Armed Forces and who is to serve in industry, agriculture, and other deferred classifications.*" (From the Prepared Budget Presentation of the Selective Service System to the Committee on Appropriations, U.S. House of Representatives, February 1, 1966.)

"*The local board is composed of friends and neighbors of the registrant it classifies. The Act is based on the very realistic philosophy that a man's friends and neighbors are far better qualified to decide whether he would be more useful to his country in a uniform or in a civilian capacity.* . . ." (From Selective Service System General Information Bulletin No. 27, January 1968.)

v

PREFACE

This is a systematic examination of the structure, personnel, and operations of the Selective Service System. We deal also with the impact of the draft and with public attitudes toward the draft and the Selective Service System. Alternative means of conscription are considered as are the problems and opportunities inherent in the principle of citizen participation. In the last chapter, we shall analyze the organization's apparent insulation from change in a context of broad empirical theories of politics in the United States.

Our study rests in part on such national data as are available, principally data from the research conducted by or for the Defense Department Draft Study of 1964 and the National Advisory Commission on Selective Service in 1966. Most of these data have been previously published, but some unpublished data were made available by other researchers. In larger part, the book uses several different kinds of data collected in a detailed field study conducted by the authors during 1965–67 in the state of Wisconsin. The cooperation of the Selective Service System made it possible to obtain month-by-month, board-by-board performance classification data for the eighty local boards of Wisconsin, and this was combined with census data on their jurisdictions to produce some indicators of the differential impact of the draft on areas of varying socioeconomic character. We also analyzed opinion and background data gathered from 314 of the 387 local board members of Wisconsin through a mail questionnaire, and supplemented these data by interviews with forty local board members from various types of local boards and interviews with thirty officers and personnel of the State Selective Service System. In addition to simply observing the operations of the State System, we analyzed internal communications such as the monthly Selective Service Newsletter and operating bulletins. Reactions to the performance of the State System and to conscription generally were assessed through opinion samples of the adult population of the state, as well as through some data from a sample of 570 registrants who were students at the University of Wisconsin. We also examined public reporting about the system in the four leading newspapers of the state. In effect, our interpretations are the result of weaving together five different images of the organization and its interaction with its environment: those of the System itself, the newspapers' version, local board members' perspectives, registrants' and general public impressions, and our own systematic observations. We have used the comprehensive data produced in our Wisconsin inquiry to provide depth and detail not available in any other way, but we have employed all available means of broadening and testing our findings, so that we emerge with interpretations which are in most respects general to the operations of Selective Service nationally.

Much of what is in this book is appearing in print for the first time, but some of our data were reported in three papers written during the course of our study: "A Social Profile of Local Draft Board Members: The Case of Wisconsin," in Roger Little, ed., *Selective Service and American Society* (New York: Russell Sage, forthcoming); "Selective Service: Present Impact and Future Prospects," *Wisconsin Law Review* (1967), pp. 892–913; "Selective Service and Military Manpower: Induction and Deferment Policies in the 1960's," in Austin Ranney (ed.), *Political Science and Public Policy* (Chicago: Markham Publishing Company, 1968). We are grateful to the publishers for permission to use portions of those articles.

This study was supported in part by funds granted to the Institute for Research on Poverty of the University of Wisconsin under the Economic Opportunity Act of 1964. We are grateful for this support, and for the equally instrumental cooperation of the Selective Service System. With the approval of General Hershey, Colonel Courtenay, Director of the Wisconsin Selective Service System, granted us access to conduct our research with the records and personnel of the System. He and his staff gave freely of their time and expertise to educate us in the operations of the System, and saved us from many factual errors. We need scarcely add that neither of these agencies of government bears any responsibility for the judgments expressed herein. Many of these judgments are critical of the operations of the Selective Service System; let us note, however, that they are chiefly reflections upon national circumstances, the decisions of national policymakers, and organizational characteristics—and made with all respect for the dedicated service of literally thousands of men and women across the nation, some tiny proportion of whom we have come to know.

We are grateful also for the opportunity to serve as consultants to the National Advisory Commission on Selective Service. In the course of a hectic six months, we benefited greatly from the hard questioning of Chairman Burke Marshall and members of the Commission, and from sharing in the research effort with members of the staff, notably Staff Director Bradley H. Patterson, Jr., Dr. John Folger, Dr. Stuart Altman, and Jacques Feuillan. Important assistance in formulating our approach was also received from the participants at the Social Science Research Council Committee on Governmental and Legal Processes Conference on Political Science and Public Policy in August 1967. Many of our colleagues at the University of Wisconsin have helped by listening to us think out loud and by reading various papers and drafts of papers. Special thanks must be given Herbert Jacob, Murray Edelman, Michael Lipsky, Ted Marmor, Jack Dennis, and James M. Gerhardt, who found time to read some or all of the final manuscript. Very competent research assistance was provided at various stages of the study by Diane Brutout, Barry Gaberman, James Thomas, and Marilyn Wenell, all graduate students in the Department of Political Science at the University of Wisconsin. James Rowen kindly made available for our use data collected in connection with a thesis undertaken with one of the authors. Our wives, Jean and Pat, have tolerated life with Selective Service for almost three years in a way which has made this book more enjoyable.

Finally, this has been the authors' joint project in every sense since its inception, and, while we would wish this book were more fully representative of the quality of the efforts which all the people named above extended to help us, we must jointly accept responsibility for what follows.

J. W. D.
K. M. D.

CONTENTS

LIST OF TABLES

Chapter I

SELECTIVE SERVICE: AN OVERVIEW

I. INTRODUCTION

This book uses the Selective Service System to explore several different subjects, but two primary purposes have guided our inquiry. We have tried first to understand the problems and operating characteristics of a highly decentralized organization in which thousands of citizen participants play a vital part. For example, we are interested in the processes of communication and control; in the responses of the organization to changes in its environment; in interactions between the organization and its most directly affected public, the registrants; in the attitudes of the general public toward its performance; and in the way in which these factors apparently combine to insulate the organization from forces making for change.

These might be intriguing questions to explore under any circumstances, using any national agency as the subject, but at the end of the 1960s, Selective Service seems an especially important one. After three decades of ignoring the draft, social scientists and journalists have recently begun to pay close attention to it. A systematic analysis of the operations and impact of the Selective Service System may well add to the still limited fund of knowledge about this vital public function. We have also been interested in Selective Service because it reveals much about American politics. The decisions made and carried out by the organization fall with great impact on the society and the economy. Heavy investments of economic interest, status aspiration, and ideology surround its goals and their implementation, and it is fundamentally associated with the capacity of the United States to act in international affairs. For these reasons, analysis of Selective Service touches almost all of the sensitive nerves of American politics.

Because our research developed considerable data on the impact of decisions made by the organization, we have sought as a second purpose to use this study as an experiment in policy analysis. We have endeavored, after tracing out the various consequences of the actions of the Selective Service System, to build a set of interpretations concerning the effects of public policies in this area. In other words, we have focused on various components of the substance of public policy and the way it is implemented, and have then sought to identify and characterize the impact on the objects of policy—asking, for example, who was affected in what ways by these policies, and why?

We have employed our findings in three different ways to illustrate the possible payoffs, for political scientists, of policy analysis. Undoubtedly, many more ambitious efforts might have been made, but we were concerned also with the boundaries of professional capacity; we have tried to show that, acting within the range of their expertise as professional students of public affairs rather than as citizens or even as informed persons in the field, political scientists could make a contribution to the understanding and perhaps even formulation of public policy. For this combination of reasons, we chose as illustrations (1) the implications of policy consequences for a general theory of politics—the processes of output, outcome, feedback, support, and output reaction, in Eastonian terms; or problems in the nexus between policy impact, public reaction, and organizational change, in more general terms; (2) the generation of some notes or benchmarks on a basic problem (and opportunity) of government organization—the problem of involving citizens in the formulation and implementation of policies affecting them; and (3) specification of the probable consequences of continuation of present policies—including issues of choosing among alternatives or outright recommendation of a preferred alternative. The considerations which lie behind each of these choices—and, in effect, the central concerns of this book—are briefly reviewed in the paragraphs that follow.

Policy Impact, Reactions, and Change

Today's Selective Service is in every essential respect the organization that was designed by military and National Guard planners in the 1930s and first enacted in 1940. Since 1940 the United States has fought two wars, become thoroughly urbanized, and experienced revolutionary changes in technology, culture, and values. In these nearly three decades, Selective Service has registered, deferred, and inducted the nation's youth with—until 1966—almost no controversy and no significant change in structure or procedure. It has grown old in the service of the nation, literally as well as figuratively: 22 percent of local board members in 1966 were over 70 years of age.

Rising draft calls in 1965 and 1966 brought the System an unaccustomed degree of attention. Charges of inequities in deferment policy and archaism in structure were aired in Congress, the press, and on campuses across the country. But when a Presidential Commission recommended changes in policy and structure to modernize the organization in 1967, the Congress brushed them aside, enacted amendments which would preserve the status quo, and extended the statute for four years. If for no other reason than its longevity and apparent insulation from forces which have made for change in every other dimension of life, careful evaluation of the dynamics of this organization is long overdue.

The task of the organization can hardly be assumed to be popular; its system of deferment and induction through more than 4,000 local boards ("Little Groups of Neighbors," to use General Hershey's phrase) is based on assumptions of a rural America long extinct; and, with almost 30,000 local citizens wielding decision-making authority in such widely decentralized units, it faces herculean problems of coordination and control. Why then has it survived so long in this form? How has it been able to supply the nation's demands for manpower, fluctuating from the total mobilization of World War II, to the partial mobilization of Korea and Vietnam, to the minimal demands of cold war—expanding and contracting its deferment and induction patterns with dramatic impact on the society—with little controversy and no significant modification?

Were we to accept the System's rhetoric, we would find the explanation in the wisdom and justice of the decisions of knowledgeable local boards, supported by the patriotic acquiescence of a responsible citizenry. Others would attribute the System's longevity and static character quite simply to the fact of its low salience, or to its structural conformity with a strongly held public ethos of decentralization, or to its ties to the power centers of Congress or to local sources of strength such as the National Guard or the American Legion. At a higher level of analysis, we might hypothesize that the System has developed sophisticated techniques of coordination which enable it to meet the challenges of the 1960s despite the handicap of the structure and procedure of the 1930s.

Our study of the operations of the System at the state and local level from 1965 to 1967 leads us to conclude that none of these is the major explanation, although each plays some part in the System's remarkable record. We see instead an intricate meshing of deferment policy and

organizational characteristics which has the combined effect of offering
alternatives to military service to the sons of the higher socioeconomic strata
while conferring the management of deferments and inductions upon
community influentials drawn from the same strata. The most politically
aware and efficacious members of the society are thus both advantaged and
coopted by the present System. Small wonder that they are then willing to
tolerate if not affirmatively support its continuation. Substantial majorities
of the lower socioeconomic levels, however, disapprove of conducting conscription through local boards. Such people are, of course, politically quiescent, at least in the short run. What may develop over time, as economic
differences become more and more determinative of military service prospects, could be an entirely different matter. Already, evidence as to the
military service experience of college and non-college young men from the
two socioeconomic levels provides an objective basis for lower-class disapproval of the draft itself. Acquiescence in conscription as it is now practiced
thus rests on the tenuous and short-range basis of advantages conferred
upon the already favored segments of the society.

Citizen Participation as a General Problem in the Organization of Government

Twenty years ago, Philip Selznick published *TVA and the Grass
Roots*,[1] a study of the consequences of citizen participation in a national
government agency that has taken its place as an early classic in modern
sociological and organizational theory. It came at the end of a period in
which several national government functions had been conducted on a
deliberately decentralized basis, with volunteers drawn from local communities participating in various ways to shape local policy applications, and it
raised some sobering questions about the attainments realized through such
experiments. In the decades which have intervened since Selznick's study,
organizational analysis has proceeded swiftly to new levels of sophistication
in understanding the internal relationships and processes of bureaucracy.
But relatively little has been done to further our understanding of the
problems and opportunities raised by what was for Selznick the stimulus
for the organizational consequences that he analyzed: the principle of
citizen participation in government. The nation is still experimenting with
various forms of citizen participation in national government activities—in
urban renewal, and in the poverty program, for example—and there is

[1] Philip Selznick, *TVA and the Grass Roots* (Berkeley: University of California
Press, 1949).

brave talk of participatory democracy, or the need to decentralize the federal government's activities to guard against excessive bureaucratization. And yet we still know very little in empirical terms about the workings of citizen participation, and less about the consequences inherent in its various manifestations.

There are serious potential conflicts in the principle of citizen participation. These center around the issues of who participates and the nature of their participation. Participation by clientele is distinguishable from that of the general public, as is participation by persons representative of the general public from that of a small selection of elites or other locally dominant persons. Participation which carries with it the responsibility to share in the making of policy by the organization is distinct from mere involvement of citizens and possible manipulation to produce their consent to programs already decided upon. At stake here are the goals of the participatory arrangement.

These goals include the democratization of bureaucracy and the securing of consent, as well as—to some extent, at least—the improvement of the participating individual. To gain such ends, and to ensure that the citizen's relationship with the organization will not degenerate into mere involvement, where he is manipulated into acquiescence in the organization's program, some degree of influence over the substance of policy seems to be essential. But this immediately raises a problem for the organization: to what extent is it prepared to yield on the substance of the program which has been entrusted to it, and how much can technical expertise give way to citizen preference? Almost by definition, there must be tension within the organization between the policy goals it holds and meaningful participation of citizens; the democratic goals of engagement, policy-shaping influence, and self-realization are ranged against the need to serve the national interest or accomplish technically necessary ends, in a microcosm of democracy's eternal problem: How can the system be structured so as to enable a major share of the people to take part in a real sense, and yet assure that the vital tasks of government are still accomplished in technically expert fashion? Different organizations reach different adjustments, of course, depending on their tasks and the manner in which they establish their priorities among the goals they seek to serve. Some end up losing control over policy determination completely, as did the TVA in some respects, but more often citizen participation is reduced to a convenient means of manipulating consent. What determines what will occur in particular circumstances? What implications are there in this experience for the principle of citizen participation generally? None of the experiments attempted seems to have been successful, although it also seems safe to say that citizen participation in the meaningful sense has never been attempted under conditions promotive of success.

Selznick saw the democratic dilemma clearly in his classic study. In that case, participation led to modification of the policy of the organization in some respects, and devolved into forms of cooptation in others. Selznick's concerns were chiefly for the organizational consequences of participation —rather than for a general assessment of the principle of citizen participation—but his analysis provides the starting point from which we shall attempt to extract some notes on the problems and prospects of citizen participation. Selective Service is not an encouraging example of citizen participation, it will be seen, but some insights are offered from its experience which may serve to render the device more productive elsewhere.

There are limitations to the teachings of Selective Service in this regard, of course, arising out of the special nature of the organization and the function it performs. But despite its special features, such as the aura of patriotic responsibility which it invokes, its threatening character in the eyes of some, or its semimilitary makeup, it is a national organization with nearly thirty years of participatory experience and almost 30,000 citizens associated with it in various forms. Few attempts to engage citizens in government have ever been made on this scale, and we think that Selective Service offers a unique opportunity to gain understanding of the problems and consequences involved in citizen participation. Combined with Selznick's findings and such data as are available from the experience of other participatory organizations, our interpretations may provide the basis for some notes on the general principle of citizen participation itself.

Alternatives to the Present System, Their Consequences and the Problem of Policy Recommendation

Among the potential payoffs from a study of public policy, the recommendation of alternative policies is at once the most obvious and the most crucial to the issue of professional role. No attempt at policy analysis would be complete without confronting this problem. Our conclusion is that the data pertaining to the operations and effects of the Selective Service System are sufficient to so narrow and so structure the range of value choice that selection among alternatives is professionally possible. We make recommendations, but we do so in a narrow range and in a possibly unique situation where data and interpretations are relatively plentiful; we do not argue that professionally responsible recommendations would necessarily be possible in other policy areas, but only that they are here. And we anticipate that some may doubt the professional quality of even the limited and narrow recommendations which we hazard. We shall not actually approach this problem again until we reach Chapter 8, but we should stress even at this early stage that the selection of evaluative criteria for assessing the merits of present performance or the probable consequences of alternative arrangements is critical to the ultimate act of judgment.

Among the possible criteria for evaluation are the organization's own stated goals and rationale. For example, the official rationale for management of the draft through local boards is that it (1) promotes local acquiescence and (2) results in better decisions because local men know their registrants and communities. We shall present detailed evidence on both of these assumptions, but for the present we may note that statewide opinion sampling of the adult population of Wisconsin in September 1966 revealed that only 52 percent of the respondents were even aware that the draft was conducted through local boards.[2] Of those who *did* know that the draft was conducted through local boards, 53 percent considered the draft to be working fairly; *but of those who did not know that the draft was conducted by local boards, 57 percent believed the draft was working fairly.* Of those who knew about local boards, 52 percent disapproved of the idea, while the others, upon being advised that the draft was conducted by local boards, disapproved of the idea by a ratio of almost two to one. These data offer no support for the first assumption. The second faces the obstacles inherent in evidence that urban board members do not in fact know their registrants, nor could they be expected to in modern cities where 20,000 registrants per board is not uncommon; in rural areas, where board members often do know their registrants, the consequences may not be wholly advantageous. The question of the existence of a "community" seems at least an open one, whether one considers arbitrarily laid out district lines in a city or a collection of farms and hamlets in a rural area; in any event, in many cases the registrant has long since moved to another part of the country and his local board has no knowledge whatsoever concerning its needs or his contribution to them. And the men who make the decisions are anything but representative of their communities.[3]

Another defense for the local board system has been that by directing

---

[2] For a full analysis of this survey, see Chap. 7.

[3] See Chaps. 3 and 4. Data on the number of registrants per local board, a critical aspect of the "Little Groups of Neighbors" concept, may be found in National Advisory Commission on Selective Service, *In Pursuit of Equity: Who Serves When Not All Serve?* (Washington: Government Printing Office, 1967), pp. 131–32. (Hereinafter cited as *President's Commission Report.*)

registrants toward employment and activities which were most in keeping with skills, capabilities, and national needs, local boards have promoted the national interest. This idea received a severe setback in February 1968 when the National Security Council suspended the lists of essential activities and critical occupations which were supposed to guide boards as to national needs. Local boards, however, were left with authority to grant occupational deferments "based on a showing of essential community need." It was made clear that community need, not national interest, was the critical matter. (Whether local boards are able to determine community need in any objective sense, is, of course, another critical question.) But even before the National Security Council suspended the lists of essential activities and critical occupations, the idea of local boards acting in the national interest in this respect was in difficulty. It was clear that many boards paid little attention to the lists that did exist and that there was substantial variability between individual boards in some states and between boards in different states. It could be argued that each board had its own notion of national interest and was allowed to implement it, or one could believe that national interest was in fact a myth and that boards were intended to protect local interests. In the face of available evidence it was impossible to demonstrate that boards were supporting a single view of the national interest.

The stated self-image of the System and its official rationale for policies and organization structure are not serviceable as evaluative standards because they are too readily shown to be undemonstrable or inaccurate. We seek our standards elsewhere. One possibility which expands only slightly from the official rhetoric of the System is to treat both public rhetoric and promulgated self-image as a means of symbolic reassurance which will allow practices of conscription to run their course without effective opposition.[4] In other words, we might hypothesize that the function of the System's self-description is neither defensive justification (which may or may not be believed by the System to be an accurate portrayal of its operations and effects), nor even an internal ideology designed to promote loyalty and cooperation among volunteers—but rather a ritualistic invocation of the symbols of equity and efficiency consistent with the preamble of the statute (". . . in a free society the obligations and privileges of serving in the armed forces and the reserve components thereof should be shared generally, in accordance with a system of selection which is fair and just, and which is consistent with the maintenance of an effective national economy"). If substantial segments of the population are content with this

---

[4] See Murray Edelman, *Symbolic Uses of Politics* (Urbana: University of Illinois Press, 1964), esp. Chap. 2.

type of assurance, acquiescence then forthcoming may permit the System to discharge its responsibilities as its units see fit. In part, this possibility presents empirical questions which we shall try to deal with later.

The implications of these considerations are that we shall have to formulate evaluative standards prior to selecting among alternative policies, and the data to be reviewed only partly prepare us for this task. We must seek to balance the identifiable achievements of the organization against the demonstrable effects of its operations on the society and the economy. Selective Service is, after all, a going organization which has staffed the armed forces for several decades without failing to meet the rapidly fluctuating demands upon it, and this is no small benefit to a world power with far-flung international commitments. But we shall see that changing conditions in its environment have put new strains on it, and there are inequities, public disapproval, dislocations within the society, and other effects which are costs of its operations. Perhaps they are necessary costs, and possibly they are outweighed by the value of the System's primary achievement. Only an empirical identification of the nature of both costs and benefits can focus this issue for judgment. The remaining question then will be not *whether* there are value-based priorities to be applied in deciding what modifications (if any) should be made in the present System, but how wide a range of choice is still possible after the data have established both facts and cause-effect relationships. On this issue rests the question of professional capacity to recommend alternatives in any given policy area.

In the course of our policy analysis experiment, much has been omitted and much assumed, but we think that enough remains to warrant our exploratory approach. Military manpower procurement is related to the conduct of foreign policy and the context of assumptions and definitions about the international environment, for example, but we have ignored such aspects of policy choices and consequences completely. Nor is conscription the only means for staffing an army: cogent arguments can be and have been made for a voluntary manpower procurement system, and they deserve the fullest consideration and perhaps experimentation. Even if (or when) conscription is accepted as necessary, it can take widely variant forms, and further policy-choice problems are involved in selecting among such alternatives; we have expressed our views on some of these elsewhere.[5] But for the purposes of our present attempts to assess policy consequences, we have assumed probable continuation of conscription as a major instrument of military manpower procurement and concentrated our analysis on the

[5] "Selective Service and Military Manpower Procurement: Induction and Deferment Policies in the 1960s," in Austin Ranney (ed.), *Political Science and Public Policy* (Chicago: Markham Publishing Company, 1968).

organizational means of implementing it in its various possible forms. Even this narrow range of policy analysis presents a substantial number of empirical, interpretive, and recommendatory problems, however, and we trust we may be forgiven for thus confining our experimentation.

Some of our findings are relevant to the ongoing national debate about conscription, its implementation and effects, though it should be clear from the above that we do not intend this study primarily as a contribution to that controversy. Although we eschew polemics, we are not reluctant about noting our conviction that our evidence establishes certain points relevant to that debate. In our eyes, this study is neither normative—in the sense of being infused with the purpose of prescribing a better means for accomplishing desired goals—nor value-free, in the sense of adhering exclusively to empirical data and interpretations and avoiding all contact with the value components of policymaking. Deferment-induction policy, and the organization and operation of the Selective Service System, are subjects thoroughly suffused with values and value-laden assumptions. Conduct of inquiry in such a value-permeated context could not but mandate concern for such questions; every finding supports or rejects value-laden assumptions and/or bears on the attainability of various goals. Our response has been to proceed as far as possible with the objective design and execution of empirical research, to submit data and interpretations to examination, and then openly to extend the implications of our findings into the value-laden preserves. We do this in part because we are reluctant to permit the impression that our data sustain any number of interpretations or policy applications, and, again, because of the special availability of data in this particular (and narrow) policy area. Let us begin with a survey of the setting of Selective Service in the 1960s.

II. SELECTIVE SERVICE: A CURRENT PROBLEM

With a few minor exceptions, every young man in the United States has a personal meeting with his government within five days of his eighteenth birthday. He is required by law to present himself at one of the nearly 4,100 local board offices around the country to register with the Selective Service System.[6] In so doing, he joins almost 45,000,000 of his fellow countrymen

---

[6] The governing statute, now known as The Military Selective Service Act of 1967, may be found in 50 U.S.C. App. 451ff. Basic data on the structure of the Selective Service System and the number of men in various classifications is best obtained from the *Annual Report of the Director of Selective Service* (Washington, D.C.: Government Printing Office, for years indicated).

on the records of the System, and for the next seventeen years (more, in some cases) he shares control of his life and career with the three to five men who make up his local board. Their policies and decisions, together with national needs and circumstances and his own physical and mental capacities, will shape his future in fundamental ways.

The process has become a familiar milestone of American life. Since the draft began in 1940, two generations of American men have followed the path to the local board and then have gone through the processes of the System. So familiar did the practice become, and so routine, that Selective Service has been taken for granted. From the end of the Korean War to the beginning of the conflict in Vietnam, the System existed at the margins of American consciousness, inducting few men and intruding little on the economy or the society. As calls rose in 1965 and 1966, however, the System's operations became salient again. Some heard for the first time, but others could recall from Korea or World War II, the conscription policy of the nation as articulated by Selective Service Director, General Lewis B. Hershey:

> A selective service system in some form is the only method of managing . . . our manpower force for defense. If the nation needs those who are trained, it should be prepared to defer them when the needs of the Armed Forces permit, and the individual continues to serve the national interest. So long as we recognize the wisdom of allocating our manpower resources to support to the greatest possible degree both our Armed Forces and our national economy, we should also recognize the wisdom of approaching this allocation problem with the best judgments we can muster, rather than by chance. . . . The Congress has made certain that the key decisions of classification shall be left to civilian boards of the registrant's community. . . . The Nation, in my judgment has no other group of citizens to compare with these men in undertaking a difficult and often unpleasant job solely for the good of the country.[7]

It was the same rationale for the same policy that had successfully staffed the armed forces for total war and for limited war over nearly three decades. To the Selective Service System, as to many others, the rising induction calls of 1965 and 1966 merely meant another shift from slack to stress conditions—one more upward turn in the recurring cycle of first low and then high demand for military manpower.

---

[7] U.S. House of Representatives, Committee on Armed Services, *Review of the Administration and Operation of the Selective Service System,* Hearings (89th Cong., 2nd Sess., June 22–24, 28–30, 1966) (hereinafter cited as *Hearings*), pp. 9621–24.

But the reaction across the country was unprecedented. Members of Congress, university presidents, and respected columnists and editorial writers joined students and others in condemning some or all aspects of conscription as it was conducted by the Selective Service System.[8] Opposition to the Vietnam War was only partly responsible, for supporters of the administration's foreign policy numbered among the draft's severest critics. For the Selective Service System (and again, for many others), a fundamental question arose: Why this criticism? What was different? Policy and organization were unchanged; did the difference lie with the intellectuals, the people, the times?

No single factor accounts for the criticism directed at the System prior to the extension of the draft in 1967, of course. But the central fact which gave rise to many of these complaints was that, although policy and organization were the same, the conditions facing the System were radically different from both Korea and World War II. The principal change lay in the much larger pool of draft-eligible manpower compared to military needs. From this vital difference, there flowed other effects not previously produced by the System's operations, not previously recognized, or not previously thought undesirable. And these effects were the grounds on which most of the criticism was based.

During the Korean War, military needs and limited manpower supply resulted in military service for 70 percent of draft-age men.[9] Only those who were unqualified or had dependent children, and a few others, did not see military service. The number of men entering the eligible age group each year increased steadily in the late 1950s and 1960s, however, and by 1965 it was more than 50 percent higher than it had been in 1950–54. By 1971, the number of men entering the prime draft age year of 19 will be more than 70 percent higher than it was in 1951. But the services have not sought proportionately more men; force levels for the Vietnam War in 1966 and 1967 were only slightly higher than during the Korean period. The result is that the proportion of men actually experiencing military service has been dropping steadily. Less than 50 percent of draft-age men, according to present projections, will actually see service during the Vietnam conflict. Only drastic expansion of the military establishment can alter these prospects. By the mid-1970s, and sooner if Vietnam War requirements permit

[8] For a digest of the substance of these complaints, together with the rebuttal of the Selective Service System, see pp. 9985–96 in *Hearings*. The index to the same volume provides a handy means of identifying the positions taken by the leading Congressional participants in the debates.

[9] Department of Defense estimates, *Hearings,* p. 10005.

lower force levels, the proportion of men required by the armed forces will be approaching one third of the age group. In the 1970s, only one in every seven physically acceptable men will have to be drafted.[10]

Such proportionately lower military needs and the existence of a manpower surplus have changed the task of the Selective Service System and altered its effects. The System was designed to produce men for the armed forces, with those exceptions which "the national interest" appeared to justify. But in recent years, its priorities were reversed; it had to find ways to defer large proportions of men, inducting only those small numbers actually required. In the process, deferment criteria lost their rationale, variability between local boards were exacerbated, and discrimination along economic lines developed. A brief survey of these several effects of Selective Service indicates the major criticism voiced in the 1966–67 debate, and establishes the context of Selective Service in the mid-1960s.

The Draft as a Means on Inducing Enlistments

Throughout its postwar existence, Selective Service has been supported in part on the premise that conscription spurs enlistment.[11] The extent to which this is true may be seen from the experience of fiscal year 1966.[12] Of the 1,090,000 men (excluding officers) who entered service in that year, 343,500 were inducted. Another 380,700 entrants enlisted *after* they were given pre-induction examinations and found qualified. A total of two-thirds of new entrants into military service thus were attributable to Selective Service in one of these direct ways: there is no way of knowing how many of the remaining 366,000 "voluntary" enlistments were draft-inspired to some extent. Confirmation of the importance of the draft to enlistments, if any is needed, may be found in 1964 Defense Department opinion studies of service personnel who had enlisted. Even in this "peacetime" army, more than 43 percent of the army respondents said that their enlistments were "draft-inspired."[13]

The services have learned that enlistments rise, particularly among technically skilled or trainable men, when induction calls are raised.[14] But

[10] Assistant Secretary of Defense (Manpower) Thomas B. Morris, in testimony before the Senate Armed Services Committee, April 12, 1967. U.S. Senate, Committee on Armed Services, *Hearings on Extension of Selective Service Act* (90th Cong., 1st Sess., April, 1967), p. 69.

[11] *Annual Report of the Director of Selective Service for Fiscal Year 1966* (Washington, D.C.: Government Printing Office, 1967), p. 43.

[12] *Ibid.*, p. 44.

[13] *Hearings*, p. 10038.

[14] Assistant Secretary of Defense (Manpower) Morris, *Hearings*, p. 9938.

this is not likely to happen unless draft pressure appears either generally high or particularly focused. This pressure may be created by using deferments generously to reduce the size of the available manpower pool, by granting bloc deferments (such as to all married men, or to all the nation's 2,000,000 male college students), or by creating the public image of manpower scarcity. Under the conditions of the mid-1960s, the Selective Service System was obliged to engage in all three practices, with the effects noted in the sections following.

Deferment as a Means of Reducing the Available Manpower Pool

Physical and mental standards of acceptability are set by the Defense Department and administered by Armed Forces Examining Stations. They are adjusted according to conditions of manpower availability and military needs. Standards are raised when military needs are low and manpower plentiful, and they are lowered again when needs increase. All other deferment criteria, and the order of call among groups of otherwise available men, are the responsibility of the President and the Selective Service System. These deferments also are granted under changing criteria which reflect military needs, and existing criteria are applied differently according to needs for men. The order of call is arranged so that some groups may be removed from immediate liability and then restored to liability when needs increase, as was done with married men in 1963 and 1965. Such manipulation of deferment criteria is effective for the purpose for which it is intended, but it may undermine the argument that the sole ground on which deferment is granted is the national interest. A concept of the national interest which proffers deferments generously during years of low military requirements and then quickly tightens standards when the nation is threatened may readily be seen for what it is: at least in part, a rationale for reducing liability for some so that it may be heightened for others.

Uncertainty Regarding the Military Obligation for Extended Periods of Time

Any registrant who is ever classified in a deferred category automatically has his military liability extended from its normal expiration date on his 26th birthday to his 35th birthday. Deferments, except for some of the unfit-for-service classifications, are normally granted only for one-year terms or less. They are subject to review and renewal by the registrant's local board. Together with the practice of calling the oldest available men first, such policies had the effect of prolonging the potential liability of men for the maximum period of time. The services prefer younger men, so that few men over age 25 were in practice ordered for induction; but the *average* age of induction was 23.7 in 1963[15]—with the implication that many men lived five or six years of what might have been productive periods of their lives under the threat of induction. In the Defense Department study, 54 percent of enlisted personnel age 22–25 reported that they had experienced difficulty in obtaining employment because of their draft-eligible status.[16]

Some degree of uncertainty is functional for the promotion of enlistments, of course. But the more emphasis placed on the possibility of military service at a relatively advanced age, and the more deferments extended through the early years of eligibility, the greater the potential social and economic impact of the draft. When the period of uncertainty is reduced, as it would be under provisions which call for inductions at age 19 (except for those who have been deferred as students or for other reasons), this impact will be reduced. But so will enlistment pressure; one is joined inextricably to the other.

Discrimination along Economic Lines

In the past, blanket deferments for college students frequently ripened into subsequent occupational deferments for the same persons, and students also were able to go from college deferment to dependency deferment. Even today, blanket college deferments permit those who are economically capable of going to college to choose their time of service, and thereby grant such men a chance to avoid the years of a shooting war. In the 1960s, service experience on the part of higher-income registrants was distinctly less frequent than for lower-income registrants, even though more low income registrants were found unfit for service. Data from the Selective Service System itself show that only 40 percent of all college graduates of age 26 in 1964 had seen military service, while—despite much higher unfitness rates —53 percent of men in all other educational levels had been in military service.[17] During one calendar year in 1965–66, college graduates made up only 2 percent of inductees into the Army, while men with high school or less education made up 85 percent of the total. These proportions existed

[15] *Hearings*, p. 10006.
[16] *Ibid.*, p. 10010.
[17] *Ibid.*, p. 10011.

even though more than 40 percent of the age group now goes to college.[18] The remainder are readily located, however: of men entering the Reserves in the same year, 16 percent were college graduates.[19] Both the Reserves and the National Guard, neither of which were drawn on for the purposes of the Vietnam War until the spring of 1968, and then in only small and scattered fashion, appear to contribute to the economic effects inherent in deferment policy.

This pattern of deferment confers special advantages upon those who are economically capable of qualifying. Summarized and reduced to its simplest terms, it means that the chances of military service for a qualified low-income registrant have been 50 percent higher than for a similarly qualified higher income registrant.[20] When the higher income man does enter the service, it is most likely to be as a Reservist or National Guardsman, with consequently reduced prospect of active duty. The liberal granting of deferments in the early 1960s had the effect of heightening the economic differentiation inherent in the deferment policies themselves, and gave substantial grounds for the allegation that the Army—and particularly the combat forces within it—was chiefly composed of Negroes and low income whites.

Racial Discrimination

Several factors have given rise to allegations of racial discrimination by elements of the System, but only some of these allegations are soundly based. Negroes are severely underrepresented on local boards in almost every state, and several Southern states in 1966 had no Negroes on their boards.[21] In these and other states, there may well be evidence to support charges of deliberate inductions of Negroes, particularly in the case of civil rights activists.[22]

A considerable problem inheres in the definition of discrimination employed in resolving other issues regarding racial discrimination. In the aggregate, Negroes are not drafted in proportions exceeding their proportion of the male population in this age group.[23] Because Negroes have drastically higher unfitness rates, however, this is a misleading datum: of

---

[18] *Ibid.,* p. 10012.

[19] Unpublished Defense Department data and research findings made available by Dr. Stuart Altman, Department of Economics, Brown University.

[20] See the analysis which supports this conclusion, Chap. 6.

[21] *President's Commission Report,* p. 80.

[22] As one example, *Newsweek,* July 10, 1967, quotes an Atlanta draft board chairman as saying, "This nigger Julian Bond. We missed him. I've always regretted that."

[23] *President's Commission Report,* p. 22.

those men who are qualified, Negroes are drafted in much higher proportions than whites. But again, this can be misleading if not explored further: qualified Negroes do not appear to be drafted any more than qualified whites of the same economic level; indeed, by virtue of the urban location of most Negroes and the quota system employed for the assignment of induction calls, qualified whites of relatively low income in rural areas are probably the most draft-vulnerable of all identifiable groups.

The data to be presented on this question will establish the foregoing, but they cannot be expected to end the argument. Negroes are as a group among the lowest income levels because of three centuries of racial discrimination, and thus they are as a group far more draft-vulnerable than whites. Negroes qualify for specialized training less frequently than whites, and therefore they end up in the combat forces in high proportions. Finally, although they do not enlist as frequently as whites, once in the service Negroes reenlist with much greater frequency than whites. Thus, at any one time both the combat units and the Army as a whole are composed of greater proportions of Negroes than is the general population, and this inevitably gives rise to the impression of discrimination in conscription. And, in a sense, there is. This is why there is no definitive answer to allegations in this area.

Variability of Local Board Decision-making

Only the local board has the legal capacity to classify a registrant or select him for induction, and this autonomy and discretion are regularly stressed by the System. Such guidelines as are provided by the national headquarters are general and declared to be "advisory only." Specific policy interpretations, if they are supplied to local boards at all, must come from the 56 state and comparable jurisdiction headquarters; necessarily, because no effort is made to coordinate the advice given by these intermediate bodies, local boards in various states receive different and frequently conflicting interpretations of national deferment policy and criteria.[24] This is one important cause of the considerable variation between boards which was documented by the research of the National Advisory Commission on Selective Service.[25]

If a state headquarters is so inclined, it can employ a variety of techniques to standardize the performance of its local boards. This has been approached in Wisconsin, where local conditions and a relatively small number of boards (80), facilitate such efforts. Where "standardization" has

[24] *Ibid.*, Appendix, Sec. VI, pp. 167–73.
[25] *Ibid.*, Sec. II, pp. 83–93.

been accomplished, however, substantial variation in the proportions of registrants in the various classifications still exists—the product of differences in the socioeconomic characteristics of the registrants in the boards' jurisdictions combined with the economic factors built into deferment policy. "Standardization" thus means only that idiosyncratic local board behavior is controlled.[26] States with internally standardized local board performance still differ from most other states, including others which are internally standardized, because the standards set are locally originated and particular to each state.

Many states make little effort to standardize performance among their boards. Variation among boards within their jurisdictions is thus based not only on the inherent differences in socioeconomic impact of deferment policies on different kinds of jurisdictions, but also on local board idiosyncrasies and discretionary behavior. The generality of the criteria for deferment, and the vagueness of the definitions of "the national interest" which have been provided, permit if they do not encourage broad and unstructured exercise of local discretion. The most conscientious local board members frequently have no basis for action other than their own understanding of the nation's or the community's interests in a particular situation, and their judgments are bound to differ in various contexts across the country. The liberality in extension of deferments mandated by the surplus of manpower in the 1960s increased the opportunities for such discretionary judgments, and hence for variation between the performance of local boards.

Three kinds of variability have been identified: variation based on differences in socioeconomic characteristics of jurisdictions; variation among states based on differences in policy interpretations provided to local boards and exaggerated by success in achieving standardization around such particular practices; and variation produced by idiosyncratic discretionary decision-making by local boards. Given the present character of deferment policies and organizational structure, such variability is inevitable. But the System's national performance is then fairly chargeable with non-uniformity of the most obvious kind: similarly situated men in various parts of the country are treated in totally different ways. Men of one age group, or a particular marital status, are drafted in one state or area, deferred in another; a group of graduate students with similar programs and records at the same institution are classified in a variety of ways by their respective local boards; teachers, artisans, social workers, and other skilled occupational groupings may be automatically deferred in some boards, challenged

[26] For the techniques by which this standardization is accomplished, and the results of such efforts, see Chaps. 2 and 6 respectively.

but ultimately deferred in others, and automatically drafted in other boards —or handled in any patchwork combination of individualized decision-making. The possibilities are almost infinite, and the criticism of the System which results is commensurate. Individual spectaculars, such as deferment or induction of athletes, civil rights figures, movie stars, and other celebrities, merely personalize a readily observable general phenomenon.

These are the major outlines of the conditions and problems which established the context of the Selective Service System in the mid-1960s. All these factors contributed to the criticism of the organization, and all are traceable at least in part to the fact of manpower surplus. Some are endemic to the decentralized character of the organization and the nature of its policies, and merely exacerbated by the abundance of manpower, while others are noticeable only in times of manpower surplus. Some aspects of these grounds for complaint might well be overlooked in times of total war emergency or in an era of less concern for equality—such as during World War II. But they could not be and were not in 1966 and 1967. Let us look first at how the System came to have its 1960s form.

III. THE DEVELOPMENT OF THE SELECTIVE SERVICE SYSTEM

The Selective Service System of the late 1960s is in many ways the System of 1917, and is in no important respect distinct from the System erected in 1940. It may best be understood through a time perspective of more than one hundred years: it was planned in the early years of the nineteenth century, fitted to the society and economy of that time, and much influenced by the experience of the Civil War draft.

Conscription has a long history in this country.[27] Every one of the

[27] For histories of Selective Service and comparisons of the various statutes, see Jack Franklin Leach, *Conscription in the United States: Historical Background* (Rutland: Charles E. Tuttle Publishing Co., 1952); the inception of the 1917 Act is particularly well covered in Edward M. Coffman, *The Hilt of the Sword* (Madison: University of Wisconsin Press, 1966), and David A. Lockmiller, *Enoch H. Crowder, Soldier, Lawyer and Statesman* (Columbus: University of Missouri Studies, 1955); the *Special Monograph Series* of the Selective Service System (Washington, D.C.: Government Printing Office, 1947–1955), containing volumes on the background, organization and administration of the System in the Second World War; *Selective Service under the 1948 Act Extended* (Washington, D.C.: Government Printing Office, 1953); Clyde E. Jacobs and John F. Gallagher, *The Selective Service Act: A Case Study of the Governmental Process* (New York: Dodd, Mead, 1967) particularly for the Congressional debates; and *Hearings,* Note 6 above, Appendix II, for the pre-1967 statute with analysis and a brief description of the Selective Service System.

colonies and later the states conscripted men for the militia, and after independence the Militia Act of 1792 prescribed militia enrollment for all male citizens of the states. Conscripts were sought under the provisions of the Federal Enrollment Act of 1863 during the Civil War, with results which are celebrated under the title of the New York Draft Riots. Nearly 1,000 persons died in five days of rioting which began when the first steps were taken to carry out a draft plan which permitted men to avoid service through payment of the sum of $300 or the provision of a substitute. This draft was conducted by the military, with a Provost Marshal in each Congressional District in charge. His responsibilities included apprehension of spies and deserters as well as registration, and these functions were often carried out through house to house canvasses.

At the end of the Civil War, a critique of the operation of the draft was written by Brigadier General James Oakes, Assistant Provost Marshal of Illinois. Perhaps the most important single formative element in the history of Selective Service (its words are still cited regularly, and its 100th anniversary was celebrated in 1966), this document called for personalized and nonavoidable obligation to serve, the elimination of the military from the local administration of conscription, and registration at a central place rather than by house-to-house canvass. When the Selective Service Act of 1917 was hurriedly drafted in the spring of that year, the Oakes Report was used as a guide and draft headquarters were established in each state, with civilian local boards in each county assigned administrative responsibilities. Relatively little public opposition developed. We can only speculate as to the reasons, but they probably include (as well as any actual preference for local boards) greater support for the war, diffusion of objects against which to react, relatively small calls, and less salient registration. In any event, this basic arrangement became the accepted model for conscription.

In 1920 the National Defense Act was enacted, with the provision that the War and Navy Departments prepare plans for manpower mobilization. The Joint Army and Navy Selective Service Committee was established in 1926 and began the preparation of a standby Selective Service Law and accompanying regulations. The Committee included among its nine members both National Guard and Reserve officers with 1917 experience, and these were supplemented in the 1930s with more National Guard personnel, including then-Major Lewis B. Hershey. In each state, the Adjutant General's office of the state National Guard also prepared plans for the effectuation of Selective Service when and if it were again enacted. Planning at all levels took place against the background of the 1917 experience, and thus when the Congress passed the 1940 Act the local board was again the basic unit. Over 6,000 of them were established, together with 250 appeal boards and 54 state or comparable jurisdiction headquarters. National Guard personnel provided the nucleus of the staffs in both national and state headquarters throughout the System.

For a brief period after World War II, the System (known as the Office of Selective Service Records), functioned solely as a recordkeeping office at the national and state levels. By 1948, force levels had dropped below 1,500,000 men and overseas commitments were rising, with the result that Selective Service was revived; the terms of the statute, and the personnel who filled the offices and functions which it set up, were the same as in the World War II organization. In many cases, the local boards were staffed entirely with men who had served on them during the War, and the state and national headquarters changed their names again to reflect the return to operational responsibilities.

The present organizational character of the Selective Service System is thus deeply rooted in the tragic experience of the Civil War and the comparative success of 1917; the extension of the 1917 experience into World War II having proved effective, the same design and practices have simply been continued into their sixth decade. Three different types of personnel are integrated into the three layers of the System: at the top, in both national and state headquarters, managerial positions are filled almost exclusively by military officers, usually National Guard or Reserve officers on active duty; at the middle ranges of headquarters and local personnel, full-time civilian men and women perform the clerical and logistical tasks; at the decision-making local board level, all positions are filled by volunteer local citizens who devote several hours per month to the job. It is a highly decentralized organization, and despite its military ethos there is little command potential over the nearly 4,100 local boards scattered across the country.

At no time has the practice of conscription in this country been anything but selective. There have always been exceptions or deferments for men in some occupations or officials whose services were deemed to be more valuable elsewhere than in the military. Conscientious objectors (under varying definitions) have always been deferred or permitted to serve only in noncombatant tasks. Student deferment was initiated during the Korean War instead of the induction and assignment to colleges which was under-taken during World War II. Childless married men were subject to induc-tion for most of the Korean War, removed from immediate liability between 1963 and 1965, and then restored to liability when needs increased. Deferments have been slackened and tightened over the years as military needs changed, and over time they have acquired an independent status. For many years in the late 1950s and early 1960s, the System was more active in extending deferments than it was with inductions, until deferment began to take on a function separate from the mere expression of the relatively greater national interest in the civilian services of a given individual for defense purposes. The System, and particularly General Hershey, began to view the overall social effects of years of deferments in a patterned form which was termed "channeling"—"that process through which registrants are influenced to enter and remain in study, in critical occupations, and in other activities in the national health, safety and interest by deferment or prospect of deferment from military service."[28]

In one sense, channeling was merely the extension of the logic of the Tydings Amendment of World War II, through which farmers were deferred as long as they stayed on their farms, but drafted as soon as they left them. General Hershey saw the System's channeling functions as important contributions to national well-being, declaring in 1966 that the System's deferment practices deserved some credit for the increases in college-educated and technically skilled men in the nation between 1949 and 1962.[29] But the assumption of responsibility for so serving the national interest was hotly contested during the debates of 1966–67 on the grounds that the System's definition of the national interest was inappropriate, that it had not been asked to assume such tasks, that the discharge of such functions required lengthy periods of military liability and consequent governmental controls over citizens, and that, in any event, many other changes had occurred of a less desirable kind for which the System might be equally responsible but for which it had not claimed credit. Using a Selective Service handout of July 1965 as a source, Jean Carper's *Bitter Greetings* turns the words of the System into a confession of totalitarianism, in one of the sharpest polemics of the pre-extension debates.[30]

IV. CONTROVERSY, PROPOSALS, AND THE CONGRESSIONAL ACTION OF 1967

The coming expiration of induction authority in June 1967 served as the focus for several studies of the draft in the mid-1960s. The first of these was undertaken by the Defense Department and became known as the Defense

[28] *Annual Report of the Director of Selective Service,* 1966, p. 16.

[29] *Hearings,* p. 9618.

[30] Jean Carper, *Bitter Greetings: The Scandal of the Military Draft* (New York: Grossman Publishers, 1967), pp. 114–15.

Department Draft Study of 1964. Its purpose was to determine whether the armed forces could be maintained in the absence of conscription; its perspective was that of the military services, and it did not undertake any assessment of either deferment policy or organization characteristics within the Selective Service System. The study employed population and employment projections, service statistics, and extensive opinion sampling both within the services and among the civilian population, the latter accomplished through the facilities of the Census Bureau and the National Opinion Research Center of the University of Chicago.[31]

Much controversy surrounds the interpretations, conclusions, and reporting of this study, though apparently not the methods or data developed. Most Congressmen appear to believe that the study has never been fully released to Congress or the public, and one author of a popular attack on the draft claims to have seen pages of the study which were altered and supplemented before parts were released.[32] Assistant Secretary of Defense Thomas D. Morris, however, officially advised the House Armed Services Committee in 1966 that his testimony and supporting documentary materials which he then provided constituted the entire Report of the Draft Study.[33] These materials make up 55 pages in an Appendix to the record of the June 1966 hearings on Selective Service conducted by that Committee.

Both sides in this controversy appear to have some basis for their diametrically opposed public positions. The study was initiated at a time when total levels of 2,000,000 or 2,500,000 men were within the range of possibility, but by the time it was nearing completion actual force levels had already risen to 3,300,000 and further increases were being considered. Conclusions concerning the feasibility of a military establishment based entirely on voluntary enlistments, and estimates of the wages necessary to produce it, are clearly dependent on the force levels contemplated. Changes

[31] Self-administered questionnaire data were received from a total of 9,593 civilian male respondents (60 percent nonveterans, 31 percent veterans in the final weighting) between the ages of 16 and 34, and combined with the responses to a similar questionnaire from 102,000 men on active military service (9 percent in the final weighting). The basic source in which these results are reported is Albert D. Klassen, *Military Service in American Life Since World War II: An Overview* (Chicago: National Opinion Research Center, 1966), many aspects of which are included among the materials presented by the Defense Department in Appendix I, *Hearings*. Several other publications from the National Opinion Research Center drew on these data; see, for example, Karen Oppenheim, "Attitudes of Younger American Men toward Selective Service" (Chicago: National Opinion Research Center, 1966).

[32] Carper, *op. cit.*, Chap. 11. James Gerhardt also says that the study has not been fully published. "Military Manpower Procurement Policies 1945–1967" Ph.D. dissertation, Harvard, 1967), see p. 618, n. 136.

[33] *Hearings*, p. 9997.

in these estimates in the face of a changing world situation might well render moot or irrelevant a large proportion of the analysis or conclusions based on such assumptions. But whether interpretations and conclusions were or should have been changed and/or released need not concern us for our present purposes; the basic data themselves appear to have been responsibly developed and are uncontroverted, and where applicable we shall employ them in our analysis of the System's performance.

The most comprehensive study of conscription undertaken in this period was that of the National Advisory Commission on Selective Service, appointed by President Johnson in July 1966 with instructions to report by January 1967.[34] Established in part to head off Congressional calls for investigation of the draft, the Commission was composed of twenty members who were private citizens with extensive governmental or other public experience.[35] Although time pressures were severe, the Commission's staff conducted considerable research into the operations of the Selective Service System and alternatives to it, and the judgments of the Commission represent the first informed, independent evaluation of conscription practices ever made. We shall summarize the recommendations of the Commission's Report shortly.

Another set of recommendations concerning conscription was put forward by a Citizens' Panel constituted by the House Armed Services Committee. Chaired by General Mark Clark and composed chiefly of retired military men, this group apparently conducted no independent research and, according to its report, heard testimony chiefly from the staff of the Armed Services Committee and representatives of the Selective Service System.[36]

Both academics and journalists were also at work on a variety of studies of aspects of conscription during 1966 and 1967. The field study of state and local operations of the System which is reported in this book began in 1965, as did a doctoral dissertation concerning the decision-making

[34] Executive Order 11289 of July 2, 1966, creating and charging the Commission may be found in *President's Commission Report*, pp. 66–67.

[35] Members of the Commission included Thomas S. Gates, Jr., former Secretary of Defense, John A. McCone, former head of the CIA and the Atomic Energy Commission, General David M. Shoup, former head of the Marine Corps, and George Reedy, former Presidential Press Secretary. Burke Marshall, former head of the Civil Rights Division in the Department of Justice, was appointed Chairman. Other members included representatives of higher education, labor, business, and Negro groups. The full list may be found in *President's Commission Report*, p. v.

[36] See Civilian Advisory Panel on Military Procurement, *Report to the Committee on Armed Services, House of Representatives* (90th Cong., 1st Sess. (Washington: Government Printing Office, 1967).

of local boards.[37] Members of the Inter-University Seminar on Armed Forces and Society initiated studies of Selective Service and its effects,[38] and several economists examined the costs of staffing the military through market wages.[39] A multidisciplinary conference including several leading academicians and other public figures was held with the help of the Ford Foundation at the University of Chicago in December 1966,[40] and several other conferences and symposiums were conducted elsewhere in the country.

Most of the popular books concerning the draft which appeared in late 1966 and 1967 argued the case for supplanting conscription with some form of voluntary recruitment program. Perhaps the best-researched of these was *Bitter Greetings: The Scandal of the Military Draft*,[41] a stinging attack on the Selective Service System's procedures and rhetoric by Jean Carper, an experienced journalist with a keen social perspective. Others included *Wrong Man In Uniform*,[42] by the young Republican activist Bruce Chapman, which helped to focus Republican support for the voluntary army argument; *Let's End the Draft Mess*,[43] a knowledgeable dissent against the System by a former officer in the national headquarters, provides some sidelights on the strength of status quo elements in that body and states the case for universal service ("national service"). A full assessment of the arguments for a voluntary military establishment[44] (or a "professional army," as others would term it) or national service[45] is beyond the scope of this book. Voluntary army proposals are attractive to a wide spectrum of

[37] The author of the dissertation, as yet untitled, is Gary L. Wamsley, currently an Assistant Professor of Political Science at Vanderbilt University.

[38] See Roger D. Little (ed.), *Selective Service and American Society* (New York: Russell Sage Foundation, forthcoming).

[39] See Stuart Altman and Alan E. Fechter, "The Supply of Military Personnel," paper presented at the Meetings of the American Economic Association, December 1966; Walter Oi, "The Costs and Implications of An All-Volunteer Force," unpublished paper; W. Lee Hansen and Burton A. Weisbrod, "Economics of the Military Draft," unpublished paper; and Milton Friedman, "An All-Volunteer Army," in the *New York Times Magazine*, May 14, 1967.

[40] See Sol Tax (ed.), *The Draft* (Chicago: University of Chicago Press, 1968).

[41] Carper, *op. cit.*

[42] Bruce Chapman, *Wrong Man in Uniform* (New York: Trident Press, 1967).

[43] George Walton, *Let's End the Draft Mess* (New York: David McKay Company, 1967).

[44] The case is made effectively in the works by Carper, Chapman, Oi, and Friedman, cited in notes 40–42 above, and is carried forward by the Council for a Voluntary Army, a Chicago-based organization.

[45] The goal of national service is advocated in publications emanating from The National Service Secretariat, Donald Eberly, Executive Director, 522 Fifth Avenue, New York, N.Y. For a representative statement, see *A Plan for National Service* (November 1966).

political opinion, but, for the reasons already set forth, we shall adopt the conclusion of the National Advisory Commission on Selective Service[46] that some form of conscription is necessary under present circumstances of international affairs and given the present level of American commitments. We may observe that not even the strongest advocates of a "voluntary army" believe that it is possible to institute such a policy during time of war or when force levels are over 3,000,000 men, and that most such advocates endorse the idea of retaining some form of conscription machinery as a backup against the need for it at some future time.

In the context of the complaints directed against the System by Congressmen, writers, conferences, and the academic world, all widely circulated and supplemented by the national news media, the recommendations of the President's Commission appear moderate indeed. Entitled *In Pursuit of Equity: Who Should Serve When Not All Serve?*, the report emphasized the theme of inequity due to economic discrimination and variability between local boards. In a series of appendices, it documented most of the characteristics of Selective Service operations summarized in the first section of this chapter. The chief recommendations that the Commission made to the President in February 1967 were:

1. Elimination of student deferments, except for officer training programs.
2. Elimination of all other deferments (including occupational and dependency deferments) except hardship deferments.
3. Induction of men on a "youngest first" basis, at age 19.
4. Selection of such men by means of a random selection system, in which their vulnerability would be limited to the year in which they were aged 19.
5. Prohibitions against enlistment into the Reserves or National Guard for those men with no prior service, unless they enlist before being classified I-A. Where such units are not able to fill their ranks by enlistment, they should be staffed by inductions under the same random selection system.
6. Reorganization of the System to reduce the number of local boards to 300–500, under a centralized arrangement with 8 to 10 regional offices and professional classifiers acting in accordance with nationally uniform classification criteria. Local participation would be cut back to the form of local boards of appeal from the actions of classifiers. Data processing equipment and methods would be instituted to maintain current uniform handling of all registrants.[47]

---

[46] *President's Commission Report*, pp. 11–16.
[47] *Ibid.*, pp. 3–10.

A considerable minority of the Commission had endorsed retention of student deferments, but with the provision that there be no further deferments granted to such persons so that student deferments did not ripen into exemption from service. There was little or no dissent from the general theme of economic discrimination, and none from the conclusion that local board operations as then conducted were promotive of variability resulting in inequity. Random selection ("lottery") was seen as the only means to establish equitable selection among qualified registrants, only some of whom were required by the armed forces; even the minority which supported retention of student deferments would have subjected students to the random selection after graduation.

In his message asking for extension of the draft the President, following the recommendation of the National Advisory Commission, asked the Congress to pass legislation granting the Defense Department authority to induct men into Reserve and National Guard units.[48] Rather than asking for the reorganization of the System, however, he announced that the reorganization recommendations of the Commission were being turned over to an interagency task force for further study. The other recommendations of the Commission were within the President's existing authority to implement and he declared his intentions with regard to them. He noted that he was instructing the Director of Selective Service to develop a random system of selection and he said that he would institute a youngest-first draft. He called for Congressional and public discussion of the question of undergraduate deferments, but said that he intended to end graduate student deferments.

The Congress rejected the Commission recommendations and the President's requests and acted to prevent the President from carrying out his announced intentions.[49] (Not surprisingly, Congressional action followed rather closely the recommendations of the Civilian Advisory Panel appointed by the House Armed Services Committee.) To the recommendation that undergraduate deferments be eliminated the Congress responded by writing into the law a guarantee of such deferment for any student in school, for four years or until age 24, whichever was the shorter period. To the suggestion that selection be by random means, the Congress responded by prohibiting such action unless the method were first approved by the Congress. To the recommendations regarding limits on enlistment in the Reserves and National Guard, the Congress responded by guaranteeing the

[48] The President's Message to Congress is reported in the *New York Times* of March 7, 1967.

[49] See Public Law 90–40 (90th Cong. June 1967), reported in *U.S. Law Week*, June 17, 1967, Vol. XXXV, No. 50.

opportunity to enlist even after induction orders had actually been issued. To the conclusions concerning variability of local boards, Congress responded by adding a specific protection for local board autonomy and discretion. To some Commission recommendations concerning the need for fixed terms for local board members (five-year terms were suggested) and maximum retirement ages in the System, the Congress did act: it set 25 years as the maximum term, and established 75 as a retirement age. Congress also went outside the ambit of recommendations by any but the Clark Panel to restrict the effects of Supreme Court decisions[50] concerning conscientious objection, to eliminate procedural and investigation requirements which delayed denial of such claims, and to provide for the speediest possible prosecution of those who maintained conscientious objector claims. The courts were prevented by the statute from inquiring into the merits of any registrants' claims concerning the propriety of classifications, leaving the local board as the only trier of the facts in such cases.[51]

Our review of the conditions and problems under which Selective Service was operating in the mid-1960s pointed out that economic discrimination and local board variability were inevitable under circumstances of manpower surplus. What are the prospects for change during the next four years, with these Congressional modifications of Selective Service policy and operations? Firm data are available on the numbers of young men who will be entering the manpower pool: a larger and larger surplus of men over military needs is in store unless service requirements radically increase in 1968–71. Thus, more and more men will have to be deferred. The guarantee of undergraduate deferment with no firm prohibition on further deferment seems bound to continue the economic discrimination that was apparent before Congress acted. College students can hope to avoid a shooting war. Occupational deferments, which go mainly to college graduates, will continue to be available. The guarantee of Reserve and National Guard enlistment will allow some college men who are under draft pressure to avoid active duty even more surely than they can now. The protection for local board autonomy and discretion will assure continued and (with the increasing manpower surplus) probably increasing variability among local boards. It seems clear that the Congressional actions of 1967 will have the effect of exaggerating all the major problems of Selective Service operations which gave rise to criticism in 1966–67. By 1971, these characteristics of the System's activities may well become so insistent that they can no longer be ignored.

---

[50] *United States* v. *Seeger*, 380 U.S. 163 (1965).

[51] See Chap. 5 below for an analysis of the effects of such amendments on the hearing and appellate process within the System.

In February 1968 two executive actions were taken that deserve comment.[52] We have already alluded to the suspension by the National Security Council of the list of critical occupations and essential activities. In our view, if this action has any real impact it will only be to heighten the variability among local boards that now exists—for now all national guidance has gone. The other step was more significant, though still minor in comparison with the Commission's recommendations. Deferments for graduate students (except in medicine, dentistry, and allied fields) were withdrawn effective June 1968. The impact of this policy, if not modified, will be substantial. Employers may benefit since many potential graduate students may choose to enter the job market and try for an occupational deferment; graduate schools will certainly experience an enrollment drop for a year or two until veterans begin to return; the temporary enrollment drop will have later effects on both education and industry; and since, at the time of writing, an oldest-first induction policy is being followed the army will be inundated with college graduates aged 22 and older. Because of the oldest-first basis of call in effect at the time such deferments were ended, college students were rapidly shunted from specially favored status to a situation of special vulnerability to immediate call. This probably undesirable set of consequences appears to stem from the limited and patchwork character of the available modifications which remain within Presidential discretion after the statutory modifications of 1967. Still open, of course, is the possibility of change in either order of call or method of selection.

Finally, it should be noted that in April 1968 the report of the task force appointed to review the organizational recommendations of the President's Advisory Commission was made public. It recommended that the local boards of the System be retained. In commenting on the task force report, General Hershey (one of three members of the task force) is reported to have said that the Advisory Commission proposal to consolidate the System was "pretty far out." For example, he declared that consolidation and professionalization of the System would have restored the Civil War System. The Commission, of course, recommended nothing approximating house-to-house registration by the military. As one press dispatch reported, "Hershey was generally scornful at an hour long news conference of the recommendations for reform made by the National Advisory Commission on Selective Service headed by Burke Marshall."[53]

[52] See *New York Times,* February 17, 1968, p. 10.
[53] See UPI dispatch of April 29, 1968. The Task Force Report is also briefly described in the *New York Times,* April 30, 1968, p. 2. According to both reports, the Task Force Report was not printed for distribution.

Part I

STRUCTURE, OPERATIONS, IMPACT, AND REACTIONS

The six chapters of Part I represent the extent of our data collection and make up the descriptive-analytical body of the study. Chapters 2, 4, and 5 are devoted chiefly to a standard analysis of the internal operating characteristics of the organization. Methodologically and conceptually, their approach will be familiar; the subjects, have not, however, been covered elsewhere. Chapters 3, 6, and 7 concern aspects of the interaction between the organization and its environment, from recruitment of local board members to patterns of deferment and induction and public reactions to them. They represent a modest advance in organizational analysis, particularly as regards impact and public response; again, the findings are substantively unduplicated elsewhere. The two sets of factors, internal characteristics and interaction with the environment, will be seen to articulate with each other in a manner which we think is revealing about the present management of the draft.

The data developed in these six chapters are intended to provide a sufficient base for the chapters that follow in Part II. Consistent with our ultimate intentions, we have sought to identify relevant variables and important relationships bearing on problems of change, citizen participation, and the consequences of various policy characteristics, but we have not gone beyond this. This Part attempts no more (and no less) than a comprehensive analysis of the state and local operations and impact of, and reactions to, the Selective Service System.

Chapter 2

ORGANIZATIONAL STRUCTURE AND PROCESSES

Selective Service is an independent agency whose Director, appointed subject to Senate confirmation, serves at the pleasure of the President. Lt. Gen. Lewis B. Hershey, a principal author of the 1940 statute, was appointed Director in 1941 and by 1968 had served five Presidents in that capacity. The System's three-level organizational structure faithfully reflects American federalism, but its processes are distinctive in that the central unit in this case has limited influence over the nearly autonomous local decision-makers. We shall sketch the outlines of formal structure briefly, and then analyze some characteristic internal processes.

I. THE FORMAL STRUCTURE

We begin where Selective Service begins: with the local boards. At the end of 1966, there were 4,087 local boards, ranging in size from 27 registrants in one board in Colorado to more than 54,000 in a Los Angeles board. Local boards consist of at least three and usually five members. They are nominated by the Governors of their states and appointed by the President, serving without compensation and, until the 1967 amendments, for unlimited periods of time. Attached to each local board, at least in the System's organizational charts, are medical advisers, advisers to registrants, and government appeal agents (usually lawyers), all of whom are volunteers also; a paid clerk and other clerical staff as needed make up the rest of the local structure. All classifications and selection for induction decisions are the exclusive prerogative of the local boards, subject to reversal by appeal boards (also composed of civilian volunteers) in those cases where appeals are taken by such authorized parties as the registrant, his dependent or employer, the appeal agent, or the State or National Director.

The placement of decisional authority in the hands of local volunteers represents a fundamental commitment within the organization, around which all its other values are organized and from which flow its distinctive characteristics. The commitment reflects past experience, and assumes a rural society; it draws further support from the conviction that popular acquiescence in conscription will be forthcoming only when local management is assured. Against such experience, assumptions, and convictions— however remote from or inapplicable they might be to the 1960s and 1970s —it is of little avail to point out as many did during the 1966–67 debates that America has moved far from pre-World War I days. Then, the rural population was slightly higher than the urban population, and the concept of local men knowing their communities or the registrants no doubt received empirical support in many if not most instances. Today, when the urban population has increased by 150 percent and outnumbers the rural population almost $2\frac{1}{2}$ to one, and some local boards have more than 50,000 registrants, the concept seems much less valid. But the System adheres to this commitment as firmly as ever, as indicated by such 1966 declarations as the following:

> It would be essential to avoid in any way interfering with the present decentralized approach of the System which has proved so successful in contrast with the centralized ones of both the Federal and Confederate governments during the Civil War. The decentralized, or local board, or grass-roots operation of Selective Service began with the First World War and demonstrated that the Nation would much more willingly support compulsory military service operated by their neighbors at home, than they would a program operated by a remote, impersonal organization.[1]

Acting under the assumptions that conscription is unpopular, and that the only alternative to the present system is operation reminiscent of the Civil War, the System has held fast to its view that local control is the key to acceptance. The Governors of the states are the only sources of nominations for membership on local or appeal boards, and the President may appoint only those who are so nominated. The Governors also nominate the State Directors of Selective Service, who serve at the pleasure of the Governor. Acting consistently with its commitment, the System has resisted any attempt to impose national standards of uniformity on local boards:

[1] *Hearings,* p. 9993.

We do not believe that more detailed mandatory criteria for local board classification guidance is desirable or would be beneficial to the registrant or to the country. At the present time local boards, subject to appeal, determine the classification of the registrant based on all the facts in the case and their knowledge of the general economic, employment, and defense situations in the country. There can be no uniformity nor is it desirable since there are no two cases that are exactly the same, whether they be students, employees, or family providers.[2]

The intermediate level within the organization consists of the 56 state and comparable jurisdiction headquarters, such as New York City, Puerto Rico, the District of Columbia, etc. The state headquarters serve as communication channels between national headquarters and the local boards, allocating induction calls received from national headquarters to the boards and occasionally interpreting national policy for the guidance of boards. Most of the managerial positions at the state level are filled by military officers: 48 of the 56 State Directors held ranks from Lieutenant Colonel to Lieutenant General in 1966, and only eight were civilians.[3] In addition to military officers each state headquarters also has a clerical staff and field "auditors" whose task it is to maintain liaison with local boards and clerks.

The key functions of the state headquarters are (1) the maintenance and supervision of the state's local boards, from staffing with board members and clerical personnel, to guidance and oversight of their decision-making, to provision for logistical support of their processing of registrants; (2) the allocation of the state's monthly induction call (received as a state total from national headquarters) to the various local boards, a complex procedure which seeks to balance the immediate availability of men with the board's proportionate share of state population and men already in service; and (3) liaison with the state's mass media, trade associations, employers, and other interest groups, and enforcement of the Selective Service statute in cases of delinquency.

In practice, there are wide variances in the size and operating characteristics of the state headquarters. Some of this is due to the variety of conditions which they face: in September 1966, Nevada had 42,216 registrants while California had 58 times as many or 2,473,184. The State Director of Delaware had at that time only five local boards to supervise, while his counterpart in Illinois had 217. State Directors are, in effect, appointed by the Governors of their states; in some states, the same man has served

[2] *Ibid.*, p. 9986.
[3] *The United States Organization Manual, 1966* (Washington: Government Printing Office, 1966).

throughout the existence of the System, but in others the post is part of the Governor's patronage and Directors come and go with elections. The primary reason for variation in the practices and priorities of the state headquarters, however, is the fact that they are not closely supervised by the national headquarters and individual State Directors are obliged to define their responsibilities and develop means of carrying them out independently.

At the apex of the System is the national headquarters in Washington, staffed almost entirely by a combination of Reserve and National Guard officers on active duty. Of the thirteen major managerial positions shown on national headquarters organization charts, only one (Research and Statistics) is filled by a civilian. Functions of greatest relevance for our purposes include (1) development and promulgation of deferment criteria and other regulations concerning the procedures of local boards, (2) allocation of calls received from the Defense Department to the states, and (3) maintenance of records on the availability of manpower. Each of these warrants further comment.

As is the case with many executive agencies, the policies transmitted from national headquarters to the units of the System are an extension of the President's basic responsibilities, and an informal sharing of authority has developed. Ordinarily, the Director issues regulations relating to the internal administration of the System while the President issues regulations relating to registration, classification, and induction. In either case regulations are likely to be drafted informally on an as-needed basis by an ad hoc task force of Selective Service personnel. In some instances Department of Defense personnel may also participate in the drafting of new regulations. If a proposed regulation is to be issued as an Executive Order it is forwarded to the Bureau of the Budget for review and there may also be consultation with interested departments such as Defense, Health, Education, and Welfare, and Labor. Changes in the regulations do not invariably originate within Selective Service. For example, the National Advisory Commission on Selective Service recommended that the time in which a registrant could take an appeal from his classification by a local board be lengthened from 10 to 30 days and the President issued an executive order to this effect even though Selective Service had opposed such a change.[4]

[4] In comments submitted to the House Armed Services Committee in June 1966 the Director of Selective Service said, "Extending the period of appeal might result in those having the right to appeal to put it off until even the longer appeal period had expired." The National Advisory Commission in February 1967 recommended, "The registrant should be able to appeal his classification to his local board within 30 days instead of the

National headquarters receives requests for men from the Defense Department and converts these into specific calls upon each state in accordance with a quota system devised from a combination of each state's share of the armed forces compared to its share of the national population, plus the relative availability of men in the various states at any given time.[5] Much was made during the 1966–67 debates of the fact that the availability of men in some states led to higher draft calls on those states and in effect punished them for having more efficient local board classification processes than other states.[6] With a population-proportionate control as the base of the system for assigning calls, however, such apparent inequity should be self-regulating over time.

The records kept by Selective Service, as in any organization, are a function of available resources (personnel, space, money), of the state of technology, and of the questions that the organization wants or needs to answer. Selective Service has frequently not been generously funded and the outmoded record-keeping technology of the System can be ascribed partially to this. No doubt this is also to some extent a result of a lack of personnel sophisticated in records management. There is also, however, a substantive problem. The records of the System reflect the questions that have been thought important. (How many registrants are there? How many are available for service? How many men are in the various classifications?) But the System has not been concerned with the impact of the draft. There are no Selective Service data available that can provide answers to such questions as: What are the socioeconomic characteristics of draftees? Of men deferred? How many men classified as available become eligible for one of the various deferments? How many men, in other words, are actually channeled into deferred categories? The location of such records as are maintained also merits note. It is common for Selective Service to point out that its files on millions of registrants constitute a valuable inventory of the nation's manpower.[7] What is not pointed out is that these files are in

---

10 days presently stipulated." On May 3, 1967, the President signed an Executive Order extending from 10 to 30 days the period in which a man could appeal his draft classification.

[5] The quota and call allocations are described in *Hearings*, p. 9636.

[6] Comparisons of Michigan and Texas draft calls, emanating initially from the office of Sen. Robert Griffin of Michigan on June 1, 1966, led to a series of exchanges among Congressmen. See the account in Carper, *op. cit.*, pp. 101–02.

[7] A press information bulletin issued by Selective Service in 1966 said that one of the four major purposes of the System was "the maintenance of a current inventory of the Nation's military manpower resources to assure quick and complete operational effectiveness under any possible conditions or circumstances." A statement submitted by General Hershey to the Subcommittee on Employment and Manpower of the Committee on Labor

thousands of file drawers in thousands of local board offices. Only very summary data are ever sent to state and national headquarters, principally data dealing with the numbers in each classification. Data on individual registrants stay with local boards, thus limiting the usefulness of the manpower inventory.

Two related factors appear to account for the predominance of Reserve and National Guard officers at the managerial levels in state and national headquarters. One is obvious: the military were historically the most concerned, and were the eighteenth- and nineteenth-century managers of efforts at conscription; no other governmental body was either in 1917 or the 1930s more appropriately the locus of responsibility, nor would conflict between civilian agencies over the locus of such power be likely. The second reason for this form of military management of the System goes deeper toward the System's nature: state National Guard planning and assistance were available without additional expense, conforming to the strong emphasis within the System on a minimum expenditure, cost-accounting ethos. Further, using Guard and Reserve personnel appears to be a way of maintaining harmonious relationships within the organization's higher echelons and yet bridging the potential gap between nation and state *and* between military and civilian elements. The National Guard is both military and civilian, and, perhaps even more important, it usually accurately reflects the facts of life in state politics.[8] The System's low-cost, low-spend ethic is not limited to

---

and Public Welfare, U.S. Senate, 88th Cong. 1st Sess., said "The records of the System are an unequaled inventory of data about a large segment of our young manpower. The Selective Service System can identify a vast number of the young men of our country who are in need of medical, educational, or vocational rehabilitation." See Part 8, p. 2816 of the subcommittee hearings on "Nation's Manpower Revolution." This statement can well be contrasted with the statement submitted by General Hershey to the House Armed Services Committee in April 1966. After first emphasizing that the System only solicited or received information that related to possible deferment the statement said, "The System, so far as funds permit, gathers information from a one percent sample of its registrant files. This information, in addition to the limitations on its reliability because of factors already discussed, does not, of course, supply any information on those non-registrants who enter service before age 18 until they leave active duty and register.

"To report and tabulate information now received on all registrants would substantially increase cost of operation. To gather, report and tabulate additional data would increase costs further.

"While all these data, now solicited from registrants, or proposed, would be helpful for other purposes, it would not contribute to the System's present function of maintaining the armed forces and supporting the civilian economy under the present scheme of deferment and the present philosophy of selective service as reflected in the law." (From 1966 *Hearings,* p. 9990.)

[8] See Martha Derthick, *The National Guard in Politics* (Cambridge: Harvard University Press, 1965).

its relationships with the National Guard: consistent with the use of volunteers at so many positions, or possibly due to this feature, local board clerks are not paid at the standard civil service rates but at specially set lower rates, and for many years a key item of internal measurement of performance was the cost in cents per registrant inducted.

Elements of formal structure, so far as they are relevant for our purposes, may be summarized briefly by reference to Figure 2.1. We have touched upon the major units of the three-level structure above, and appeal boards will be the subject of a subsequent chapter. The advisory committees at the national level and, so far as we know, at the various state levels also, appear to be operative; at the local level, however, as will shortly be described, the advisory appendages of the System are likely to be more clearly evidenced on the organizational charts than in actual practice. Of greater importance, however, are the interchanges which take place within the organization.

II. DISINTEGRATIVE FORCES AND INTEGRATIVE MEASURES

All organizations face problems of cohesion and integration, but Selective Service is peculiarly threatened by centrifugal forces. Structural decentralization and legal autonomy of local units are supported by the dominant grass-roots ethos of the entire organization and the physical isolation of many boards; accordingly, only the most general instructions are given to subordinate elements, and this in turn fosters independent and idiosyncratic definitions and applications by state and local units. Also potentially disintegrative are the norms or practices that develop in the many units of the System. If Selective Service is viewed as a system and its state headquarters and local boards as subsystems, the risk is that the subsystem may develop practices that are unrelated or contradictory to the requirements of the system as a whole. Finally, the personal preferences and values of individual organization members are disintegrative forces. No member of any organization is a member *only* of that organization. Local board members particularly belong to a variety of other organizations, are pressured by work situations, experience potential conflicts of interest, etc. In short, they are only marginally subject to the influence of Selective Service in their overall life situations.

With all these disintegrative forces at work, it is clear that national headquarters faces substantial problems. One route toward integration is

FIGURE 2.1.   OFFICIAL ORGANIZATION CHART OF SELECTIVE
SERVICE SYSTEM

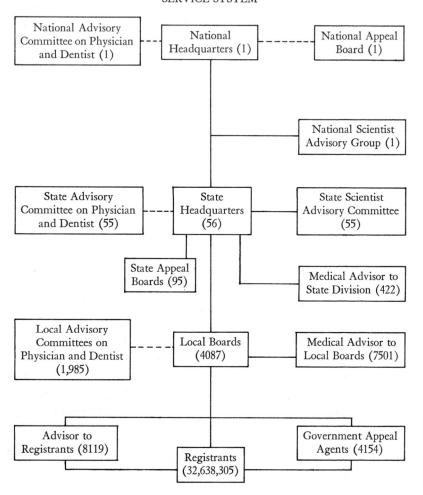

Organization of Selective Service System 30 June 1966. Taken from *1966 Annual Report*, p. 4. Numbers in parentheses are numbers of personnel or units.

through formal communication channels. National headquarters issues a variety of publications designed to inform state headquarters and local boards of current regulations, current problems, current practices, and to some extent these may counteract the disintegrative forces in the system.

Operations Bulletins, Local Board Memoranda, State Director Advices, Administrative Bulletins, and letters on special problems flow from the national headquarters to the state headquarters and to appeal and local boards. Although there is substantial overlap, these different series have somewhat different purposes. State Director Advices and Administrative Bulletins deal usually with routine organization matters, ranging from savings bond purchases by employees, to warnings about political activity by civil servants, to the care and disposal of records. Operations Bulletins and Local Board Memoranda are more likely to deal with matters relating to classification and induction. Operations Bulletins cover a variety of topics, but most of them detail the procedures to be used or standards to be applied in granting a. particular classification. Hardly distinguishable from Operations Bulletins, Local Board Memoranda describe the action that a board (in fact a clerk) should take in particular situations that may arise. Local Board Memorandum 14, for example, describes the steps to be taken when a registrant refuses to submit to physical examination or mental test or fails to report for or submit to induction. Local Board Memorandum 71 describes the public information policies that a local board may follow. This memorandum illustrates national headquarters sensitivity to state headquarters desires and an unwillingness to intrude into a state headquarters bailiwick:

> There are no restrictions imposed by the Director of Selective Service upon the release or publication of lists of names of registrants nor upon the time such lists may be made available for publication. In the absence of any restriction imposed by a State Director of Selective Service upon the local boards under his jurisdiction such local boards may publish such lists of registrants as they in their discretion may deem appropriate.

In other words, national headquarters is telling local boards that they may publish names of men selected for induction, unless they have been told not to by their respective state headquarters.

In spite of all the mailings that the national headquarters sends out, state headquarters and local boards may not receive timely information. Indeed, when national headquarters makes a public announcement of consequence, the press may be informed before either state headquarters or local boards. The result is that some board members complain that, like their neighbors, they must depend on the local newspapers to find out what is happening. The directions of the System are also often quite general and leave much to the interpretation and discretion of state headquarters and local boards. While this can and does lead to substantial variation in performance, it is also true that this may be functional for the organization. When boards can read what they want to into a directive they may be more agreeable and less likely to resist it. An observation recently made by Harold Guetzkow is to the point here: "Because ambiguous messages are open to multiple interpretations, meanings more agreeable to the receiver may be attached. Although at times ambiguity results in slippage between sender and receiver, such slippage also may promote consensus and agreement, which have important value for organizational activity."[9] Of course, what may be functional or advantageous in an organizational context may not appear constructive in a larger context.

The main thrusts of the System's efforts to counteract the centrifugal forces that it faces consist of promotion of a distinctive organizational ideology and a personal loyalty to the Director. Organizational employment of ideology and justification has often been noted by social scientists. Philip Selznick has made this point clearly in his book on the TVA: "Among the many and pressing responsibilities of leadership, there arises the need to develop a *Weltanschauung,* a general view of the organization's position and role among its own contemporaries. For organizations are not unlike personalities: the search for stability and meaning, for security, is unremitting."[10] Daniel Katz and Robert Kahn make much the same point when they remark that the values of a system, its ideology, may provide a justification for the activities and functions of the system.[11] Selective Service, however, has developed its internal ideology well beyond other organizations studied; it, more than many organizations, may be in particular need of justification, both for the benefit of a potentially uneasy membership and for the benefit of a potentially doubting public. The problem may be to convince both members and the public that what is being done is both right and necessary. (In contrast a hospital or a school may not need an elaborate justifying ideology since what such organizations do is generally accepted.)[12]

Beyond justifying the organization, an ideology may also help secure

[9] Harold Guetzkow, "Communications in Organizations," in James G. March, *Handbook of Organizations* (Chicago: Rand McNally, 1965), p. 557.

[10] Philip Selznick, *TVA and the Grass Roots* (Berkeley: University of California Press, 1949; the quotation is from Harper Torchbook ed., 1966), p. 47.

[11] Daniel Katz and Robert K. Kahn, *The Social Psychology of Organizations* (New York: John Wiley & Sons, 1966), pp. 51–52.

[12] On this point see Anthony Downs, *Inside Bureaucracy* (Boston: Little, Brown, 1967). Downs points out that bureaus for which "communication and consensus play crucial roles have the greatest incentive to develop and use ideologies," p. 245. His chapter on "Bureaucratic Ideologies" is insightful.

conformity and loyalty. Selective Service in particular may have to rely on ideology to obtain conformity and loyalty since there is so little else it can rely on. Amitai Etzioni has suggested that organizations can be differentiated along the lines of their compliance or authority structure.[13] Some organizations are coercive, others utilitarian, and still others normative. With regard to its members, as opposed to its registrants, Selective Service is surely a normative organization. It does not pay its board members and certainly cannot coerce them. It must therefore rely on normative appeals and the manipulation of symbols to obtain the behavior it requires. In its ideology it must emphasize personal commitment to the organization if it is to counteract the disintegrative forces in the organization.

In its stress upon ideological justification and promotion of personal loyalty to the director, Selective Service is unrelenting. The chief vehicle is the monthly newsletter entitled *Selective Service,* which is mailed from Washington to every employee, board member and other participants. In every issue the Director has a personally signed column which by turns justifies, exhorts, and directs. The System is justified in several ways. As the following representative selections show,[14] it is viewed as necessary to the strength and survival of the nation; military service is a right, an obligation, and beneficial in any event:

> It has been my observation that most of the American people have an image of the Selective Service System as a necessity to insure survival of all.

> Military service is a privilege and an obligation of free men in a democratic form of government. It follows that the induction of a registrant is not, and cannot be, a punishment.

> Armed forces can contribute to the development of youth.

> Any survey of governmental agencies possessing capabilities of training, especially in consciousness of individual responsibility, would place the Armed Forces high on the list.

Nor do board members merely draft men. By deferring others they protect the national interest and encourage enlistments. They act, above all, with fairness, justice, and in the best interests of the nation:

[13] Etzioni has made this point in *A Comparative Analysis of Complex Organizations* (Glencoe, Ill.: The Free Press, 1961) and in *Modern Organizations* (Englewood Cliffs, N.J.: Prentice-Hall, 1964).

[14] The quotations from the newsletter are not individually cited, but all come from issues appearing between January 1965 and December 1966. Any issue will yield illustrations of the System's ideology.

Education has been considered a process which increases the value of a citizen to this nation.

Deferment is not for the convenience of the individual registrant, although the Nation's interest may at times coincide with the registrant's desires.

The numbers who have enlisted from the examined and accepted pool illustrate the major dependence of the recruiting service on the Selective Service System.

The Selective Service System earned through a quarter of a century a reputation of fairness, knowledgeability, and effectiveness in operation.

The principles of decentralization of authority, local autonomy, and participation of the Governor in each state have created an image of the Selective Service System that creates confidence in Congress, which has been a large factor in the extension of the Selective Service law, each successive extension being accomplished with less opposition.

Direction and exhortation also appear regularly in the Director's column, occasionally in the form of a eulogy of a deceased member whose performance is set forth as an example for others:

The personnel of the Selective Service System has adapted well to the everchanging winds of events. Their problem now is to remain alert to the degree of readiness required to be prepared to pursue our present course, to reduce our procurement for the service, or to increase these numbers to some degree or substantially.

There will be a change in the nature of the decisions; more discretion will be required.

Local Board members have the knowledge, the experience, and the common sense to make sound judgments. They will make them, remembering that our regulations are adequate.

It must remain clear always that it is the Selective Service System, through its local boards, which determines classifications.

Besides conveying the values of the System to the members of the organization the newsletter is used also to give members of the system factual information and to tell them about each other. Space is taken up with lists of official notices issued during the month, articles on current problems, information about manpower calls, and figures depicting the current classification picture. Special events or activities (for example training meetings being held for Reserve officers) may also be publicized. The newsletter contains much material dealing with the personnel of the System, material best described by the title to a column that began appearing in June 1966: "The Human Interest Stories of People Who Make Up the Heart and Sinew of the Selective Service System." Awards given to members of the System and their visits to national headquarters are duly reported. Particular local boards may rate a story for one reason or another and occasionally an exemplary registrant (one who overcomes obstacles and hardships to register) will gain attention. In general, a homey-folksy air pervades the newsletter and it is easy to conclude that it tries to give the impression that Selective Service is rather a close-knit family.

The newsletter also makes a point of telling members of the System about the Director. In 24 issues of the newsletter, from January 1965 to December 1966, there were 22 articles focused on General Hershey, independent of his signed column. Several of the articles dealt with Hershey giving or approving awards to System personnel and others dealt with Hershey receiving awards. Several articles showed Hershey giving information to various Congressional committees and other articles provided general information about his activities and opinion. Articles were complemented by pictures: General Hershey appeared in almost half of the 26 pictures printed in 16 consecutive issues. In his columns, he expresses convictions which are likely to be shared by board members:

> Patriotism, belief in our country, standards of integrity, and respect for the religion of others, have not been superseded by education. If they have, it is the wrong kind of education.

> It is a hope supported by some reasonable expectancy that the changing international situation will cause our public to demand more responsible conduct by our registrants and less liberality by our courts toward those failing to perform their obligations.

> It weakens the nation when dissent is within legal limits and can be but a termite gnawing at the foundation of government when defying the laws.

> Some would turn over to computers the task of fairness and of uniformity, depending more on card punchers than dedicated, unpaid local board members.

The strength of the personal loyalties effectively developed through this and other routes is evident in interviews with board members. There seems little reason to doubt that the Director has made up in personal influence for some of his lack of formal coercive capacity. Amitai Etzioni has phrased the same observation in these terms: "Power used by an organization to control its participants derives either from specific positions or from personal qualities. Personal power is almost always indentitive power, it is based on the manipulation of symbols and it serves to generate commitment to the persons who command it."[15] Hierarchial power is of little use when it comes to local board members—they are volunteers. State Directors are appointed by the Governor and other employees are either appointed by the State Director or are covered by civil service. Since General Hershey's position thus has little coercive power, personal power is required if he is to influence the behavior of other members of the System and counteract the many centrifugal forces.

The foregoing analysis of integrative measures shows that national headquarters has taken at least some steps to counteract the System's disintegrative forces. The grass-roots structure and ethos, for example, may be to some extent counteracted by attempts to portray the organization as a single close-knit body and by attempts to get members to identify with the Director. National headquarters does issue regulations and general guidelines. But perhaps persuaded by its own rhetoric, and in effect a victim of the System's emphasis on decentralization, national headquarters has not done a great deal to counteract disintegration. In this it contrasts starkly with an organization like the Forest Service, of which Kaufman writes: "The Forest Service has made decentralization its cardinal principle of organization structure, the heart and core of its 'administrative philosophy.' "[16] But Kaufman also describes the number of measures that have been taken to neutralize the risks of decentralization. Detailed rules, preformed decisions, official diaries, reports, inspections, transfers—all these techniques and more are used to keep Forest Rangers acting predictably and according to requirements.[17] Virtually none of these techniques is used by Selective Service national headquarters; it does not in any meaningful sense supervise, control, or review the actions of state headquarters and their local boards. Uniform action is not a goal[18] and national headquarters has not

---

[15] Amitai Etzioni, "Organizational Control Structure," in March, *op. cit.*, p. 659.

[16] Herbert Kaufman, *The Forest Ranger* (Baltimore: Johns Hopkins Press, 1960), p. 83. See also Part I for a discussion of "Tendencies Toward Fragmentation."

[17] Part II of Kaufman's book is entitled "Techniques of Integration," and contains a detailed analysis of the measures taken by the Forest Service to ensure that the Forest Rangers behave uniformly and predictably.

[18] General Hershey regularly takes the position that uniformity is impossible. For example, in testimony before the Senate Armed Services Committee he said: "Well, in the first place, of course, uniformity is something that everybody talks about and nobody knows what they are talking about when they say it. I don't want to be critical but that is a fact. And we have it no place in public life. I don't want to be tried by the judicial

developed performance standards or systematically collected the data required to measure and evaluate either system performance as a whole or the performance of various units. And, of course, there has been no systematic comparison of the performance of different units. Directions are issued and in effect forgotten. What are the criteria that different boards have used in granting deferments? How consistent are the state headquarters in their interpretations and instructions? How much variation is there? These are questions that national headquarters did not find it important to answer, at least until after the National Advisory Commission on Selective Service reported its findings.[19]

III. THE ROLE OF THE STATE HEADQUARTERS

Despite the lack of direction from the top, some State Directors of Selective Service have tried quite actively within their own state systems to counteract the centrifugal forces at work, and have brought a semblance of uniformity and predictability to their own organizations. This statement is supported both by National Advisory Commission findings[20] and by what we have learned of the operation of Selective Service in Wisconsin. In some states, of which Wisconsin is one, the State Director is aware of the disintegrative forces in the System and has taken such steps as are available to him to counteract them. A State Director is clearly limited in his actions by the overall system structure, regulations, and norms, but within these constraints he may if he chooses try to control his organization. What tactics are available? The case of Wisconsin offers some illustrations.

First, the Director takes a personal interest in appointments to the

---

courts of the United States, but if anyone feels that there is a uniformity in the decisions of the courts of the United States, even with all the decision of the courts of the United States, even with all of their decisions published and everything else in the world done, it just doesn't exist, for two or three reasons.

"One is that we have the tendency to look at two people 19 years of age, and we take one and we don't take another and somebody says that isn't uniform. Well, uniformity has nothing to do with it. Their cases are entirely different. I have looked at thousands, maybe tens of thousands, probably hundreds of thousands of files, and I have never seen two alike."

[19] In the *President's Commission Report,* see especially Sections III, IV, and VI of the Appendix. These sections deal, respectively, with local board, appeal board, and state headquarters variability.

[20] The National Advisory Commission found that while in some states there was high variability among boards in jurisdictions with similar socioeconomic characteristics, in other states there was low variability among boards in similar jurisdictions. See the evidence in Chapter 4.

compensated staff of the state system as well as an interest in appointments to local and appeal boards. Officers at state headquarters, selected from among military Reserve officers with mobilization assignments in Selective Service, have been personally (and to all appearances carefully) chosen by the Director. In addition to these officers and other state headquarters personnel the compensated staff includes six state auditors and the local and appeal board clerks. The auditors, who might more accurately be called field supervisors and personal representatives of the State Director, are civil service employees and most have served as clerks before being appointed auditors by state headquarters. The auditors in turn are responsible for the selection of local board clerks from civil service lists and are responsible for their supervision and training.

Local board members are initially selected in a variety of ways that are detailed in the next chapter, but every appointment must go through the Director's office and be approved by him before it goes to the Governor for recommendation to the President. If a proposed board member does not fit the State Director's image of a proper board member he will be rejected. Board members must be respected citizens of their communities, men likely to instill confidence in those who know them or come in contact with them, dependable, and generally representative of their community. If the State Director thinks that one more American Legionnaire, or one more farmer, or one more city man is one too many for a particular board, that could mean rejection of a proposed member.

The goal of the Director is to get board members who will do what he thinks ought to be done. Perhaps more accurately his aim is to get board members who without being told (he recognizes that they are relatively autonomous volunteers) will act in ways he thinks proper. If the state System is viewed as a coalition with a number of members or participants the importance of recruiting is emphasized.[21] Careful recruitment is one way to prevent conflict within the coalition, a way to protect against sharp disagreement among the members on preferences and goals, a way to hold the coalition together. It is important here to remember that the State Director has few resources with which to bargain in order to resolve conflicts; he must therefore do all he can to prevent them. The most

[21] Cyert and March in *A Behavioral Theory of a Firm* (Englewood Cliffs: Prentice-Hall, 1963) suggest (p. 27) viewing the organization as a coalition in order to emphasize (1) that it may be composed of diverse individuals and groups with diverse goals and (2) that organizational goals are the product of bargaining. Since a State Selective Service Director has few resources with which to bargain it would seem to be in his interest to limit the diversity of his organization unless he is content to let each local board do what it wants, rather than what he wants done.

important thing a State Director can do then is select board members who will want to make the System work. It is not too much to say that if the organization is going to function it must be because most of the members think it ought to.

Important as it is, careful recruitment is not all that is important; recruits cannot be forgotten. Socializing men into the organization and motivating them to remain are also important.[22] Socialization is perhaps most important when recruitment is unselective, and heterogeneous personnel are drawn in. It is less important when recruiting is selective and personnel who already have the characteristics of existing organization members are recruited. Because this is the case with local board members, not a great deal of effort need be devoted by state headquarters to their socialization: new members are mainly introduced to the organization by their senior colleagues on their respective boards. Board members are rarely if ever brought to state headquarters and almost never meet with members of other boards.

More attention, however, is paid to motivation. Through the use of psychic or nonmaterial rewards the State Director tries to bind the local board members to the System. The state staff takes every opportunity to boost the egos of local board members, they are protected and defended from criticism, the sacrifice their job entails is emphasized, and so is the importance of their work. (Here clearly the state staff is acting in accordance with System norms.) In communications with board members the state staff emphasizes that it cannot decide individual cases, and that the final decision is in the hands of board members. But here there is a problem. As with the members of any coalition, volunteer board members may threaten to withdraw whenever they cease to get what they want, so the State Director must see that they get what they want—a sense of doing something that is important and challenging, a sense of self-importance perhaps, a sense of independence. But not only must board members get what they want; national policy must also be carried out. These two demands must be continually balanced.

State headquarters staff officers, as we have said, are drawn from an earmarked military reserve which is required to complete correspondence courses relevant to Selective Service and military manpower procurement and every year must serve a two-week period of active duty in a state headquarters. Recruiting staff officers from this source as the State Director

---

[22] A useful treatment of organization socialization is Chap. 5, "Making the Organization Man," in Caplow, *Principles of Organization* (New York: Harcourt, Brace & World, 1964) p. 62.

does means that he gets men who in a sense are already part of the System. Local clerks, however, must be socialized after recruitment. They are mainly trained by the auditor or field supervisor responsible for their jurisdiction. During training they are visited frequently to ensure that they are following proper procedures and to allow them to ask any questions they may have. As they become experienced they will be visited less frequently, but they will not be forgotten. All clerks whether new or experienced are periodically brought to state headquarters for training sessions. Here they are briefed on current problems by staff officers and they get a chance to talk to each other; they meet both in formal sessions and in informal gatherings. These various activities have the effect of making the clerks into a relatively cohesive group loyal to the organization and the State Director.

A supplementary route to understanding of the role of state headquarters in the operation of the System and its relation with local boards is through examination of the communications process in the state system.[23] The primary communication links run between state headquarters and the local board clerks, but an important back-up system runs from headquarters through the auditors to the clerks. It is important to note that direct communication between state headquarters staff and local board members themselves is rare; usually headquarters communicates with the board through its clerk. But occasionally there is direct communication between state headquarters staff officers and local board members. If a board is uncertain about a new policy it may request the State Director or a member of his staff to come to a board meeting to explain matters. Or, if a board appears to be acting contrary to state headquarters wishes, a headquarters representative may attend a board meeting. But these examples make an important point—direct communication between state headquarters and local board members is exceptional, not routine. (It is indeed so exceptional that some board members say that they do not hear directly from state headquarters as frequently as they would like to.) In general it is the clerk to whom board members turn for information. Members apply law, regulations, and facts to particular cases; but they learn their law, regulations, and indeed on occasion their facts from the clerk.

[23] For discussions of communications in organizations see, among other sources, Katz and Kahn, *op. cit.*, Chap. 9, Peter Blau and W. Richard Scott, *Formal Organizations* (San Francisco: Chandler, 1962), Chap. 5, Harold Guetzkow, "Communications in Organizations," in March, *op. cit.*, and William V. Haney, "Serial Communication in Organizations," in Sidney Mailick and Edward H. Van Ness (eds.), *Concepts and Issues in Administrative Behavior* (Englewood Cliffs: Prentice-Hall, 1962), pp. 150–65.

In the field the clerk is, in effect, the sender and receiver of all communications with state headquarters, but in state headquarters the identity of the sender or receiver depends on the content of the message. General instructions and interpretations go out over the signature of the State Director himself. Matters of administration—need for more space, more file cabinets, more help—are handled by the Executive Officer. Another member of the staff handles calls for men and the transportation of registrants to Armed Forces Examining and Induction Stations. Other matters are handled by other staff officers.

It should be emphasized that communication between state headquarters and local clerks is very much a two-way affair. Headquarters is in frequent touch with the clerks, but the clerk also frequently initiates contacts with headquarters. Some of the communication back and forth is regularized and predictable. A monthly call for men goes to the board (clerk) and the clerk sends monthly reports to state headquarters. A summary of each board meeting (minutes of action) which records what cases were considered and what disposition was made of each is forwarded as is a report listing the number of men in each classification. There is also much ad hoc communication, from headquarters to clerks with specific instructions and interpretations and from clerks to headquarters with requests for help on particular problems. The clerk is also expected to report any unusual action taken by a local board or any action that she thinks is questionable so that state headquarters will be prepared for possible complaints. Much of the communication in both directions is formal and written, but much is also ad hoc and oral. Clerks do not hesitate to phone state headquarters for advice on urgent questions and, as we have said, they are periodically brought to headquarters for briefing sessions.

Another element in the process of communication between state headquarters and local boards is the management of the appeals system in the state. Unlike the practice in many states where appealed cases and files go directly from local boards to appeal boards and back again, appealed cases in Wisconsin go through the state headquarters on their way to and from appeal boards. Acting as relay provides state headquarters with an additional opportunity to learn what local boards are doing and what kinds of actions are being appealed. Naturally it can learn which boards are most frequently challenged and it can learn which boards are rarely challenged, and it may learn whether boards are conforming to directives or deviating from them.

The auditors in the state system have been mentioned in our discussion of communication, but their most important role is inspection. During a visit to local board offices and inspection of the records the auditor can detect deviation from established practices (on the part of both clerk and board), ascertain the reasons for it, and in many cases suggest corrective action. Perhaps a rule or new directive was misinterpreted or its intent was not understood; the auditor can set matters straight. Perhaps a clerk has become lax in record keeping or answering mail. The auditor can report the fact and suggest appropriate action. To be sure there are some things an auditor cannot do. If a board has decided to stop deferring schoolteachers or takes a negative approach to conscientious objectors there is little an auditor can do even though his experience suggests the action is unwise. But he can report the trend of board activity to state headquarters and perhaps suggest that a visit by a headquarters staff officer to the board would be appropriate.

The broad scope of the auditor's job is succinctly summarized in the words of one of the auditors:

> I supervise the offices, hire the clerks, train them, supervise and direct them. I see to the physical equipment and office space. I investigate and sign up new local board members for nomination by the Governor. I work with local board members, carry policy to them and mediate disputes that arise in the board and between the board and registrants.
>
> Every two years I have to audit every board in my area; the state rule is that every board be audited at least every two years. I go over the records to see how many are in each classification and see that state and local records agree. I have to see that every registrant is accounted for and that the files are documented. But I get to see the boards at least every four months and some much oftener. How often depends largely on the clerk, whether she is an experienced dependable girl or a new one with little experience. On a typical visit I go through the file of pending cases, check the I-A file and check any critical files—such as the CO's. And I may check a certain group. Right now I am checking I-D classifications.

The auditors meet together four or five times a year to discuss policies and problems. Whenever state headquarters officers are in the field they see auditors as well as clerks and board members, and occasionally an auditor may work in state headquarters for a week or so at a time. The auditor is also required to make a weekly written report to state headquarters that indicates what he has found in his visits to local boards.

In effect, the auditors extend the eyes and ears of the State Director; without them he would be blind to much that goes on in his organization. The desires of headquarters can be misinterpreted or ignored in the field; events in the field can be misreported or ignored in messages to headquarters. But the auditor can reinforce the desires of headquarters, can check on compliance, suggest corrections, and report conditions. Even with the auditors, however (and the Wisconsin State Director devotes more resources to inspection than most other State Directors), the Director is at best an executive with one arm tied behind his back. He may direct local clerks and other compensated staff; after all he controls their grade and salary. But he can only recruit local board members carefully and then keep them informed and content.

The National Commission finding that Wisconsin is a "low variability state" supports the conclusion that the State Director has done what he could with some success. It is difficult to think of more that might have been done given the present structure and norms of the System. But we would emphasize that there are State Directors who, because of particular definitions of their responsibilities, have done much less, have been less concerned with recruiting, have given their boards less information, and have paid less attention to inspection. We describe Wisconsin as an example of how a state system may work, not as an example of a typical state. National headquarters allows the State Directors so much leeway that it might be hard to find a typical state system. It would indeed not be inaccurate to say that there are in fact 56 Selective Service Systems—one in each state.

Chapter 3

"LITTLE GROUPS OF NEIGHBORS": LOCAL BOARDS AND COMMUNITY CONTROL STRUCTURES

The structure, ideology, and operating characteristics of the Selective Service System are all shaped by the organization's paramount commitment to decision-making through decentralized, autonomous units. Local boards, limited in public visibility but high in impact, are thus the key to understanding the System. They are the First Principle from which all else has been designed; they are the System's most unique feature, and its only point of contact with registrants and public; in short, local boards are both its strength and its principal weakness. This chapter and the next seek to answer two vital questions about local boards: What sorts of men are drawn from their local communities to serve on these nearly 4,100 local boards, and what are the implications of their existence for the organization and for the publics which are affected?

These questions are critical for understanding the System's internal operations and for assessment of its interaction with its environment. Beyond such immediate purposes, however, lies the prospect that we may gain some insight into the reasons for the organization's apparent insulation from forces making for change and some basis in data for evaluating the problems and opportunities inherent in the idea of citizen participation in government. The latter point requires some elaboration.

Supporters of citizen participation have seen it as a route toward several goals. To some, it is a means of democratizing bureaucracy—of assuring that citizen preferences will receive consideration along with technical expertise and efficiency in use of resources when the organization

54

seeks to implement policy. To others, citizen participation is both essential to the attainment of certain policy goals and vital for the purpose of engaging the citizen, heightening his commitment and sense of participation in the functions of government. Among others, Richard Goodwin has strongly advocated citizen participation and decentralized responsibility; terming the idea "practical and politically realistic" and "the decisive issue of the 1970s," he insisted in 1967 not only that all three of these goals were attainable but that broadly employed citizen participation with these purposes in mind was mandatory to the attainment of governmental ends in contemporary America.[1]

Such enthusiastic advocates—and Goodwin is only one of several—seldom pause to identify problems of implementation. This chapter and the next raise two major issues concerning citizen participation. First, which citizens are to serve as participants in decisions which apply national standards and policies to the circumstances of the local situation? Local elites or their representatives? Representatives of affected publics, or of the general public? If the latter, how will the consent and support of established local elites be gained and held? Second, what is to be the manner of the citizen's participation? Is he to be admitted into a policy-shaping role? If so, can the organization sufficiently employ its technical expertise to fully discharge the tasks of national policy confided to it? If the citizen is to be kept from a policy-making role in order to assure the attainment of organization goals, is not his participation merely involvement, with the ultimate effect of extracting from him a consent he might otherwise not have given willingly? Data describing the Selective Service local boards suggest that there are serious problems in designing participatory arrangements which can realize the goals that are so optimistically stated by the advocates of various forms of "participatory democracy."

Selective Service, of course, did not place a high priority on the goals of citizen participation, and therefore its failure to attain such goals—it can be argued—cannot be charged to inherent difficulties in the principle itself. But this is just the point we seek to make: citizen participation is a means of attaining a variety of ends, some of them conflicting with the benevolent aspirations of its advocates, and this is precisely why care must be taken to face up to its problems before setting out to carry participation into effect. The architects and founders of Selective Service were willing to pay almost any price for local acquiescence in conscription, and it appears that the price

---

[1] Richard N. Goodwin, "The Changing Shape of American Politics," *Commentary* (June 1967).

was high. Administration was conferred upon the states' National Guards and local political structures, together with a policy role for local decision-makers which left the national organization practically without capacity to assert any but the broadest outlines of policy. The price was probably not as high as similar action would be for other national instrumentalities, however, because the tasks of Selective Service are less specific: the System fulfills its mission by producing a specified number of men at the induction stations, but it is immaterial to the System which or what kinds of men the local units order for induction. By not asking such questions, the System can take advantage of its more general task assignment and accommodate itself to a complete policy-making role at the local level more readily than might other organizations. Acknowledging such special factors in the case of Selective Service, there is still much insight to be gained into the problems of citizen participation by careful analysis of its experience. When the data have been reviewed, comparisons with the experience of other participatory organizations can be employed to deepen our perspective.

One other preliminary consideration should be borne in mind. We know from a series of voting studies stretching from the earliest days of panel and survey research to the present that electoral activity is characteristic chiefly of the middle and upper classes.[2] Voting, campaign activity, and financial contributions—indeed, every measure of participation developed in these studies—decline among lower classes as compared to the upper classes. Measurement of other forms of political participation, such as voluntary association membership, attendance at local political meetings, use of media for acquiring political information—at both the national and community levels—show similar patterns.[3] Participation in public affairs is a middle class characteristic. Our focus in interpreting the data which follow, then, should be on such matters as the extent rather than the fact of lower class exclusion, on which particular segments of the middle class are represented on local boards, and on the extent of the distance between local boards and the control structures of their jurisdictions. Selective Service, after all, entered local-level America hurriedly in 1940, under circumstances which eliminated practically every consideration except its need for men; it was only partially reconstructed in 1948, so an intimate contact with local elites is to be anticipated. What is crucial is the extent to which present practices of themselves foster such a relationship, and what degree of

---

[2] Angus Campbell et al., The American Voter (New York: John Wiley & Sons, 1960).

[3] See, for example, the compilation of such evidence in Lester W. Milbrath, Political Participation (Chicago: Rand McNally, 1965), Chap. 5.

detachment may be maintained under varying circumstances. These are the kinds of considerations which will enable us to identify the lessons flowing from the experience of Selective Service and to make maximum use of the data involved.

I. THE MAKEUP OF LOCAL BOARDS

The System declares that local boards are "little groups of neighbors on whom is placed the responsibility to determine who is to serve the nation in the armed forces and who is to serve in industry, agriculture and other deferred classifications."[4] Table 3.1 summarizes some of the basic character- istics of the 16,638 males who were serving on local boards in October 1966. Nearly half were over 60, and a similar proportion had served for ten or more years on their boards.[5] Almost two thirds of all board members were veterans; a few (3 percent of all board members) were Korean War vet- erans, but one in three had his service experience in World War I. The net result of this age pattern is that, on the average, each local board will include three veterans (one of whom will be a veteran of World War I), and that at least one board member will be over 70; only one board member will be under age 50.

The educational level of board members is comparatively high. Only 12 percent of the male population over age 25 had four or more years of college in 1960, according to the Census Bureau, while over 30 percent of the board members had this much education. The educational level of board members varies sharply between urban and rural areas, however, with college degrees held by almost twice as many board members in urban areas as in rural areas. Less than half of the 9,532 board members in nonmetropolitan areas had been to college at all, and less than a quarter of them held degrees.

Only 1.3 percent of board members were Negroes in 1966, as compared to about 11 percent of the total U.S. male population. Four southern states with high proportions of Negroes in their populations had no Negro board members, and others had only a few; underrepresentation also was the case in Northern cities with concentrations of Negroes in their populations. In New York City, for example, 3.3 percent of board members were Negro,

---

[4] See the prepared testimony of General Hershey in *Hearings before the Subcommittee on Independent Offices of the Committee on Appropriations*, U.S. House of Representa- tives (89th Cong., 2nd Sess.), Part I, p. 19.

[5] These and the remainder of the data reported in the ensuing four paragraphs are drawn from the *President's Commission Report*, Sec. I, pp. 73–81.

TABLE 3.1. PERCENTAGE DISTRIBUTION
OF LOCAL BOARD MEMBERS BY AGE, LONGEVITY,
AND EDUCATION, 1966

Age	Percentage
30–39	5%
40–49	24
50–59	26
60–69	23
70 & over	22
	100%
	(N = 16,535)

Length of Service	Percentage
Less than 10 yrs.	53%
10–19 yrs.	39
20 yrs. & over	8
	100%
	(N = 16,440)

Education	Percentage
Less than high school graduate	15%
High school graduate	31
Some college	22
College graduate or more	32
	100%
	(N = 15,644)

Source: National Advisory Commission on Selective Service, *Who Serves When Not All Serve?* Data recomputed from Appendix, Sec. I, pp. 73–74.

as compared to 14 percent of the population. Not one state had a proportion of Negro board members comparable to the Negro proportion of the male population, with the exception of Delaware, which had five Negro board members out of a total of 26, yielding a proportion of 19 percent against a Negro proportion in the population of 14 percent.

The concept of a local board being a "little group of neighbors" in the representative sense is brought into question by the data presented above, but data concerning the occupations of board members raise even stronger doubts. Table 3.2 presents a comparison of the occupations of local board members with those of employed males in selected states and in the United States as a whole. Two occupational groups dominate membership on local boards: professionals, and proprietors-managers-officials. Three and one-half

OF EMPLOYED MALES, IN SELECTED STATES AND THE UNITED STATES

	No. of Board Members	Professionals Lawyers	Professionals Total	Proprietors, Managers, Officials	Farmers, Farm Managers & Workers	White-Collar (Sales, Clerical)	Blue-Collar	N.A.
United States								
Board members	15,738	7 %	21%	34%	16%	14%	9%	6%
Employed males		0.5	10	10	8	14	53	5
California								
Board members	618	10	28	35	7	18	7	5
Employed males		0.4	14	12	5	15	49	5
Florida								
Board members	340	9	19	44	9	17	5	6
Employed males		0.5	10	14	6	14	50	6
Massachusetts								
Board members	614	16	32	28	1	13	15	11
Employed males		0.6	13	10	1	16	5o	5
New York City								
Board members	454	31	43	33	—	16	5	3
Employed males		0.9	11	12	—	20	50	7
North Dakota								
Board members	213	0	6	17	61	12	5	—
Employed males		0.3	7	11	42	10	29	1
Pennsylvania								
Board members	662	10	36	37	2	15	8	2
Employed males		0.4	10	9	3	15	59	4
Washington								
Board members	125	9	36	41	3	10	3	6
Employed males		0.4	12	12	7	13	53	3

Source: National Advisory Commission on Selective Service, *Who Serves When Not All Serve?*, Appendix, Sec. I, pp. 76–79. Data on state male populations from U.S. Bureau of the Census, *Census of Population, General Social and Economic Characteristics* (Table 57) and *Detailed Characteristics* (Table 121), 1960.

times as many proprietors, managers, and officials serve on local boards as appear in the male population as a whole, while professionals and farmers are represented by double the proportion of their incidence in the employed male population. This overrepresentation occurs at the expense of blue-collar workers, who make up six times as large a share of the employed males as they do of local board members.

Table 3.2 also permits an assessment of the variation in occupational backgrounds of board members in several states. The occupations represented bear little relationship to the occupational characteristics of the population. Instead, they appear to be the result of the interaction of state headquarters policies with the general political ethos of the state. The states are distinguishable by the particular occupational groups from which they draw their board members, some emphasizing proprietors and managers much more than others (Florida and Pennsylvania, for example), and some including much larger shares of the blue-collar population than others (Massachusetts vs. Washington, for example). Some jurisdictions have apparently established a policy of seeking lawyers as members of local boards, such as New York City (31 percent of all board members), while others, such as North Dakota (not a single lawyer serves) have decided to exclude them completely.[6] We doubt that these patterns emerge by chance, and we speculate that they may be rooted in the recruitment policies employed. No systematic data are available concerning the practices employed in the 56 state or comparable jurisdictions, but scattered reports indicate that each state's approach to recruitment is distinctive. In all cases, nominations are forwarded by the Governor to the President for appointment, but the means by which the Governor arrives at his recommendation differ between states and within states over time. In California, for example, nominations are made by Superior Court judges and forwarded to the

---

[6] A touch of irony appears in the case of those jurisdictions which emphasize lawyers as board members. The Selective Service statute prohibits registrants from having an attorney with them at personal appearances before their local boards, and in response to Congressional suggestions that counsel be permitted, General Hershey has said: "The selective service classification procedure involves a determination with respect to the availability of a registrant for military service, made by a board composed of the young man's neighbors who are generally without legal training. . . . It has been our feeling through the years that procedures should be kept so simple that it would not be necessary to have legal counsel at a hearing . . ." (*Hearings,* p. 9987). Both the board and the registrant, of course, have access to the assigned Government Appeal Agent for legal advice. But if the classification procedure is so simple that the registrant needs no attorney in his lone appearance, it is difficult to see how a state may consistently conclude that its much more experienced board members should as a matter of policy include one or more attorneys.

Governor; in Texas, the recommendation is usually made by a local committee which includes a county judge; in some other states, the recommendation appears to come to the State Director of Selective Service through the local political party organizations.

This brief profile of board members indicates that they are as a group unrepresentative. In terms of sex, race, age, military experience, education, and occupation, board members are not representative of the general population, and they are not in this respect "little groups of neighbors." But no body of decision-makers is representative in the sense of reproducing characteristics of the population. The United States Congress, for example, is made up almost entirely of members drawn from the same two occupational groups which dominate local boards, and the average state legislature or city council is only slightly less so. Such other bodies are, however, representative in other ways: they are elected by their constituents in elections in which all may take part, they are accountable to those same constituents at the next election, and their actions are visible and subject to public review and criticism. Local board members, on the other hand, are appointed, unaccountable, and low in visibility and public oversight; in addition (and perhaps unfortunately) the System has billed them as "little groups of neighbors" who are said to embody their communities. Under such conditions, concern for representativeness may be more than mere political naïvete.

In any event, these data led the National Commission on Selective Service to recommend changes in the eligibility standards and nomination practices in order to render local boards more representative, particularly regarding sex, age, and race.[7] The Commission urged that:

1. Boards should represent all elements of the public in their jurisdictions.
2. Terms of service should be set at five years.
3. A maximum retirement age should be established.
4. The President's power to appoint members should not be limited to those nominated by the governors of the states.
5. Women should be eligible to serve.

Congressional action in 1967 accomplished only the elimination of the sex limitation. Congress did provide that no board member should serve longer

[7] The Commission's intent apparently was to refer to the representativeness of the board members with respect to the entire community, not to the public actually "served," i.e. the registrants. Issues of citizen participation were not part of the Commission's deliberations. The recommendations are found on page 5 of the *President's Commission Report*.

than 25 years, or after he reached the age of 75—amendments with fairly limited effects. No action was taken with regard to the racial composition of boards or the presidential alternative appointment power which was intended to implement it. The changes, in short, were minimal and unlikely to work major changes in the character of national membership just described.

Further understanding of the reasons for—and implications of—this form of unrepresentativeness was gained from our field study in Wisconsin. In particular, we sought to explore two major aspects: the problem of age, longevity, and low turnover among board members, and the nature of the recruitment processes as they operate to produce the distinctive makeup of the local boards. In part at least, our findings indicate that participatory organizations have special problems in each area.

Age, Longevity, and Low Turnover

Wisconsin board members closely parallel the national averages in age, length of service, and education.[8] In an effort to identify those who had come to adulthood in World War II or after, we set up special age groupings, as shown in Table 3.3. In Wisconsin as in the nation, local board members are distinguished by being older than members of other similar

TABLE 3.3. AGE OF LOCAL BOARD MEMBERS
COMPARED TO STATE POPULATION AND
SELECTED OTHER OFFICIALS

	Local Board Questionnaire Respondents, 1966	Wisconsin State Population, 1960[a]	Wisconsin State Legislators, 1966[b]
Age Group			
30–44	16%	38%	30%
45–59	40	33	41
60–69	18	17	21
70 & over	26	12	8
	100%	100%	100%
	(N = 314)	(N = 960,305)	(N = 117)

[a] Source: U.S. Census, 1960 (male population over 30 used as base).

[b] Source: Wisconsin Blue Book, 1966 (N = 117 because 16 members were rejected because under 30 or age unknown).

[8] The data on Wisconsin local board members are drawn from a mail questionnaire which elicited 81 percent response from the 384 board members of the state.

bodies of decision-makers or the state population. More than twice as many are over 60 as are under 45; 26 percent are over age 70, and, on the average, a local board is likely to have two retired (post–65) men for every member whose experience dates from World War II or after. We found that men stay on as local board members long after they have retired from their jobs, and some have even come on to their local boards at that point in life.

The problems created for the organization by superannuation and longevity are particularly visible in Wisconsin, where board members have served longer than the national averages. A total of 57 percent of board members have served over ten years, as compared to 47 percent nationally; more than 10 percent have served over twenty years. Agreement is general throughout the System that superannuation is a problem, but it is not easily handled in this kind of organization. For one thing, board members do not find the job a taxing one except when draft calls are high, and almost to a man they say that they find high satisfaction in doing a job that has to be done and which they think is an important one. For many, this service seems to be a means of participating in something that extends beyond their own community and gaining a sense of integration with the nation as a whole. They are proud of their job and some feel that they gain status from being on the local board. Only rarely do board members willingly retire under these circumstances.

For several reasons, the System may find it desirable to encourage long service from board members. It is not always easy to recruit new members, and there is some uncertainty involved in adding new men. Another reason for encouraging longevity is that it makes the job of the State Director simpler. Low turnover increases the chances that he can predict the actions and reactions of board members whom he has come to know, and that he will have experienced men on the job in times of stress. Paradoxical as it may seem, it may be that encouraging long service is a way of coping with the stress of new pressures on the System. A further reason for promoting longevity is defensive: it avoids conflicts within the organization. The state headquarters cannot easily detach men who have volunteered their time for several years and who find that attending board meetings gives them a sense of usefulness in their later years. Headquarters is faced with legally autonomous volunteers whose cooperation is essential, and within this delicate relationship it must accomplish its work through tactful suggestion and invitation. It cannot issue orders, and it may be just too costly in terms of continued working relationships to precipitate a confrontation with respect to an elderly member.

In any event, Selective Service has made long service into an organizational norm, operative from national headquarters down to the local board level. General Hershey began as Director in 1941, and there are State Directors and local board members who have held their posts as long. No retirement age had been applicable in the System until the amendments of 1967, even though fixed maximums had long been in effect elsewhere in the federal service. The System has also done much to reward long service: ceremonies and awards regularly take place for men who have reached the levels of 10, 15, 20, and 25 years of service. State Directors make every effort to prevent resignations by board members, to the point where they may, as in Wisconsin, go to considerable lengths to avoid creating the impression of challenging the judgments of local boards.

Some of these characteristics may be the result of not having prescribed terms of service in the original appointments of board members. But at least in part they appear to be endemic to participatory organizations which depend upon volunteers for decision-making, in the sense that the organization must avoid conflict with them where possible. And the costs of such concern for the sensitivities of the volunteer may be high. Low turnover can lead to an inflexible organization and excessive support for the status quo. It may result in local board members becoming increasingly less representative of their communities: men appointed in the early 1950s (to say nothing of the 1940s) may not reflect the area's population patterns in the 1960s or 1970s. And low turnover which yields an organization disproportionately composed of elderly men may mean commensurate dependence on the local board clerk. Even if the newly imposed retirement age were lowered and/or terms of service were limited, the System's need to maintain the cooperation of its decision-making volunteers would probably lead it to acquiesce in if not actively promote long service, low turnover, and consequent superannuation.

Recruitment

Recruitment practices contribute to this age and longevity situation, but their greatest importance flows from the impact they have in structuring the occupational and sociopolitical composition of local boards. Again, the participatory nature of the organization appears to be partly responsible for some of the special features of the recruitment processes, and thus some of the resulting distinctiveness of board composition may be a general characteristic of citizen participation in government.

Wisconsin board members proved to be better educated than the average of the state population in about the same proportions as the national averages would suggest. Where 22 percent of board members held college degrees, for example, only 8 percent of the male population over 25 had reached that level; only 19 percent of board members had failed to complete high school, as compared to 61 percent of the male population. Wisconsin board members were slightly higher than the national averages in proportions of nonveterans (38 percent), although veterans still appear among board members in proportions which far exceed their proportion of the male population. Seventeen percent of all board members were veterans of World War I, as compared to 4 percent who were veterans of the Korean War. Racial minority groups (Negroes and Indians) are represented on each of the four boards where the minority group constitutes 10 percent of the population, and in rough proportion to that group's share of the population.

Our analysis of occupational groupings was shaped by the actual distribution, and a comparison with the male labor force is presented in Table 3.4. When classified in this way, a profile of a relatively narrow

TABLE 3.4. OCCUPATIONAL DISTRIBUTION OF WISCONSIN LOCAL BOARD MEMBERS, COMPARED WITH EMPLOYED MALES IN STATE POPULATION, 1966

	Local Board Members	State Population[b]
Occupation[a]		
Managerial, sales	26%	16%
Self-employed, not professional	13	3
Professional		7
Lawyers	4	
Others	2	
Government	10	9
Post Office employees	8	
Education	4	1
Agriculture	23	14
Blue-collar workers	10	47
	100%	97%
	(N = 314)	(N = 1,011,324)

[a] Occupational categories were shaped to fit the pattern found, e.g., post office employees are listed separately because of the relatively high number found.

[b] Proportions reconstructed from U.S. Bureau of Census, *Census of Populations, Detailed Characteristics*, Table 121, 1960 (3% not reported).

segment of the middle class emerges. The character of the businesses is distinctive, although the proportion of businessmen involved is generally consistent with studies of influentials in other communities.[9] There are few bankers or managers of larger corporate enterprises among local board members, most of whose businesses are of the local retail or service variety. The kinds of occupations represented are those in which the man is associated more or less permanently with a particular site, such as a farm, a store, or a family enterprise; few board members are drawn from the more mobile occupations. The relatively frequent presence of post office employees is the product of a particular form of recruitment practices: from time to time, field personnel of the State Selective Service System are obliged to locate new board members, and when they know of no candidates in the county or area they turn to the local postmasters for help—and on occasion find it at the first stop.

The recruitment of new board members in Wisconsin has been left to the State Director by a succession of Governors, Republican and Democratic, with the single exception of one two-year term in which a Democratic Governor made his own appointments. The actual processes by which the State Director secures nominees for recommendation to the Governor usually follow one of two basic forms. The first is selection by the local board itself, perhaps limited by local understandings about geographic or occupational representation on the board. The retiring member, another member, or the Chairman may secure the approval of the other members for a man he proposes and send the name on to the state headquarters for forwarding to the Governor. Of our 314 respondents, 39 percent said they had been recruited by the local board and 43 percent said the newest member had been recruited by the local board.

Thus many boards are essentially self-perpetuating bodies. The second major selection pattern is through the efforts of state headquarters personnel, usually the field staff known as auditors. Occasionally, a local board

[9] One trans-community study which may serve as the closest comparative work here is William V. D'antonio, William H. Form, Charles P. Loomis, and Eugene Erickson, "Institutional and Occupational Representations in Eleven Community Influence Systems," *American Sociological Review*, XXVI (June 1961), 440–46. This study compares six southwestern United States cities with data from Floyd Hunter's *Community Power Structure* (Chapel Hill: University of North Carolina Press, 1954) and Delbert C. Miller, "Industry and Community Power Structure: A Comparative Study of an English and American City," *American Sociological Review*, XXIII (February 1958), 9–15. It finds businessmen dominant in all cities, with financiers and manufacturers well represented. It also notes the presence of newspaper editors along with lawyers, but our inquiry did not turn up a single member of any communications industry.

may decline to choose a replacement and fairly often it has difficulty finding one; sometimes the state headquarters may seek to change the character of the board. In these cases, the auditor—normally responsible for liaison with local board clerks and oversight of their operations—takes on the additional job of locating a new member. The standard sources are the local postmaster, service and veterans' organizations, and prominent local people. In some instances, officers of the state headquarters themselves may take part in the selection process. Eleven percent of our respondents said they had been chosen by the state headquarters in some way, and 32 percent said the most recent addition had been selected in this way. Many board members are unaware of the manner in which they or others were selected, so that these totals are rough approximations only.

Recruitment processes vary over time within local boards, they vary between boards, and, as we have noted, between states. National headquarters exercises no guidance, and the resulting diversity of practices is testimony to the variety of political traditions in the nation. One constant feature, however, appears to be the propensity to rely on the remaining board members to locate replacements—and thus some degree of self-perpetuating character may be characteristic of the citizen participation organization. The new man will be integrated into the organization more effectively if he is socially acceptable to the established members. The costs (in reduced cooperation from his volunteers) to the State Director of imposing his own choice upon board members are such that it will not normally be undertaken unless considered essential. And, in all probability, the state headquarters feels that it can rely on board members to select "right-thinking" men like themselves to carry on the functions of the organization as well as or better than men it might be able to locate in the community. Only very determined action over sustained periods would enable the state or national levels to disengage selection processes from local control. Some further sense of the implications of these characteristics of citizen participation organizations will be gained from the analysis in the following section.

II. LOCAL BOARDS AND COMMUNITY CONTROL STRUCTURES

The data just reviewed indicated that board members are drawn from the locally situated entrepreneurial segment of the middle class. By means of three other measures—their number of associational memberships, their level of activity in community affairs, and their public officeholding experience—we find that board members must also be recognized as at least "community influentials," and perhaps more frankly as extensions of established local control structures.

Board members are quite remarkable joiners: Table 3.5 indicates that more than half belong to three or more voluntary associations, and there were as many board members who belonged to seven or more groups as belonged to none. This seems the more noteworthy in the light of national data indicating that a very small proportion of adults in the United States

TABLE 3.5. NUMBER AND TYPES OF GROUPS
TO WHICH BOARD MEMBERS BELONG

	BOARD MEMBERS WHO BELONG
A. *Number*	
None	5%
1 or 2	37
3 or 4	35
5 or more	25
	100%
	(N = 314)

	BOARD MEMBERS WHO BELONG	U.S. ADULT POPULATION WITH SUCH MEMBERSHIP, 1960*
B. *Types*		
Church and religious	60%	19%
Veterans	46	6
Fraternal	39	13
Business and professional	35	8
Community service	21	14
Service clubs	17	—
Social and recreational	13	13
Farm	12	3
Unions	3	15

Total exceeds 100% due to multiple memberships.

* National data are drawn from Gabriel Almond and Sidney Verba, *The Civic Culture* (Princeton: Princeton University Press, 1963), p. 247. Entry under our "community service" combines their "charitable" and "civic-political" categories. All other categories in the two studies bore the same labels.

belonged to two or more associations.[10] Board members belong to geographically localized groups which normally participate in the daily public life of their communities. Absent from their lists are reform groups, unorthodox associations, minority group organizations, and unions.

The intensity of the actual engagement of these board members in such community activities as are indicated by the foregoing is demonstrated in Table 3.6. As was suggested by the group membership data, they are highly involved, particularly in church and religious affairs. Other public service activities follow closely, but politics is lowest on the list. More board members say "never active" in this category than in any other, and fewer say "fairly often active" than in any other. This is consistent with the state headquarters' attempt to avoid selecting as board members persons who are identified with partisan political activity and to discourage continuation as a board member when a man begins to engage in partisan affairs.

The fact that board members are generally not active in partisan politics does not mean that they are not part of the sociopolitically dominant elements in their communities. It means only that they are drawn from the less visible, less openly political strata which nevertheless may be effectively part of the local control structure. A total of two thirds of all board

[10] While authorities differ, it seems clear that a number of memberships held by these board members is distinctive. A comparison of recent studies of the U.S. adult population is illustrative:

	Wisconsin Local Board Members, 1966	(1) U.S. Adults, 1960	(2) U.S. Adults, 1954	(3) U.S. Adults, 1955
Number of Memberships				
None	5%	43%	45%	64%
One	14	25	30	20
Two	22	14	16	9
Three or more	60	18	9	7
	100%	100%	100%	100%
	(N = 314)	(N = 970)	(N = 2000)	(N = 2379)

Sources: (1) Gabriel Almond and Sidney Verba, *The Civic Culture* (Princeton: Princeton University Press, 1963), p. 264; (2) an American Institute of Public Opinion survey; (3) a National Opinion Research Center survey, both of which are reported in Murray Hausknecht, *The Joiners: A Sociological Description of Voluntary Association Membership in the United States* (New York: Bedminster Press, 1962), p. 23. While local board members are all males, and males show slightly higher incidence of associational memberships, this can hardly account for these totals.

TABLE 3.6. COMMUNITY ACTIVITY OF LOCAL BOARD MEMBERS

Activity[a]	"Fairly Often Active"	"Occasion- ally Active"	"Never Active"	No Response[b]	
Youth work	36%	27%	14%	23%	(100%)
Charity work	43	35	7	15	(100%)
Church affairs	58	23	7	12	(100%)
Service clubs	32	20	26	22	(100%)
Politics	21	26	32	21	(100%)
Business and professional	26	23	29	22	(100%)
					(N = 314)

[a] Higher percentages in regard to activity than to memberships (Table 3.4) are assumed to be the result of the cumulative nature of the question which is the basis of this table and the fact that some of these activities would not require group membership.

[b] "No Response" category was created to distinguish these respondents from the more convincing affirmative indications in the "Never Active" column, but lack of response is assumed to be the equivalent of "never" in most instances.

members have held some form of public office during their lives, a proportion which clearly indicates their elite status. Table 3.7 presents the data concerning the public office experience of these board members. For the most part, their offices are appointive or "good government" offices, and only a small proportion have held a partisan office. The recruitment processes thus appear to have emphasized "the right kind of people"—civically active merchants and managers—who are heavily engaged in all but the partisan politics of the community.

Not unexpectedly, rural board members differ from urban board members, not only in background characteristics but also in degree of involvement in their communities. The urban boards reflect the industrial occupations of their areas, and also have more attorneys and other professionals, higher levels of education, and a number of Negroes proportionate to Negro population in the major city of the state. Outside the highly urbanized areas there is not much difference in board members' backgrounds. And there is little difference between urban and rural boards as to the age of members, length of service, veteran status, or number of organizational memberships.

There are some noticeable differences between urban and rural board members which are not quite so predictable as those so far noted. For example, although there are no differences in the number of groups to which members belong, nor any differences in the proportion who are

TABLE 3.7. PUBLIC OFFICES HELD BY
LOCAL BOARD MEMBERS

Type of Office Held[a]	PERCENTAGE OF ALL RE-SPONDENTS WHO RE-PORT HAVING HELD THIS OFFICE
County Board	13%
City Council	9
School Board	26
Appointive Boards	18
Post Office	6
Civil Service	5
Other public office[b]	32
	(N = 314)

[a] Of these offices, only the County Board is normally filled by partisan election, and in several counties there is no contest in the final election. City Councils are normally nonpartisan, although this may be only form in some cases. School Boards, while elective, are almost always nonpartisan in fact as well as form.

[b] These positions include a wide variety of employment, such as County Veteran's Service Officer, public utility engineer, state employees, local government employees, and so on.

veterans, there is a distinctly greater tendency for rural members to be members of veterans' organizations. Only 28 percent of urban board members are members of veterans' groups while twice that many, or 57 percent, of rural members are; we surmise that the local veterans' groups are instruments of recruitment in rural areas but not in the urban areas, although veteran status is still thought desirable in the urban areas.

Another decisive difference may be noted in regard to the public office experience of board members. Rural board members are much more likely to have held public office, perhaps reflecting the relatively larger number of offices available to capable and active members of the rural community. This effect is particularly noticeable in regard to that office most commonly held by draft board members, the School Board. There are relatively many urban residents per available School Board office, of course, and this is part of the explanation for low public office experience. The urban board member may be as active, but his activity probably takes more of a youth work, charity, or professional orientation and less of a community governing form. Aside from these differences, the profile of board membership shows considerable homogeneity across the state, as might well be expected under a self-perpetuating and standardized recruiting system. And yet, because of the availability of public office opportunities, the image of elite membership (in the sense of governance) is stronger in the case of rural board members. The complexity of the urban environment means that urban members are not only more removed from their registrants but also from participation in public affairs. They have different backgrounds of associational activity and more professional backgrounds to draw on for what we hypothesize to be a more impersonal, standardized application of deferment and classification policies. They are not representatives of the major influentials in the large city; they are anonymous, and for the most part invisible.

In looking at rural local boards and their environment, one is repeatedly struck by the parallels with the conditions described in *Small Town in Mass Society*.[11] One finds, as in Springdale, the self-image of neighborliness and self-reliance, the domination of the community by small businessmen, and unrecognized but pervasive politics. As might be expected in a Springdale, in some rural areas the draft has been converted (perhaps unconsciously) into part of the social control system of the community. Some board members will promptly and enthusiastically reclassify a man when a change in his status coincides with a violation of community norms—as in the case of failure to keep up child support payments, leaving one's family, or not getting a job in timely fashion.

The very low turnover of board members and their large number of other localized activities and memberships leads to the impression that draft boards become the permanent property of lifetime residents who represent the community control structure; thus local elites become, in effect, the managers of the national government's function. Once again we are reminded of Springdale, this time in regard to the way in which local political forces took over the making and administration of agricultural policy. The takeover in the urban area is more personalized and less in the name of the locally dominant, and therefore less systematic, but it is nonetheless a removal from national hands.

III. SOME IMPLICATIONS OF LOCAL BOARD MEMBERSHIP PATTERNS

We shall explore the decision-making processes and effects of local boards within the System in the next chapter, but some implications of these membership patterns are already visible. We must ask now whether what

---

[11] Arthur J. Vidich and Joseph Bensman, *Small Town in Mass Society* (Garden City, N.Y.: Doubleday, 1958), esp. Chap. 2 and pp. 111, 136, 104. The extent of the conflict between assumption and reality is emphasized in Maurice Stein, *The Eclipse of Community* (Princeton: Princeton University Press, 1960), pp. 289–94.

may be seen as penetration of the organization by local elites is attributable to the System's origins, policies, or other unique features, or whether it may be a characteristic of citizen participation organizations generally.

When local boards were first staffed, state National Guard personnel had to find board members in each local area quickly; in many cases, they did so by asking officials of local governments to suggest names of men who might serve. Where choices were made by county clerks, judges, or committees of local officeholders, it seems likely that local boards were made up of men who, if not representative of local social and political structures, were at least known by and acceptable to them. The revival of the System in 1948 drew heavily on those same men who had served in World War II, and recruitment (as we have seen) has tended to be on a self-perpetuating basis throughout the history of the organization. But there have been nearly three decades in which the System's recruitment processes might have evolved into more independent form, with the result that new members might be less closely related to local elite structures than those who joined the organization in the past. If this were the case, the implication would be that the System had freed itself somewhat from the local elite management which was mandated by the exigencies of its early needs. Nothing in our evidence, however, suggests that this has happened. So far as we are able to tell, men coming to local board membership in the last few years have not been distinguishable (in terms of associational memberships or public office experience) from those of the past. We conclude that the System's recruitment practices have continued to draw in men essentially representative of local elites; in other words, the dominance of local elites is not simply the product of the System's origins, but of its present recruitment policies as well.

Nor are these membership patterns necessarily characteristic of citizen participation organizations generally. Perhaps the closest governmental analogue to local draft boards is provided by the case of the local rationing boards of the Office of Price Administration during World War II.[12] Although these boards were set up very rapidly by agencies of the states in a time of grave national emergency (and in an era when concern for representativeness was probably lower than it is now), the data in Table 3.8 suggest (so far as they are comparable) that the OPA of the mid-1940s was more representative of the public at large than the Selective Service System of the late 1960s.

These data and classifications are very limited, and as such they typify

[12] The data in this and the ensuing two paragraphs are drawn from Emmett S. Redford, *Field Administration of Wartime Rationing* (Washington: Government Printing Office, 1947), pp. 18–22, 91–110.

TABLE 3.8. OCCUPATIONS OF MEMBERS OF LOCAL BOARDS, OPA 1944 AND SELECTIVE SERVICE 1966

	OPA	SELECTIVE SERVICE
Occupational Grouping		
Professionals	16%	21%
(Lawyers)	(5)	(7)
Proprietors, Managers, Officials	32	34
Farmers	13	16
Blue-collar	12	9
White-collar	No Entry	14
Housewives	27	0

Source: OPA data from Emmett S. Redford, *Field Administration of Wartime Rationing* (Washington: Government Printing Office, 1947), p. 102 (reports data on 70,901 members). Selective Service data: see Table 3.2.

the state of our knowledge about citizen participation in national government activities. The local rationing boards of OPA are, however, to some extent comparable to local draft boards, in that they were made up of citizen volunteers whose decisions affected their fellow citizens in the name of the national government. Although established by the state and local authorities at the request of the national government, the OPA rationing boards gradually came under increasing federal control as the war went on and additional tasks were conferred upon them. National standards for inclusiveness of membership were asserted on at least two occasions in order to achieve membership first for labor and then for Negroes. By August 1944, there were almost 600 Negroes serving on local rationing boards, about 1 percent of the total membership, a figure which compares favorably with the 213 Negroes (1.3 percent of the total) serving on local draft boards in 1966. The absence of any entry comparable to our "white-collar" category is probably due to the broad inclusiveness with which OPA treated the category of proprietors and managers; this was broken down into "merchant" types, and we may assume that some proportion of this category corresponds to the sales and clerical personnel who make up our white-collar group. Within the ranks of professionals, OPA engaged the services of clergy (2 percent of total membership), doctors (2 percent), and educators (7 percent), all of which are only negligibly represented among the professionals on local draft boards. Selective Service has instead leaned toward inclusion of men working for government (5 percent of the total membership, and the next largest group among professionals after lawyers), such as

County Agents or County Veterans' Service Officers or other local officials. The character of the OPA data permits us to say this much: as far as local board membership is concerned, there is nothing foreordained or inevitable about the patterns of participation within Selective Service. The particular social backgrounds which characterize local draft boards must be in part due to the System's toleration if not encouragement of a restrictive set of recruitment and membership standards at the state and local level. Under conditions of wartime emergency, when much was accepted in the name of the war effort, and in an era when the nation saw fewer dimensions to equality and representativeness, the OPA engaged a broader segment of the citizenry in the discharge of equally onerous but much more visible responsibilities. We conclude that the character of membership on local draft boards is at least as much the product of the operations of the Selective Service System as it is the result of environmental or other conditions external to the organization.

This view gains some support also from comparison with an organization having citizen volunteers who are recruited on a completely undirected and self-perpetuating basis, the National Foundation for Infantile Paralysis.[13] Although this is a nongovernmental organization, it is national in character and operates through 3,000 local chapters, which provide services and programs the year round and serve as the nuclei of the annual March of Dimes fund drive. Only incomplete data are available regarding the social and economic characteristics of the chapter volunteers, but fragmentary reports suggest close parallels with Selective Service. There were some 12,000 members of the 3,000 local chapters in the 1950s, most of whom were active in other civic or community type activities. The chapters were small, self-perpetuating bodies which secured new members chiefly through invitation. Perhaps for this reason, they were seen as homogeneous membership groups who "spoke the same language" even though they had different occupations. The chapters were originally organized in 1935 around the postmasters of the local communities in order to share in the promotion of fund-raising from the President's Birthday Ball. They drew on locally situated business people rather than socially prominent or professionally high status persons in order to promote maximum engagement with and continuity of the organization. The similarities in makeup and recruitment practices (essentially self-perpetuating) between the two organizations suggests that, in the absence of standards or direction from above, participatory

---

[13] This account relies on David L. Sills, *The Volunteers: Means and Ends in a National Organization* (Glencoe: The Free Press, 1957).

organizations may to a considerable extent reflect patterns of community activism.

We come then to the speculation that the efforts of the national directorship of OPA played an important part in opening local rationing boards to a relatively broad segment of the local publics. Undirected and self-perpetuating recruitment opens the organization chiefly to community activists. Selective Service, however, seems to have gone beyond merely accepting the results of self-perpetuating recruitment practices to the point where it affirmatively seeks men who are in effect representatives of local elites. This appears to be the import of its recruitment processes, and its emphasis on local board autonomy, on the need to avoid standardization, and on the "little groups of neighbors" concept. For better or for worse—a judgment we cannot make until all the evidence has been examined—Selective Service has purchased the willing cooperation of local dominants by conferring management of its vital local functions upon their nominees and representatives.

We should make clear that we do not envision Selective Service as subject to the calculated actions of unified local elites. Board members are, after all, a special segment of local elites: they are not necessarily in contact with or receiving orders from a body of decision-makers who are a "power elite" in the community. Instead, they are merely one part of a network of similar nonpartisan offices with overlapping occupancies distributed among active members of the communities in which they are located. We know of no studies which compare the background characteristics of appointive, nonpartisan officeholders such as these across several communities, but the existing literature suggests obliquely that the explanation for the appearance of these men lies in some configuration of the opportunity patterns, social structure, political cultures, and motivational contexts within their communities.[14] They really could not be members of a single unified elite, if only because their constituencies diffuse their contacts: rural board members act for units of county size, while their elite status is most often with reference to a town within the county; urban board members act with reference to subcity areas which have no particular identity or integrity such as to

---

[14] For a distinction between the motivations of those who seek elective office and those who seek appointive office, in this case the school board, see Rufus P. Browning and Herbert Jacob, "Power Motivation and the Political Personality," *The Public Opinion Quarterly*, XXVIII (Spring 1964), 75–90, esp. 86–87. Linton C. Freeman, Warner Bloomberg, Jr., Stephen P. Koff, Morris H. Sunshine, and Thomas J. Fararo, *Local Community Leadership* (Syracuse University, University College Paper No. 15, 1960), make some useful suggestions about the relationship between societal complexity and specialization of leadership in several communities.

generate an independent elite—nor are they necessarily subject to the city's dominant groups.

What board members share with the controlling elements within their jurisdictions is the same occupational and class status and values; they participate in similar activities and may be personally known to several leading figures in the community; over time, they become known to key employers and major activists within the community. What develops, as we shall see in Chapter 7, is a sharing of responsibility for the successful operation of requisite functions which promotes confidence particularly among the members of the influential and active groups. Those local men who are most significant politically are most likely to know and trust the draft board members, while those who are not intimately involved in local affairs do not know board members; but they realize that board members travel in a different milieu, and therefore they may distrust them. Selective Service's particular brand of elitism appears to lead to these results and to some others which require the further analysis of the next chapter.

Chapter 4

LOCAL BOARDS IN ACTION

The operating characteristics of local boards—and their impact on registrants—represent the other half of the "little groups of neighbors" image. Not unexpectedly, the Selective Service System has provided chiefly this generalized and favorable self-characterization,[1] and has not sought to verify it.[2] There are few studies extant which examine the role of part-time volunteers in *any* formal organization, and fewer still which assess relations between an organization and those affected by it. As Blau and Scott have pointed out, "One serious shortcoming of most organizational research, including our own, is that there is no investigation of the publics related to the organization. Studies of organizations have not included within the scope of their analysis the publics directly in contact with the organization, let alone the larger public which is potentially in contact."[3] Such issues, however, are critical to our understanding of Selective Service. We seek in this chapter to understand the role of the board member within the organization, and particularly the extent of integration of a citizen-participant into the organization; and we shall also begin to detail the attitudes toward local boards of their most immediate public, the registrants.

---

[1] On the matter of organizational self-idealization, see Francis E. Rourke, *Secrecy and Publicity* (Baltimore: The Johns Hopkins Press, 1961) and Erving Goffman, *The Presentation of Self in Everyday Life* (Garden City, N.Y.: Doubleday Anchor Books, 1959).

[2] On the difficulty of withholding information once collected see Walter Rosenbaum, "The Burning of the Farm Population Estimates," Inter-University Case Program 3 (Indianapolis: Bobbs-Merrill, 1965).

[3] Peter M. Blau and W. Richard Scott, *Formal Organizations* (San Francisco: Chandler, 1962), p. 74.

I. THE LOCAL BOARD AT WORK

In most localities the office of the local board is open daily, and the clerk who is present registers young men turning 18, provides information to registrants and other interested parties, reviews the files of registrants, and prepares the agenda for the regular meetings of the local board. Actions for which the local board members themselves are responsible, namely classification of registrants and ordering registrants to report for induction, are carried out only during meetings of the board. The frequency and length of these meetings is governed by the number of eligible age men registered with the board, the level of induction calls, and the number of requests which the board receives for personal appearances by registrants. In 1966 the average board in Wisconsin with from three to six thousand eligible age registrants and with three or four registrants appearing personally at each meeting, met once a month for three or four hours and handled 250 to 300 classifications per meeting.

From 10 to 30 percent of the cases up for classification at any one meeting may involve major issues of discretionary judgment, and consume a substantial amount of time. But the majority of the cases are nondiscretionary and routine (a man has entered the service, or been discharged, or becomes 35, or is rejected at an Armed Forces Examining Station). These cases the clerk will have set aside before a meeting so that the board can dispose of them quickly. Often the board will only spot check her recommendations. But except for these routine classifications, board members we have interviewed in Wisconsin maintain that they are the sources of judgment; they insist that they decide the discretionary cases, and clerks support this position.[4] Indeed it was apparent that board members were jealous of their decision-making powers and some of them had on occasion cautioned clerks about intruding into the preserve of board members. But the clerk does set the agenda for meetings, and she is an important source of

---

[4] This finding, of course, does not necessarily contradict Congressman Chet Holifield's statement: "the bulk of the work, I would say 85 percent of the work of screening and classifying these boys, [is] done by civil service clerks, and then when the board meets that night, they hand it to them, and they run through them and the clerk says 'this bunch on the top ought to go,' so they sign their names and they go." *Hearings*, p. 9764. In fact it is clear from our research that if on a given night 85 percent of the cases to be acted on are nondiscretionary the board will not spend much time with them; it may well spend a lot of time with the remaining 15 percent. The real problem is whether clerks decide the discretionary cases. They do not in Wisconsin, but this may well vary among states.

information about changing regulations and practices. These are not insignificant functions, and they clearly are sources of influence.

The materials available to the local boards which they may use in making decisions are of two types. First, there is material furnished by the System: regulations, operations bulletins, State Directors' advices, and a variety of other series emanate from both national and state headquarters. Many board members admit frankly that they do not try to keep up with these documents and that they rely on the clerk to keep them informed. ("After all, that's what she's paid to do.") Second, there is material furnished by the individual registrant. Every man must, when he registers, fill out a personal data questionnaire and if he is a conscientious objector he must fill out an additional questionnaire. In addition to the questionnaire(s) a registrant may submit to the local board such letters or documents as he wishes to or are required by the local board. A registrant wanting an occupational deferment would normally submit letters from his employer, a college student would submit evidence of college attendance, a prospective father must submit a doctor's statement, a Reservist must submit a DD Form 44 (proof of service), and so on. The board may, if it chooses, actively seek information; for example, from a welfare department in the case of a claim for hardship deferment or from a police department if a criminal record is in question. In small towns and rural areas board members may also draw upon their personal knowledge of a registrant and his family in making a decision. Lest it appear otherwise, it should be emphasized that the information at the disposal of the board is normally sketchy and in fact on occasion appeal boards have sent files back to local boards when they appear so thin as not to support *any* classification at all.

In addition to considering files, local boards may also see registrants personally.[5] Either the registrant or the board may request a personal appearance which consists of an informal question and answer session, during which the registrant is normally able to present both written and oral statements in support of his claim for a particular classification. The board may allow the registrant to be accompanied by another person (parent or employer), but legal counsel is not permitted. The number of registrants that a board personally sees depends primarily upon the number of conscientious objectors among the previous classifications, and secondar-

---

[5] Our information is based on interviews with 40 local board members but not on observation of meetings. For the account of sustained observations, see Gary Wamsley, "Local Board Behavior," in Roger Little (ed.), *Selective Service and American Society* (New York: Russell Sage, forthcoming). For another account see Calvin Trillin, "The War in Kansas," *New Yorker*, April 22, 1967, pp. 101ff. Trillin reports on a visit to Local Board No. 71 in Topeka, Kansas.

ily upon the level of grievances among other recently classified registrants. Most boards find that personal appearances are sought as a preliminary to an appeal (though it is not a necessary prerequisite), and then chiefly by those who have had guidance or advice either from an employer or a religious group.

The cases presenting the most difficult decisions for local board members are the borderline hardship cases (III-A) and occupational deferment cases (II-A and II-C). In these categories there is an absence of clear standards or requirements and there is often also a lack of relevant information. The result is that board members reach decisions in a variety of ways. It was found in a participant-observation study of local boards conducted in one urbanized area that board members were inclined to fall back on evaluations of the registrant's personal appearance or choice of words in a letter. Commenting particularly on occupational deferments, the author contrasted the criteria which board members were instructed to employ with the lack of adequate specific information concerning the nature of national needs or the occupational skills which were in short supply. The Department of Labor Critical Skills List, for example—supposedly the basis of such determinations—was not used at any meetings of the boards studied. Board members were observed to have *asked a clerk* on two occasions whether an occupation was on the list. Most clerks had heard of the list but neither they nor their boards had found reason to make use of it. Instead, decisions were based on board members' newspaper reading, individual assumptions, or private prejudices. The version of the list available to most boards was published in 1955 and had by 1965 actually been outdated by several subsequent revisions. There seems no reason to believe that this group of local boards was distinctive in its non-utilization of the national-interest criteria for deferment.[6]

The criteria available to board members regarding other discretionary deferments are not much more clearly defined. Thus, unless state headquarters takes upon itself the responsibility of providing local boards with detailed guidelines, board members are often on their own. A problem develops for the conscientious board member in these circumstances: How

[6] Wamsley, *op. cit.* The Department of Labor List of Currently Critical Occupations was rewritten in 1962 and amended in 1965. In a letter to Congressman Thomas B. Curtis dated September 12, 1966, Secretary of Labor Willard Wirtz stated, "The 'List' was reviewed by the Labor Technical Committee several times between 1962 and 1965, and since the fall of 1965 the committee has had the list under almost constant review and discussion." See pages 2085–86, 1967 House *Hearings on Extension of the Draft.* The point that suggests itself is that the boards that Wamsley talked to did not know the list had been revised; in any event it is clear that board members often pay no attention to the critical occupations list. This latter point was emphasized in February 1968 when the list was formally abandoned by the National Security Council.

can he develop or find general principles that can remove the need to make ad hoc decisions for every registrant whose case is not automatic? A study of 121 local board members in the New York area at the close of World War II found that most tended to seek out guidance early and to respond readily to even the slightest hints from above.[7] But the urban area study found that when guidance was not received, boards developed their own decision rules based on middle class values (thrift, education, morality, nativism, etc.), a "Legionnaire" outlook created by a predominance of veterans on boards, and the use of personal evaluative judgments.[8] In addition, the boards themselves come to value consistency for its own sake.

We should, of course, note that in Wisconsin the state headquarters does assume responsibility for promulgating standards and operates skillfully to standardize local board decisions as much as possible. Most notably with regard to farm deferments the state headquarters has reduced uncertainty for local board members by means of an elaborate set of methods (developed by state headquarters in conjunction with professors from the University of Wisconsin School of Agriculture) for measuring productivity on farms and allocating deferments accordingly. But even though the state headquarters tries to achieve uniformity there are still occasional instances where local boards depart from national, state, or even adjoining local board standards. Some rural boards, for example, regularly grant occupational deferments to milk tank truck drivers or cheesemakers, although neither occupation was on the critical skills list; other boards in similar farming communities do not do so. One reason for this is that local board members in rural areas are sufficiently well known that they may be informally requested by local employers to act in particular ways. Moreover, boards are authorized to permit employers to appear with registrants who are seeking occupational deferment, and many employers regularly do so. Farm organizations also frequently urge particular concerns on local boards, and school principals and superintendents try to get their teachers deferred.

The President's Commission sought in its research to measure the extent to which boards' decisional processes varied from the suggested national norms. Examiners surveyed the files of registrants in a sample of 199 local boards around the country, and the highlights of their findings indicate that the essentially arbitrary process so far described is characteristic of the System as a whole.[9] Within these 199 local boards, for example,

---

[7] Donald D. Stewart, "Local Board; the Place of Volunteers in a Bureaucratic Organization" (unpublished Ph.D. dissertation, Columbia University, 1950).

[8] Wamsley, *op. cit.*

[9] *President's Commission Report,* Appendix, Sec. III, pp. 95–106.

"about half of the registrants actually classified into II-A were in neither a critical occupation nor an essential industry as defined by the Department of Labor."

One illustration drawn from Commission data may serve to portray the two major forms of variability among local boards. Figures 4.1A and 4.1B compare the performance of local boards in two major acts of classification —originally assigning I-A classifications to new registrants and shifting men from II-S to I-A—in two groups of states. The boards were specially selected because of their socioeconomic similarities, in order to present situations where manpower characteristics would be as much alike as possible: six low-income, low educational level, rural, county boards were chosen at random in each of several states in the cotton belt and again in the corn belt.

The key finding vividly documented in the highlights presented in Figures 4.1A and 4.1B is that there are two forms of variability: variability

FIGURE 4.1.   LOCAL BOARD VARIABILITY IN ECONOMICALLY SIMILAR COUNTIES

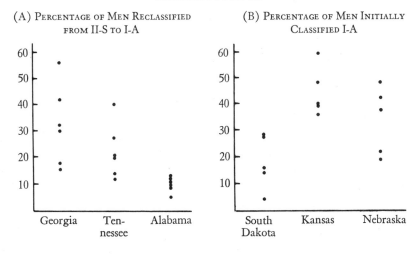

(A) Percentage of Men Reclassified from II-S to I-A

(B) Percentage of Men Initially Classified I-A

COTTON BELT STATES

Note: All boards are in areas with less than 30% urban population; $2000–$3000 income; and less than nine median years of school completed.

CORN BELT STATES

Note: All boards are in areas with less than 30% urban population; $3000–$4000 income; and between 8.5 and 10.5 median years of school completed.

Source: National Advisory Commission on Selective Service, *Who Serves When Not All Serve?* (Washington: U.S. Government Printing Office, 1967), Appendix, Section II, pp. 85–86.

within a state, between its boards; and variability *between* the boards of one state and those of others. All of the boards in Figure 4.1A, for example, are similar in socioeconomic character. But those in Tennessee vary widely, while those in Alabama are barely distinguishable, suggesting that the Alabama State Selective Service System standardizes effectively. And boards in Tennessee vary around a median which is drastically higher than that of the Alabama boards. The same is true in the corn belt states with regard to initial I-A classifications (Figure 4.1B). Purely tactical considerations on the part of individual boards might account for some of the variability in Figure 4.1A ("Classify them all I-A—that will bring in the documentation we need to justify a II-S"), but it would not explain all of the within-state variation, nor the differences between states, in Figure 4.1A, and it would not explain the variability evidenced in Figure 4.1B. The conclusion seems inescapable: local board autonomy implies both *within* state and *between* state variability, even among socioeconomically similar board jurisdictions. (The third form of variation, not identified in these figures, is that occurring between local boards with jurisdictions of differing socioeconomic makeup. We shall concentrate on this feature of Selective Service impact, which is not so much local board variability as it is differential impact of deferment policy according to jurisdictional characteristics, in Chapter 6.)

The Commission also found that some boards never reclassified men with deferments in effect, and some boards did so regularly. Registrants who had moved to another city or another state since their registration (but who always remain subject to their original board) were found to be assigned I-A classifications at consistently higher rates than similarly situated men who were still resident in the boards' jurisdictions. Boards ranged widely in the extent to which their classifications were supported by evidence in the files, with some following the suggested requirements for documentary support almost uniformly, and some having evidential support for relatively few of their actions. The Commission was not able to conduct observations of local board meetings but these data suggest that the decisional processes of boards and the criteria employed are variable and, in all probability, as individualistic as the case study descriptions would indicate.

II. LOCAL BOARDS AS PART OF THE SELECTIVE SERVICE SYSTEM

The Selective Service System has in effect reinforced the legal autonomy of local boards by refusing to become concerned about the diversity present in the system. General Hershey has consistently resisted the suggestion that clear and precise national standards be laid down for the guidance of local boards.[10] The one clear demand that is placed upon all local boards is the necessity of providing a specified number of men at the induction centers on the dates scheduled. But for any individual board and for board members generally the lack of national guidance may create difficulties. Many board members do not relish the idea of personal responsibility for the granting of deferments or selection for induction, and, as we have said, board members may seek guidance for their decision-making. In addition, unaware that they cannot apply a national policy because of its vagueness or generality, board members may try to carry out what they think they perceive in the instructions from national headquarters. Many board members think they should follow some rules.

The position of the board member is, however, ambivalent. He seeks guidance, but he is also repeatedly told that he has discretion and the System's effectiveness depends on the exercise of his independent judgment. What is more, he believes in the propriety of this principle. He derives a considerable personal satisfaction from doing a job which has to be done in the nation's interest, and he would not find it satisfying if he thought he were merely a "rubber stamp" for the policies of others. He also believes, and has evidence for, the argument that local humanizing of rigid national rules frequently has beneficial results. In short, he may seek guidance, but he values discretion. This is the dilemma of a participatory organization, from the citizen's perspective; for the organization, of course, the problem is one of permitting citizens a policymaking role but still accomplishing organizational goals.

So far we have only spoken generally of boards seeking guidance; how common is it in fact? Among other aspects of its research into local board operations the President's Commission sought to measure the contact be-

---

[10] The following exchange between Congressman Schweiker and General Hershey is illustrative:

> Mr. Schweiker: General Hershey, what is your objection to having national standards in terms of priority in deferments? Why do you not advocate that to resolve some of these inequities?
>
> General Hershey: Well, Mr. Schweiker, I suppose part of it is the fact that I don't know what people are talking about when they talk about national standards. You always find them on paper, but when you start applying them, then—for instance, people would like to take everybody born in a certain month of a certain year on a call for a certain month and the first thing you know you get so much detail that you don't get any men.
>
> Now this inequity is relative, and you get your balance sheet only from time to time, but I have never had faith that you could, from a central place, set up a detailed standard that would not handicap the local boards more than it would help them. (From *Hearings*, p. 9633.)

tween local boards and their state headquarters.[11] In questionnaires directed to all local boards and answered by the boards as units, boards were asked if they had consulted with their state headquarters about the classification of any cases during the past year, and if so how many. A full 60 percent of all boards had not consulted with their headquarters more than ten times, which suggests a substantial degree of independent decision-making or isolation, or both. Only ten percent of all boards had been in touch with headquarters on more than forty cases (an average of a little more than three per month), and most of these boards were located in metropolitan areas, where the number of registrants (and problems) tends to be highest.

Local boards were also asked if they would prefer more specific state and national directives, or whether they considered the present situation about right. Only a negligible proportion wanted *fewer* specific directives, while 46 percent wanted more in regard to occupational deferments, 40 percent in regard to student deferments, and 29 percent in regard to hardship deferments. These data are congruent with one of our observed responses to the ambiguity and complexity of the board member's problem: the search for guidance from above. Another observed solution to the problem—rigid adherence to locally established rules—may be seen from board members' responses to the question, "Do you think that local boards should be consistent in their judgments, even if it occasionally means that a registrant with a borderline claim to deferment must be denied?" Eighty-six percent of all local boards indicated agreement with that position.

The ambivalence of the board member may be explored further from our Wisconsin data. With respect to regulations and other policy statements from national and state headquarters, 60 percent of board members agreed that there should be more specific, more detailed, and less vague instructions. Only 20 percent disagreed. With respect to state headquarters personnel, 52 percent agreed that they "should provide more guidance so that local boards are not required to guess at what they should be doing," and only 26 percent disagreed. At the same time, 78 percent agreed that "the discretion which local boards have is a valuable factor in tailoring regulations to individual registrants' situations." Only 8 percent found it possible to disagree with that cornerstone principle of the System. Board members apparently want it both ways—testimony to the ambivalence of their situation. These board members also endorse the principle of rigid application of locally established rules (the same question as was asked in the Commission's study) by a margin of 68 to 13 percent. While responses to

[11] *President's Commission Report*, Appendix, Sec. VII, pp. 177–96.

the Wisconsin inquiry were obtained from individual mail questionnaires answered in the board members' homes rather than by majority vote as boards at a regular meeting, they are essentially comparable to the Commission's results. Board members on the whole want to have specific guidance and detailed rules, and they want to be consistent—but they also want to be able to depart from those rules when they see fit, and to feel that they have the capacity to depart from them whenever they feel they should.

This ambivalence, together with the natural fractiousness of volunteers operating at sometimes great distances from headquarters in widely variant settings, presents the higher echelons of the System with problems of adjustment of their own. Some states' headquarters adapt to their local boards by limiting themselves to serving as conduits for transferring information back and forth between national and local levels. When they do so, it is likely that the output will vary from board to board and the overall performance of the state's Selective Service System will show high internal variability with regard to who gets inducted and who gets deferred. In other states, varying levels of effort may be expended by state headquarters in attempting to encourage uniformity of criteria and performance by local boards. Board members do seek guidance, and if it can be provided without appearing to threaten their independence, their actions may be standardized at least within the limits set by the character of national deferment policies themselves. Too much assertiveness on the part of the state headquarters, however, would probably lead to reaction—or nonaction—by many local boards.

The task of standardizing requires subtlety and political sophistication. Fortunately for our understanding of what can be done within this type of participatory organization structure, the effort has been made in Wisconsin, and with considerable success. The political ethos of the state, which supports nonpartisan adminstration of government according to rule, concern for uniformity, and consistency, has provided an environment in which skillful administration could bring about substantial uniformity of performance. The state headquarters has acted at all levels of the System's operations within the state to achieve uniformity, from careful recruiting to personal attention to board members' sensitivities throughout their period of service, from selection and training of clerks to imbuing them with loyalties to the state headquarters, from providing many services to boards through the employment of unusual numbers of field personnel to conducting frequent and thorough inspections of board records. No single technique would have been sufficient in itself. It is only the combination of many methods tactfully and resourcefully employed that has permitted the state headquarters to accomplish its ends. We are not suggesting that the Wisconsin experience could be a model for other states in the System; it may be too personalized and dependent on local conditions. What it does demonstrate is the flexibility of the System, and the extent to which adroit adaptation can accomplish desired policy ends in harmony with real citizen participation in decision-making. Nor, even if the other states suddenly achieved the degree of standardization which has been attained in Wisconsin, would it remedy the serious problem of nonuniformity within the national System. Each state would still be uniform around an idiosyncratic state standard, and only national standards articulated and enforced can begin to standardize the System's performance across the nation.

III. LOCAL BOARD MEMBERS AS REPRESENTATIVES OF THE PUBLIC

We have already reviewed characteristics of board members with regard to age, occupation, educational attainment, and so forth. Are there differences in attitudes toward Selective Service and the task of a local board member which correspond to differences in socioeconomic characteristics? The short answer is no. More precisely there are not many striking variations in board members' opinions which are traceable to background characteristics. Certain correlations, however, as well as some of our negative findings, are directly relevant to the issue of what difference it makes who serves on local boards. We found a distinct association between the extent of board members' education and their attitudes toward deferment of college students and graduate students. Table 4.1 eliminates "don't know" responses and presents attitudes by educational attainment. Those who are themselves college graduates or who have had some graduate training are more likely to attach some degree of importance to student deferment and are less likely to be opposed to such deferments. The same pattern of attitudes exists in regard to graduate student deferment although in less decisive form.

We found another minor example of board members' "looking out for their own" in regard to agricultural deferments. Members of farm organizations were more likely to think farm deferments very important than other rural board members and even than other unorganized farmers generally. In absolute numbers there are relatively few farm deferments in the state, however, so that this could have little impact in any event.

The negative side of our findings is revealing in itself. Such factors as age, length of service, occupation, public office experience, and organiza-

TABLE 4.1. ATTITUDES TOWARD STUDENT DEFERMENT BY
EDUCATIONAL LEVEL OF LOCAL BOARD MEMBERS

	EDUCATIONAL LEVEL			
	LESS THAN HIGH SCHOOL	HIGH SCHOOL GRADUATE	SOME COLLEGE	COLLEGE GRAD. AND GRADUATE TRAINING
Attitude toward Student Deferment				
Very important	24%	23%	23%	29%
Fairly important	25	31	30	49
Should not defer	21	11	12	2
Depends	30	35	35	20
	100%	100%	100%	100%
	(N = 59)	(N = 97)	(N = 77)	(N = 66)

tional membership or activity seemed to have no systematic effect on
attitudes in the areas we have discussed. Not even veteran status, which we
had expected to correlate with stricter attitudes toward deferments, gave rise
to any clear contrast with nonveteran attitudes. Nor did those most active in
church affairs show any greater sympathy for the conscientious objector
than the inactive members; only tenths of a percentage point differences
between the two groups were visible in most categories.

The implication of these largely negative findings is that, in general,
the background which a member brings to local board service does not
carry over into clear distinctions as to his attitudes toward deferments and
other aspects of the draft. Of course, we have not probed every attitude that
may be relevant, but we have touched upon enough to lead us to this
tentative conclusion. We have noted only two minor exceptions. These
limited (though still probably important) differences in attitudes suggest
that socialization into Selective Service has proceeded to the point where
board members have developed considerable consistency of viewpoint. Perhaps, of course, they were inclined to many of the same views before they
came on their boards. Considering the nature of the recruitment processes
this possibility should not be discounted.

Our negative findings were largely repeated when we examined the
relationship between local board area variables (percent urbanized, median
income, and so on) and the attitudes of local board members. Board
members in cities did prove to be distinctly more sympathetic to conscientious objectors than were rural board members. In the urban areas,

26 percent of board members felt that it was fairly important or very important to defer conscientious objectors, while 39 percent thought they should not be deferred; in the most rural areas, only 4 percent could see it as fairly or very important, while 74 percent said they should not be deferred. Perhaps this reflects the greater experience of urban boards with such claims, but it suggests that tolerance of the unorthodox is significantly higher in the city.

We have noted some differences in attitudes of board members which seem to correlate with their backgrounds and life experiences, but for the most part we have seen homogeneity of attitude within the organization. The recruitment processes or the socialization effects of service on local boards seem to have led to the development of generally shared views toward the System and its operations. This analysis does not preclude the possibility of the existence of sharply deviant individual boards, but it does suggest that such would be an exception rather than the rule.

In some respects, however, board members hold attitudes which depart from officially promulgated interpretations within the Selective Service System. National headquarters has regularly defended the System against charges of economic bias in its deferment policies, and it has also supported the need to allow registrants to enter the Reserves or the National Guard as an alternative to the draft. Both of these arguments are vigorously championed in the Selective Service Newsletter and elsewhere. Nevertheless, when presented with the flat and perhaps challenging statement, "Registrants from wealthier families are less likely to be inducted under present policies than registrants from less favored families," board members agreed by a margin of 47 percent to 40 percent. The margin is not great, but it comes in a context of systematic argument to the contrary. In the light of our findings that deferment policies have indeed produced severe economic discrimination, perhaps we should wonder at the 40 percent who accept the official view. The absence of all economic data within Selective Service and the lack of contact with other boards may contribute to this result.

Board members also reacted with strong agreement to the statement "The Reserves and National Guard are frequently a means whereby registrants successfully avoid the draft." The margin here was 74 percent to 13 percent, one of the largest found on any question we raised. These two responses suggest that board members retain a capacity for critical judgment based on their own experience, at least as far as their experience departs from such bald interpretations issued from national headquarters. Board members keep well-informed about controversy concerning the draft, avidly following charges and actions taken in the national media. They are thus informed about public opinion, and in certain areas they have outside standards available with which to evaluate the positions taken by national headquarters.

These data may be harmonized by suggesting that board members have been socialized into acceptance of the general standards and criteria and procedures of the state System (hence the general irrelevance of background characteristics), but that they retain independent judgmental capacity against broad national headquarters' interpretations of the actions of Selective Service. Of course, it could be that background characteristics such as we employed are simply irrelevant to the mechanics of Selective Service activities, and that board members are attitudinally representative of the general public from which they depart for only three or four hours per month. The issue is a critical one, not just for the interpretation which should be placed on the data so far presented, but for the whole problem of the extent of detachment of citizen participants' views from those of the public they presumably represent. Stated another way, how much does socialization into and commitment to the goals and practices of the organization in which the citizen participates lead him to become the agent of the organization rather than of the public?

The data in this case support the initial interpretation of the last paragraph and go on to shed considerable light on this critical issue of citizen participation. Table 4.2 compares the attitudes of Wisconsin local board members on five issues of deferment policy with the views of a sample of the adult population of Wisconsin on the same issues. We may note initially that the relatively greater proportions of "depends" answers from board members probably occur because of the existence of Selective Service criteria for evaluation of cases in each category on an individual basis. Furthermore the System discourages classification by group rather than individual characteristics. The possibility that socioeconomic characteristics are simply irrelevant must be dismissed in the light of the distinctly different attitudes expressed by various occupational groupings. Such characteristics are clearly associated with attitudes in the case of the general public, but they were not in the case of local board members. We think that it is the fact of serving as a local board member, adopting the attitudes and accepting the policies of the organization, which have made the difference. In these respects, socialization has occurred.

Local board members are also attitudinally distinct from the statewide sample taken as a whole, and from each component occupational grouping.[12] (Professionals and farmers have been presented separately despite the

---

[12] The state sample has been broken down into occupational categories here because this proved to be the independent variable with the closest relationship to opinion on Selective Service issues (see Chap. 7).

TABLE 4.2. ATTITUDES TOWARD SELECTED DEFERMENT POLICIES, LOCAL BOARD MEMBERS AND GENERAL PUBLIC, WISCONSIN, 1966

	Local Board Members	General Public					
		Total	Pro-fessionals	Farmers	Proprietors, Managers, White-Collar	Blue-Collar	House-wives
College Students							
Important to defer	55%*	37%	46%	17%	43%	35%	38%
Should not defer	10	33	28	53	24	35	30
Depends	30	25	26	14	31	21	27
Graduate Students							
Important to defer	36	38	50	28	43	32	40
Should not defer	20	33	30	50	28	23	31
Depends	38	21	16	8	25	24	20
Farmers							
Important to defer	37	46	38	50	48	49	44
Should not defer	6	26	34	19	25	25	28
Depends	44	24	28	31	25	22	24
Fathers							
Important to defer	60	66	68	45	68	66	69
Should not defer	4	10	10	17	9	10	9
Depends	29	15	14	22	16	16	12
Conscientious Objectors							
Important to defer	12	13	24	6	14	9	17
Should not defer	55	68	66	69	69	78	58
Depends	24	11	8	8	12	7	15
	(N = 314)	(N = 607)	(N = 50)	(N = 36)	(N = 130)	(N = 203)	(N = 188)

* Percentages in each deferment category do not total 100% because "No Answers" have been eliminated.

Source: Wisconsin Survey Research Laboratory, clustered area probability sample of adults in Wisconsin, September 1966 (same month as mail ques-

relatively few representatives of each group, in order to demonstrate illustrative ranges between groups. Inclusion with other groups in proportions sufficient to approximate the makeup of local boards would not affect the point just made.) Once again, we have evidence that service on local boards is associated with differences in attitudes. Members support the deferment of college students, for example, in substantially greater proportions than any other group in the state sample, and at a 50 percent higher rate than the sample as a whole. On this issue, they are detached from the entire spectrum of opinion in the society.

But when the emphasis within the organization is less strong, such as in the case of graduate students, board members resemble the cross-section of the public. They were not as supportive of graduate student deferment as were professionals, nor as antipathetic as farmers. In the absence of a strong policy position on the part of the organization, the personal policy preference begins to enter, and we may speculate that it will take shape according to the makeup of the boards. The data suggest that board members are representative of the general public as well as responsive to the policies of the organization. In the deferment of fathers, which is an established Selective Service policy, board members reflect the enthusiasm of the general public for the practice. The margin between disapproval and approval in this case was 56 percent, where as for student deferment (equally a policy of the System, but less approved by the general public) the margin was only 45 percent. The "depends" category in the two cases was almost identical, and we conclude that board members are reflecting general public attitudes as well as responding to the System's position.

In the case of what appears to be strongly held and generally shared disapproval of the deferment of conscientious objectors (again a System policy, though not as strongly emphasized), board members are more closely aligned with the attitudes of the general public. Still, some withhold judgment as the System has taught them to do. The extent to which the board member holds to the organization's position appears to be the result of the intensity with which both organization and citizenry hold their views, as well as the directions in which they lead.

Thus, we have some evidence that the citizen participant represents the public and the organization both, and that the pressures on him form an equation between intensity and direction of preference and policy on the part of each. The organization does draw the citizen participant into attitudes representative not of the public but of the organization; but it probably cannot do this unless a strong and fundamental policy of the organization is at stake, and it may not be able to do it at all where the preferences of the general public (which are normally felt also by the citizen participant) run strongly in another direction. The citizen participant does bring much of the general public with him into the organization, but not so much as to threaten its important goals except when they run counter to strongly held views of the citizenry. It would be tempting to add, amen. But these data are too limited to build more than a negative conclusion, i.e. that in this situation and with careful handling it is not impossible to reach some harmony of organizational goal-attainment with policy-involved citizen participation. But this is only one limited aspect of the effects of such participation, and much more remains to be assessed.

IV. BOARDS AND THEIR REGISTRANTS

How does the participation of local citizens as board members affect their special public, the registrants? In exploring this relationship, we encounter several dimensions of the System's self-image as "little groups of neighbors." One indicator of the validity of the little groups of neighbors image might be the extent to which local board members reside in the local board area. The study by Wamsley found that fully one third of local board members did not live in their jurisdictions and only a few lived in a location that could be loosely construed as "in the area."[13] In Wisconsin, on the other hand, every local board member resides in the jurisdiction in which he functions. The former situation, of course, does not preclude the possibility that the board members "know" their areas, any more than the latter situation assures that they do. Perhaps more important, particularly in the case of urban areas, is the question of whether the area has a unity and a character that can be "known" by a board member. A geographically defined district in a city, following 1948 ward or precinct lines or based on some even less relevant boundaries, may have little socioeconomic integrity or few "needs" which board members could use as standards for classification of registrants. Indeed, in urban areas most registrants probably work elsewhere in the metropolitan area, and in every board substantial proportions of registrants have moved away; either permanently or to college or jobs elsewhere, so that knowledge of the immediate jurisdiction carries only limited returns. Nevertheless, to be valid, the concept of a "little group of neighbors" would seem to require knowledge of the area, or of the registrant (preferably of both), together with the presence of the registrant in that area.

---

[13] Wamsley, *op. cit.*

Another indicator of the validity of the "little group of neighbors" image of local boards might be the extent of contact between board members and registrants outside of the regular board meetings. Table 4.3 shows the responses of Wisconsin board members to an inquiry designed to measure this contact. Members of the large city boards are not nearly as likely to have frequent or occasional contact with registrants as are other board members. Part of the explanation could lie in the fact that the urban boards are the largest in number of registrants in the state. But the rural boards have the lowest numbers of registrants, and yet rural board members have less contact than the small town members. Possibly there are two explanations for these patterns: detachment and lack of contact are characteristic in the urban area, but outside of these areas it depends to some extent on geographic proximity and associated communication. Board members in all areas experienced greater contact the longer they had been on the board, the more local organizations they belonged to, and the more they had held public office in the community. These characteristics no doubt render them more widely known and accessible than other members, and registrants react accordingly.

The attitudes of registrants represent the other half of the "little groups of neighbors" image—for if the local boards are *perceived* as groups of neighbors it matters little whether their character as such can be documented in other ways. In connection with the Wisconsin study, 570 regis-

TABLE 4.3. BOARD MEMBERS' CONTACT WITH REGISTRANTS, WISCONSIN, 1966

	DEGREE OF URBANIZATION			
	CITY (95% URBAN)	SMALL CITY (40–70% URBAN)	SMALL TOWN (20–39% URBAN)	RURAL (BELOW 20% URBAN)
Contacts with Registrants[a]				
Frequent	3%	15%	19%	13%
Occasional	26	47	55	48
Rare, never[b]	72	37	26	39
	(N = 39)	(N = 91)	(N = 100)	(N = 84)

[a] Measured by response to question: "Some local board members frequently see registrants or get phone calls from them. Others hardly ever have contact with registrants except at board meetings. Would you say that you have contact with registrants (either in person or by phone) Rarely—Occasionally—Frequently?"

[b] Includes negligible number of nonresponses which are taken to be negative answers.

trants at the University of Wisconsin were questioned concerning their feelings toward their local boards.[14] Caution is required in the use of data obtained from students by means of mail questionnaires, particularly when other students are known to be involved in the data collection, but some perspective on registrants' views of local boards may still be afforded by such data. The most striking finding was that knowledge about local boards was very low: less than one percent of all respondents knew the number of members on their boards. Table 4.4 summarizes responses concerning basic mechanics of board operations according to the area in which the respondent was registered. Not surprisingly, Wisconsin rural and small town registrants were more likely to know the names of one or more of their board members, although the proportion with such knowledge was not high. Similar proportions of such registrants knew their clerk's name, again exceeding the urban registrants. About one third of the registrants in each group had had some form of recent contact with their boards, but the experience had little effect on their knowledge about or favorable perceptions of their boards. Those having contact with their boards were somewhat more likely to see them as important policymaking bodies within Selective Service, and they were somewhat less confident of their impartiality. They were a little less willing to leave their names with their boards, somewhat more apprehensive as to the possible effects of nonconforming behavior. There is no evidence that this is because of their experience with their local boards, of course, for it may well be that it is particularly those in jeopardy who are likely to have had contact with their boards and to be more apprehensive about them.

Two items in the table attempt to measure respondents' perceptions of the cooperativeness of the board and the utility of the information available there. For most respondents, the actual basis of judgment in these respects was their original registration (which requires a personal visit) and transactions involved in completing the Selective Service questionnaire and establishing student status, either of which could be done entirely by mail. Once again, the closer contact of rural and small town registrants seems to be reflected in more favorable perceptions of the clerk's interest and the helpfulness of the information gained. Almost one third of *all* registrants, however, rate the clerk as uninterested in their cases, and even more consider the board's information as not helpful—hardly an endorsement of

[14] These data were collected by James Rowen in connection with a senior thesis written under the supervision of one of the authors at the University of Wisconsin and have kindly been made available by him. The data have been re-analyzed for the purposes to which they are now put.

TABLE 4.4. ATTITUDES TOWARD LOCAL BOARDS,
UNIVERSITY OF WISCONSIN STUDENTS,
BY SIZE OF AREA OF REGISTRATION, 1966

	WISCONSIN SMALL TOWNS AND RURAL AREAS (BELOW 60% URBAN)	WISCONSIN CITIES (OVER 60% URBAN)	NEW YORK METROPOLITAN AREA
Knowledge of board members' names:			
None	70%	98%	93%
One	15	2	2
Two	5	0	0
No answer	10	0	5
	100	100	100
	(N = 328)	(N = 89)	(N = 118)
Evaluation of clerks' attitude:			
Very interested	7%	1%	2%
Interested	34	25	20
Uninterested	22	25	25
Very uninterested	4	10	8
No answer	23	39	45
	100	100	100
	(N = 328)	(N = 89)	(N = 118)
Helpfulness of local board information:			
Helpful and very helpful	51%	46%	37%
Not very helpful, not helpful at all	38	45	46
No answer	11	9	17
	100	100	100
	(N = 328)	(N = 89)	(N = 118)
Willingness to leave name with local board when seeking information:			
Very willing	20%	13%	9%
Willing	48	55	39
Unwilling	21	18	32
Very unwilling	7	12	20
No answer	4	2	0
	100	100	100
	(N = 328)	(N = 89)	(N = 118)

the closeness and assistance which might be expected to come from a group of neighbors. Registrants were also asked a relatively objective question (concerning their willingness to leave their names when seeking information from the clerk or board) which sought to measure the confidence generated by the local board. Again, greater rapport appears to exist in the rural and small town areas, but substantial proportions of registrants would be unwilling to give their names before receiving an answer to their questions. More than half of the respondents from the New York area, for example, indicated such an unwillingness.

This general apprehension about becoming known to one's board may be the product of an understandable desire for anonymity, but it also seems to reveal an inherent lack of confidence in the impartiality and procedural regularity of the boards. Table 4.5 presents responses of a more frankly subjective and hypothetical nature, asked as part of an attempt to explore just such vague images of impartiality. The data support the hypothesis that the respondents would have mild expectations of bias, and that they would be slightly higher in the urban areas than in the rural and small town areas. (Perhaps the more important datum under the circumstances is the relatively high proportion of "no preference" responses.) The New York area respondents anticipate less impartiality in regard to religious differences, but more in regard to racial distinctions. All respondents share expectations of sharp biases when the basis of distinction is the simple socioeconomic one of a steelworker's son versus a banker's son. In response to other questions, more than half of all respondents declared that they believed that influential members of their local communities could bring effective pressure to bear to obtain a student deferment or prevent the drafting of their sons. Other indications of apprehension concerning the actions of local boards in response to entirely legal activity were found. Thirty-eight percent of all respondents believed that their student deferments would be withdrawn if they lost an appeal to be reclassified as a conscientious objector, and almost that many thought peaceful picketing in protest against the Vietnam War would bring the same result.

These and other findings suggest that the board-registrant relationship contains elements of tension and expectations of partiality. This is not surprising in the discharge of a function which carries so much threat, but it does cast further doubt on the validity of the benevolent "little groups of neighbors" image. There is little or no real contact between boards and registrants, except in some rural areas, and what there is does not lead to mutual understanding or confidence. Instead, there is a definable gap

TABLE 4.5. IMAGES OF LOCAL BOARD IMPARTIALITY,
UNIVERSITY OF WISCONSIN STUDENTS,
BY SIZE OF AREA OF REGISTRATION, 1966

	Wisconsin Small Towns and Rural Areas (below 60% urban)	Wisconsin Cities (over 60% urban)	New York Metropolitan Area
"If the following pairs of applicants, otherwise equally acceptable for the draft, came up coincidentally before your board, which from each pair do you feel would be drafted first by your board?"			
A farmer	24%	29%	30%
A social worker	46	33	36
No preference	24	34	26
A Negro	21	18	43
A White	2	3	2
No preference	68	63	47
A Protestant	3	2	9
A Jew	14	15	12
No preference	76	71	69
A steelworker's son	43	38	45
A banker's son	1	0	3
No preference	50	60	44
	(N = 328)	(N = 89)	(N = 118)
"No answer" ranges:	6–9%	2–13%	8–12%

between board and registrant and considerable apprehension on the part of the clientele of the System.

It is clear now from the data presented in Chapters 3 and 4 that the mythology of local boards is one thing, the reality quite another. This is not surprising, but our growing knowledge of reality and its distance from the myths of the System raises an important question: What explains the perpetuation of the myths? Perhaps the mythology rests in part on the widespread public ignorance and also in part on the support of those political activists who are represented on local boards. We shall explore these possibilities in subsequent chapters.

Chapter 5

THE APPELLATE PROCESS

I. THE APPELLATE SYSTEM: PURPOSES AND STRUCTURE

Within the decentralized structure of the Selective Service System, appeals from the classification decisions of local boards may be taken to decentralized and relatively autonomous appeal boards.[1] There are 115 appeal boards and panels (at least one in every federal judicial district), which classify anew the registrants whose files come to them. Potentially discordant goals and purposes underlie the System's appellate structure and procedure. One purpose that influenced the design of the appeals system was the desire to do justice to the registrants. In order to do this, there had to be some minimum standards of procedural fairness for the registrant in his encounters with the System. But another purpose was the need to expedite the delivery of men to the armed forces,[2] and here it was recognized that a high

---

[1] No effort has been made to document the authorities for each aspect of the description of structure and powers of units of the Selective Service System presented in this chapter. Unless otherwise specified, these have been drawn from the *Universal Military Training and Service Act,* as amended (P.L. 759, 80th Cong., 50 U.S.C. App. 451 *et seq.*) or the *Regulations* of the Selective Service System (32 C.F.R. 1622 *et seq.*). For a comprehensive, step-by-step description of the registrant's progress through the stages of processing within the Selective Service System and its appellate processes, which includes extensive documentation to these two sources (and others), see Charles H. Wilson "The Selective Service System: An Administrative Obstacle Course," *California Law Review,* 54 (1966):2123–79. The interpretations contained herein on the other hand are entirely the responsibility of the authors, based on their field study in Wisconsin, except as indicated.

[2] The Congressional statement of "Policy and Intent" at the outset of the Universal Military Training and Service Act declares (50 U.S.C. App. 451[c]): "the obligations and privileges of serving in the armed forces should be shared generally, in accordance with a

degree of concern for the niceties of procedure could be dysfunctional. Recalcitrant registrants might delay their inductions; aggressive attorneys might intimidate the isolated and unsophisticated citizens serving as local board members in rural areas; and the courts might intrude into the selection process, hindering the prompt procurement of men for the armed forces.

Clearly, the protection of the registrant and his prompt induction can be contradictory goals, and the contradiction may account for most of the distinctive structural and operating characteristics of the appellate system in Selective Service.[3] The balance between these two goals was struck in favor of an internal appellate system which was insulated by law from the threat of legalistic and procedural delays.[4] Attorneys were prohibited from appearing with registrants before their local boards, and the entire System was exempted from the usual court review. Registrants have no basis for challenging classifications or induction orders until they have undergone every step in the selection process right up to the point of taking the oath of induction as a member of the armed forces. Upon refusing to submit to induction, a registrant may be prosecuted, and his prospects if he is wrong in his claim are five years in jail and/or a $10,000 fine.

When the courts do finally look at the grounds for the local board's actions, they do so on the basis of a form of review which one court called "the narrowest known to the law." The courts normally demand "substantial evidence" for the actions of administrative agencies, they enforce standards of procedural fairness, and they require preparation of a record showing in detail the steps taken by the administrative body. In the case of Selective Service, the courts require only that there be "some basis in fact" for the actions of local boards. Procedural standards do not apply, and registrants are not entitled to cross-examine persons providing information

system of selection which is fair and just, and which is consistent with the maintenance of an effective national economy." Section 455(a) provides that "selection . . . shall be made in an impartial manner. . . ." At the same time the actions of the Selective Service System are exempted from the requirements of the Administrative Procedure Act by Section 463 of the statute, perhaps in furtherance of that part of the policy statement which stresses the need for maintenance of "adequate armed strength" (Section 451[b]).

[3] Selective Service is the only administrative agency dealing with the public which is not subject to the Administrative Procedure Act. For a review of the normal procedures, see Kenneth C. Davis, *Administrative Law* (St. Paul: West Publishing Co., 1958).

[4] For the nature of the insulation, see note 3 above. The exclusion of attorneys is accomplished by the *Regulations* (32 C.F.R. 1624.1[b]). A full account of the registrant's legal situation may be found in Selective Service System, *Legal Aspects of Selective Service* (rev. ed.; Washington, D.C., 1957). For a discussion of the scope of review, including the difference between "some basis in fact" and "substantial evidence," see Wilson, *op. cit.*, note 1 above.

to boards, to see documents, to be represented by counsel, or to be told the reasons for board actions. No record is kept, except as the local board chooses, concerning the registrant's testimony at a personal appearance (if there was one), nor does the board have to state reasons for its actions. Any errors or omissions at the local board level are considered by the courts to have been cured by appeal board actions, even though the registrant is not allowed to appear before the appeal board and that board has only the registrant's file from the local board on which to decide.

It may well appear that the government's needs predominate in this arrangement. The registrant's needs are reflected in the existence of the appeal boards, but such "rights" as he acquires thereby seem to be more form than substance. The registrant gains but a second classification opportunity;[5] it is distinguishable from the first one only by the fact that the five men are different, and they act without knowing any more about him than he and his local board can convey through documents in the file.

A third purpose influencing the design of the appellate system seems to have been the desire to protect the national interest, defined as the interests of employers, or perhaps the economy, of appeal board areas.[6] Appeal boards are required to have one member each from industry, labor, and ("where applicable") agriculture, plus a doctor and a lawyer. Although registrants must always remain subject to the local board in the area in which they resided at the time of their original registration, they may have their appeals heard by appeal boards in places of their current residence or occupation. Employers are authorized to appear with registrants before local boards, and they are empowered to appeal cases on behalf of registrants. As will be seen, employers make use of this opportunity, and appeal boards respond with alacrity to protect their local economies against the classifications of out-of-state local boards.

The itemization of these purposes serves to render the structure and powers of the units of the appellate system somewhat more understandable. At the local board level, government appeal agents are assigned the tasks of reviewing local board actions, recommending reconsideration or taking

---

[5] Selective Service itself makes this clear. *Selective Service under the 1948 Act* (Washington: Government Printing Office, 1951), p. 76.

[6] The general purpose of the Congress in regard to the national economy is declared in the policy statement quoted in note 2 above. Congress has also provided for the transfer of jurisdiction (at the option of the appellant) to the board having jurisdiction over the place of employment (Sec. 458[n]). The statute applies this provision only to occupational deferment claims, but some other classifications are also transferable in practice.

appeals where appropriate, and generally representing both the rights of the registrant *and* the interests of the government. Normally, the appeals agent is an attorney. Appointment is by the President on the recommendation of the Governor, which means in effect by the same selection processes as determine local board membership. No national data are available to establish a social profile of appeal agents, but data from Wisconsin indicate that they are as a group slightly younger than board members; interestingly, less than half were veterans, perhaps because many were recruited as appeal agents during World War II and have continued to serve.

The responsibilities assigned to the appeal agent[7] reflect the tension involved in the effort simultaneously to do justice to the registrant and serve the needs of the government. At one moment he is taking appeals on behalf of registrants whom he felt to have been wrongly classified by the board, and at the next, acting as impartial counsel to advise the board about the interpretation of new regulations. He could be asked by either board or registrant to be present at a registrant's personal appearance, or to render advice in the privacy of his law office. The rationale for assigning the appeal agent "neutral" responsibilities derives from the System's premise that the established selection and deferment processes do not create an adversary relationship;[8] originally asserted to legitimate the prohibition against appearance of attorneys with registrants, this rationale spread to cover assignment of multiple functions to appeal agents as well as the absence of procedural requirements for local boards.

For several reasons, appeal agents almost never accomplish the goals for which the position was created. In the first place, few appeal agents are active in any significant way. Frequently it is not easy to find attorneys, particularly in rural counties, who have time to take on additional tasks. The position is uncompensated, but the job of keeping up with changing regulations and the decisions of the courts on this subject, and attending lengthy personal appearances and advisory sessions, can be extremely time-consuming. By 1966, most appeal agents were such in name only, and frequently even their names were unknown to board members and clerks. This was partly due to a second reason: for several years, the System had experienced low calls for induction and there were only limited uses for

---

[7] Provisions regarding government appeal agents are found chiefly in the *Regulations*. See 32 C.F.R. 1604.71 *et seq*.

[8] Selective Service has maintained that its regulatory (rather than criminal) character obviates the necessity for counsel, and the courts have upheld this view. See *Legal Aspects of Selective Service*, pp. 35–57.

appeal agents. In any event, the rise in calls at the outset of the Vietnam War, with its attendant tightening of deferment practices, clearly revealed the absence of active appeal agents.

Another major reason for the nonfunctional status of appeal agents is the duality of purposes involved in the creation of the office. The national headquarters of the Selective Service System put the matter succinctly if innocently in an official publication: "A cordial relationship was necessary between the local board and the government appeal agent."[9] Two likely ways for maintaining this "cordial relationship," and the routes actually followed in Wisconsin, are either (a) for the appeals agent to remain in the background unless actually flushed out by a registrant, in which case the appeal agent still usually remains a passive information-giver, or (b) for the appeal agent to function as an arm of the board, helping it in its primary purpose of securing men for the armed forces by enabling it to build the tightest case for a particular man's induction. These adjustments occur in order that the social relationship between board and agent remain tolerable. The agent was, in most cases, at least "checked out" if not actually selected by the board, so that the prospects of some accommodation acceptable to the board would be good; an agent who caused delays or created problems could always be circumvented through the (authorized) appointment of an associate appeal agent, and the channeling of official business through him. In rural areas, the problem of the social relationship between board and agent is particularly acute, because there are fewer attorneys and the agent is likely to be a person of higher social status and educational level *and* one who holds some position of public responsibility. In such cases, the board's fear of being intimidated or overawed may prevent it from making use of the appeal agent or inviting his use by registrants.

The nonfunctional character of appeal agents means that registrants must obtain information about appeal procedures and appeal rights from other sources. Formally, advisers to registrants are attached to local boards, but in 1966 no such advisers were functional within most of the states, and in some states they had not even been appointed.[10] Local board clerks sometimes provide information, and many local boards informally advise registrants of their appeal rights during personal appearances. In any event,

[9] *Selective Service under the 1948 Act,* p. 52.

[10] *President's Commission Report,* pp. 28–29. No advisers existed in Wisconsin in 1966. Advisers were reported to exist in most states, but no confirmation of their activity came to light in independent inquiries. After receiving vigorous criticism on this point from the National Advisory Commission, the Selective Service System moved to correct this deficiency.

the Notice of Classification card contains a written notice of appeal rights, and the System has observed the practice of accepting even ambiguous notices of desire to appeal as an exercise of a registrant's rights.[11] The absence of the appeal agents from active participation in the appellate process probably affects the incidence of appeals less than it does the merits of the claims involved and the quality of the evidence presented. It is one thing to learn of the existence of an appeal right at a point which is still timely for the exercise of the right, and quite another to be prepared in advance with knowledge of the standards established by the statute and regulations (which are not generally available), as well as of the documentation which can best support a registrant's claim. Only the previously well-informed registrant is able to choose grounds for a claim to deferment and to present the written evidence that will advance his position with a decision-making body which will not hear him personally.

The appeal boards occupy a position coordinate with—not subordinate to—the state headquarters in the basic System.[12] Their members are selected by state Selective Service personnel and recommended by the Governor to the President for appointment. The requirement for representation of industry, labor, agriculture, medicine, and law on each appeal board is the only criterion (in addition to the usual age, citizenship, and non-reserve status standards) which the state headquarters must meet in staffing the appeal boards. An imaginative and motivated state headquarters thus has an important opportunity to create a cooperative appeal board, and trusted local board members may be raised to appeal board membership for this reason.

The selection process is the major, though not the only, point where cooperation may be promoted or the policy views of appeal boards shaped by those state headquarters so inclined. Some interchange may also occur in regard to interpretations of national policy directives, or with respect to particular conditions or problems within the state. For example, the state headquarters may inform the appeal board in writing (or through the attendance of an officer of the state headquarters at their meetings) as to its instructions to local boards in the state. The appeal board may choose to be guided by such directives and apply them in its decision-making. The state

[11] Selective Service System (National Headquarters) public information release (mimeographed, undated, circa November 1966), confirmed by field interviews in Wisconsin. No form of notice is prescribed by the *Regulations*, and boards are advised to abide by the "spirit" of the provision.

[12] Appeal Board provisions are found principally in the *Regulations*, 32 C.F.R. 1604 *et seq.*

headquarters may also bring before the appeal board reports on problems or conditions which they feel ought to be taken into account by the board in reviewing appeals from local boards. Again, the appeal board will choose the extent to which it wishes to be guided by the understanding and interpretations of the basic System.

For the most part, appeal boards set their own course. They are as fully imbued with the decentralist and local autonomy ethic as other units in the larger System, and their uncompensated personnel also find their satisfactions partly in the exercise of personal discretionary judgment. Apparently, relatively few states' headquarters have sought to achieve much integration with the relevant appeal boards, and even where they have (as in Wisconsin) the results are not indicative of much progress toward uniformity. The appeal board is free to interpret national policy as it sees fit, and its views may run directly counter to those of the state headquarters. The required representation of occupational groupings on the board lends emphasis to the needs of the employers and the economy of the board's jurisdiction, a basic orientation which diverges from the state headquarters' primary concern with providing the manpower to meet calls. And there are limits beyond which even the most cooperative appeal board member will not accept guidance from the most tactful state headquarters. The appeal board member is not only an uncompensated volunteer, but also an invisible one; there is thus no status to be gained from his membership, and he must find his satisfaction in a private sense of public service or in the group's interactions. In neither case can he afford to think of himself as a "rubber stamp," and he is inclined to jealously guard his prerogatives in order to foreclose such a self-image. In Wisconsin, the two appeal board chairmen are personal friends of the State Director. In the case of one board, officers of the state headquarters attend every meeting and conduct informal briefings. Law clerks in the state headquarters prepare briefs of the facts in each appealed case. The boards nevertheless operate quite differently and produce contrasting results which are attributable only to their decisional propensities and not to variations between their respective local boards.

At the apex of the appellate system is the National Selective Service Appeal Board, composed of three Presidential appointees, apparently actually selected in the White House and not by the Selective Service System.[13] They serve at the pleasure of the President, present members being a

---

[13] National Selective Service Appeal Board provisions are found principally in the *Regulations*, 32 C.F.R. 1627 *et seq.* This section draws also on an unpublished study conducted by Jacques Feuillan, Legal Assistant to the National Advisory Commission on Selective Service, in 1966.

Connecticut probate judge, a Massachusetts Commissioner of Veterans' Services, and an Ohio surgeon. They are compensated at an hourly rate. Most of their decision-making is done by mail from files forwarded to them with briefs of the facts and suggested classifications drawn up by national headquarters legal officers. About once a month, the board meets in Washington and takes up particular problems or discusses cases on which the members were not unanimous in their independent classification decisions. At such times, the National Appeal Board frequently meets with state directors, national headquarters personnel, or representatives of other governmental agencies, both to hear of special problems or needs and to gather information concerning particular cases. Representatives of businesses, institutions, or organizations with particular needs are also heard, but no registrant is allowed to appear.

Registrants are entitled as of right only to one appeal, and they may appeal to the National Appeal Board only if there was a split decision by the appeal board which decided their case; the severity of this limitation is mitigated by the willingness of many appeal boards to deliberately arrange such a vote in cases where they feel there might be a legal issue or a marginal question involved. Both the state and national directors are authorized to appeal to both the decentralized appeal boards and the national board at any time. The workload of the national board fluctuates according to the level of calls for induction, but it is regularly made up chiefly of occupational deferment issues involving sensitive government employment or critical private employment. Partly for this reason, and probably due also to the individualized nature of its decision-making, the attainment of uniform standards of classification performance is not seen as a function of the national board. In the absence of records concerning the actions of appeal boards around the country, and with a heavy workload as well as shifting manpower needs and deferment standards, it is difficult to imagine how the national board might serve to induce uniformity.

II. APPEALS AND THE REGISTRANT

Everytime a registrant is classified by his local board, he is sent a Notice of Classification card which contains along with his classification a printed notice of his right to appeal.[14] He must exercise that right within a specified time limit, and his employer or dependent may do it independently or

---

[14] The best description of the process from the point of view of the registrant and with particular regard to fairness of procedures is Wilson, *op. cit.,* note 1 above.

jointly with him during the same period. If he should fail to act in timely fashion, he may still be the subject of an appeal if the appeal agent or the state director can be induced to appeal on his behalf. In some instances, the mere notification of desire to appeal may cause the board to review his file or accept new evidence which results in a changed classification. In other cases, particularly conscientious objectors, a personal appearance will be held as the first step in the appeal process. The personal appearance, may be demanded by the registrant or invited by the board, and the registrant must then be advised anew of the board's action and granted a new right of appeal.

The problem for the registrant in effectively making use of the appellate process is chiefly lack of information. The situation may be illustrated with the example of the possible conscientious objector. In the absence of active advisers to registrants, the young man may not even be aware that such a right is open to him at the time of his registration. The single major exception is the member of a pacifist religion, who will probably have received guidance from a minister prior to his eighteenth birthday and his registration obligation. Information distributed at registration includes little except statutory provisions and admonitions about reporting requirements.

Prior to 1967, the statutory criteria authorized boards to grant conscientious objector classification to those men who, by religious training or belief in a Supreme Being whose commands were superior to the acts of men, were opposed to service in all wars. In a landmark case decided in 1964 the United States Supreme Court had ruled that a man who, because of a moral code which was for him the equivalent of a religious belief, was in conscience opposed to service in all wars, was also legally entitled to objector status.[15] These are criteria which the average registrant has little chance of understanding without outside guidance and advice. He may or may not meet the standards, but he will probably not know of them, or of changes in their specific terms, either before or after his registration.

But if the registrant does not file the special form for conscientious objector claims when he first registers, he may for practical purposes have waived his chance to have his claim decided without prejudice. Board members, as we have seen, do not look with favor on the objector deferments, and their distaste is fed by the inordinate amount of time each individual case consumes in personal appearance and appeals. Board members too suffer from lack of information in this kind of a case—a lack of

[15] *U.S. v. Seeger*, 380 U.S. 163 (1965).

information which would permit them to decide the case on objective evidence about the registrant. Faced with the need to act in some way, they tend to accept the claims of those men who are members of the recognized pacifist religions and who have filed the standard conscientious objector form at the time of their registration.[16] Others are usually rejected and the case in effect left to the appeal board. The personal appearance then becomes a session in which the board members ask the registrant questions phrased in the words of the statute or other criteria which they believe to be presently applicable, in order to obtain responses that will make the board's statement of reasons persuasive with the appeal board. Board members frequently are not well informed about the current criteria, and their inquiry may descend to the personal level in search of some basis which can be used to support their denial of the claim.[17] The registrant who has filed his objector claim at some point after registration, or who has not been advised in advance of the personal appearance, is unlikely to receive much consideration.

The mutual information problem was alleviated somewhat under the provisions of the 1948 Act by a requirement of Department of Justice assistance to the appeal board. The appeal board consideration of the file, assuming the registrant has invoked the appellate route after denial of his claim, is in effect a new classification rather than merely a review of the local board action. Thus new evidence would be relevant and could become a factor in the decision. The Department of Justice was statutorily obligated to conduct an investigation of the facts in the case of each registrant whom the appeals board felt should not be granted objector status, and a hearing was held before a hearing officer at the close of the investigation. For the first time, facts were developed through careful investigation. The registrant was permitted to add to the report such evidence and interpretations as he saw fit, as well as to present his case before the hearing officer, who then made a report to the appeal board. The appeal board was still free to act as it saw fit, but the report at least was before it for consideration.

In the amendments which accompanied the extension of the draft in June 1967, the Congress eliminated all of the foregoing provisions for investigation and hearing.[18] The registrant who appeals now must accept

---

[16] Robert L. Rabin, "Do You Believe in a Supreme Being—The Administration of the Conscientious Objector Exemption," *Wisconsin Law Review*, Vol. 1967 (Summer 1967).

[17] Gary L. Wamsley, "Local Board Behavior," in Roger D. Little (ed.), *Selective Service and American Society* (New York: Russell Sage, forthcoming).

[18] Public Law 90–40, 90th Cong., June 1967, amendments to Section 12 (50 App. U.S.C. 460[g]).

the decision of the appeal board, made on the basis of a record containing the local board's interpretation of the reasons for denial of the claim and its description of the registrant's personal appearance; the registrant may submit documents of his own, but no investigatory agency serves as a third party to the disagreement between him and his board. The alternative to accepting the appeal board's action as final is to refuse the oath of induction. If the registrant chooses that route, his risks are high: the Congress also provided in 1967 that the Justice Department should prosecute all such cases as expeditiously as possible (if it does not do so in some case, it is required to report the reasons therefore to the Congress), and it provided further that all such cases should be automatically advanced to the top of the calendar in any trial or appellate court in which they might rise.[19] If the court, which is statutorily permitted to decide in behalf of the registrant only if it finds "no basis in fact" for the local board's classification, should convict the registrant, the penalty for having been wrong is five years in prison and/or a $10,000 fine.

The weight of power placed behind the discretionary actions of the local boards is substantial, particularly in view of the fact that the local boards have little factual base for their decisions. The situation is less acute for occupational or hardship deferment applications. Board members and clerks are more inclined to volunteer assistance to farm boys or hardship cases than they are to conscientious objectors, and employers with experienced personnel officers may assist other employees with their claims. In such cases, the registrants might be enabled to meet the standards for deferment. If they found it necessary to invoke the appellate process, the appeal board could be relied upon to respond to the economic dimension in their claim, although there would be wide variance in the definitions of national interest which appeal boards employed. Such men would thus be subject to some but not all of the problems faced by the conscientious objector.

Under these circumstances, perhaps some of the antipathies felt by registrants toward their local boards become more understandable. Not many registrants are aware of their appeal rights before they receive classifications which they do not want; less than 10 percent of our student sample had any clear idea of facts pertaining to the right of appeal such as the time limit within which the right must be exercised. But nevertheless students from all areas felt strongly that they would have a "fair chance" if they were to begin an appeal from a local board classification by appearing

[19] *Ibid.*

before their local boards. Table 5.1 presents these data. More than two-thirds of all respondents believed they would have a fair chance, and only among New York area respondents did as many as one quarter feel that appeal would be a mere formality. From what we have seen in the previous chapter of knowledge about and trust in the Selective Service System, these results can hardly be due to informed respect for either their local boards or this particular appellate process. It is much more likely to be an uncritical endorsement of the principle of appeal, in the abstract and generally benevolent sense that legal recourses are considered "good." Perhaps this is a clue to one of the primary functions of the existence of this appellate process: as a kind of symbolic reassurance for the registrant and the public that any incidental arbitrariness or irregularity by a local board is capable of being put to right by the appellate body with jurisdiction. If this is the case, the mere existence of the right of appeal serves the purpose, and the actions of appeal boards become only secondary. Some evidence in support of this

TABLE 5.1. ATTITUDES TOWARD FAIRNESS OF STEPS IN INITIATION OF AN APPEAL, UNIVERSITY OF WISCONSIN STUDENTS, BY SIZE OF AREA OF REGISTRATION, 1966

	WISCONSIN SMALL TOWNS AND RURAL AREAS (BELOW 60% URBAN)	WISCONSIN CITIES (OVER 60% URBAN)	NEW YORK METROPOLITAN AREA
"If you were to appear before your local board to appeal loss of a deferment, would you feel that the hearing was a mere formality and board members' minds were already made up _____; or, with a well presented case, you would have a good chance of winning your appeal?"			
Mere formality, minds made up	15%	17%	27%
Good chance with well presented case	78	74	64
No answer	7	9	9
	100%	100%	100%
	(N = 328)	(N = 89)	(N = 118)

Source: Mail questionnaire, December 1966.

possibility is also found in the patterns of use of the appellate process, in that they appear to be random and determined more by local patterns as to the use of legal recourses than by the actions of either local boards or appeal boards.

III. WHO APPEALS? WHY?

The appellate system is a passive system, much like the courts. It must be invoked by aggrieved parties, and it can have no impact except as such use permits. In fiscal year 1966, there were 43,681 appeals taken to the various appeal boards, chiefly by registrants.[20] Table 5.2 shows the proportions of appeals initiated by the various possible appellants, both for selected states and the United States. It is apparent that the states vary considerably in the proportions of appeals taken by various parties. In California, for example, a very small share of appeals are taken by employers, while in Connecticut and Wisconsin nearly half of all appeals are by employers. The proportions of appeals taken by relatives, or by the government appeal agents, are very

TABLE 5.2. SOURCES OF APPEALS TO APPEAL BOARDS,
U.S. TOTAL AND SELECTED STATES, 1966

	TOTAL No. OF APPEALS	APPEALS TAKEN BY:				
		GOVT. APPEAL AGENT	REGIS- TRANT	EM- PLOYER	RELA- TIVE	OTHER
U.S. total	43,004	—	80%	17%	3%	—
California	12,018	—	95	4	1	—
Connecticut	675	—	58	41	1	—
Illinois	3,488	1%	78	18	3	—
Mississippi	69	15	54	23	9	—
New York City	2,165	—	78	18	4	—
Tennessee	71	—	75	17	9	—
Utah	54	2	59	24	15	—
West Virginia	72	3	49	28	11	7%
Wisconsin	1,187	—	56	49	4	—

Source: National Advisory Commission on Selective Service, In Pursuit of Equity: Who Serves When Not All Serve?, Appendix, Sec. IV, Table 4.3, pp. 114–15. ("Other" category indicates appeal by State or National Director.) Table includes double entries in cases of joint appeals; total of appeals, therefore, exceeds total actually decided.

[20] President's Commission Report, Appendix, Sec. IV. All of the data in this and the subsequent paragraph are drawn from Tables 4.1 and 4.3 of this Section.

low in all but a few states with relatively small numbers of appeals. Only one-half of one percent of all appeals in the nation were taken by government appeal agents, a figure which supports our previous characterization of the inactivity of the appeal agents. Even fewer appeals are taken by State or National Directors. In Wisconsin, the State Director almost never appeals a case, partly because he wishes to avoid the direct confrontation this would provoke with the local board, and partly because he is generally more successful in gaining his ends through other means. The import of this pattern of appeals is that information possessed by the registrant is vital to the initiation of appeals—for the government only rarely institutes appeals. At least some of the variation among states in incidence of appeals may be a reflection of the level of information about the appellate process in those states.

The National Commission on Selective Service found wide variations among states and even among appeal boards in the same state in the ratio of appeals to number of registrants. The range was from one appeal per 109 registrants in California to one appeal per 7,134 registrants in Tennessee; in general, the urban states were highest in incidence of appeals and the Southern and Mountain states were lowest, but the Commission reported that no correlations could be found between the incidence of appeals and the decisional performance of local boards or appeal boards. Appeal boards with very high proportions of reversals of local boards did not have higher proportions of appeals than those appeal boards which reversed local boards only rarely. In view of the fact that appeal board actions are not known to more than registrant and the affected local board, this is not surprising. But what then accounts for the sharp and generally consistent variation in incidence of appeals between states? We can only speculate that the origins of appeals lie in the general orientation of the state's political or social culture toward the use of legal recourses. This speculation finds support in the rankings of states by incidence of lawsuits arising out of automobile accidents, which were drawn from insurance company data by a recent study.[21] The same general distribution of states at the high and low extremities of the rankings may be observed, suggesting that the employment of legal recourses is a consistent feature of a state's political makeup.[22] Too few Selective Service cases have been litigated to make correlations between appeals and actual litigation, but nothing in the litigation experience runs counter to these speculations.

[21] Hans Zeisel, Harry J. Kalven, and Bernard Buchholz, *Delay in the Court* (Boston: Little, Brown, 1959), p. 226.

[22] *Ibid.*, p. 234.

TABLE 5.3. RANGE OF APPEALS FROM, AND ACTIONS
TAKEN ON, SELECTED LOCAL BOARDS BY APPEAL BOARDS,
WISCONSIN, 1966

| | APPEAL BOARD A | | |
Local Board	No. OF ELIGIBLE AGE REGISTRANTS	No. OF APPEALS	NEW CLASSIFICATIONS
a	4,200	18	28%
b	4,100	34	41
c	9,500	21	10
d	9,800	56	21
e	2,100	17	53

| | APPEAL BOARD B | | |
Local Board	No. OF ELIGIBLE AGE REGISTRANTS	No. OF APPEALS	NEW CLASSIFICATIONS
f	7,500	54	59%
g	13,600	16	13
h	6,100	5	0
i	4,400	12	25
j	14,700	33	49

Source: State headquarters records.

Wisconsin ranks tenth among the states in ratio of appeals to registrants,[23] and findings as to the origins of appeals on a board-by-board basis
seem to bear out the state-based conclusions of the Commission. There is a
wide range between local boards in the incidence of appealed cases, as Table
5.3 illustrates, but it is not related to the number of registrants (which is
considered to be indicative of the number of classification actions taken
during the year) or to the decisional performance of the appeal board. In
some cases, it is clear that appeals were generated by particular policy
departures on the part of a local board, such as classifying all teachers I-A,
or taking a particularly hard line with engineers or students. The ten urban
boards of the state were very low in incidence of appeals. But beyond these
rather obvious observations, we are left with the same speculations as before.

In keeping with the relatively high proportion of appeals in Wisconsin
which were taken by employers, almost half of all appeals in the seven years
of the 1960s were for occupational deferment (II-A). During this period,
the two appeal boards decided a total of 1,647 cases appealed from Wiscon-

---

[23] President's Commission Report, Appendix, Sec. IV, Table 4.1, p. 110.

sin local boards and 151 cases from out-of-state boards. Appeals occur in direct proportion to the level of calls for induction, for 63 percent of all the out-of-state appeals, and 65 percent of the in-state appeals were received in fiscal 1966, the last year of this period.

Only a few of the out-of-state appeals were for any claim other than occupational deferment, and it seems clear that the transfer option provided for registrants is used chiefly as a means for local employers to seek protection from the perhaps uninformed or unsympathetic actions of out-of-state local boards. Some of the same function is noticeable in appeals from Wisconsin local boards in rural areas as well; such local boards are frequently obliged to act on deferment claims from registrants who have moved to jobs in industrial areas of the state, and local board members freely admit what is assumed by the appeal board members, i.e. that they have little knowledge about the kind of job held by the registrant or its utility to the national interest. The state headquarters cooperates with employers around the state, pointing out ways in which their actions can enable a registrant to meet the policy guidelines for deferment and even showing them how to improve the documentary support they provide for registrants. The quality of advice given to registrants is probably highest for employees of major companies in the state, and this expertise on the part of businesses is reflected in the high proportions of II-A appeals. Assistance in the form of advice is most relevant for the registrant from an out-of-state board, because it is not generally known that an appeal can be transferred to an appeal board in the state of new residence. Farm and educational organizations and institutions also receive guidance from the state headquarters as to the criteria which should be met in order to qualify a registrant for deferment.

Patterns of use of the appellate process, and particularly the approach taken by the state headquarters, suggest that one of the major functions of the appellate system is to impose a control on the operations of the System on behalf of the more vocal employers of the state. Perhaps we should say that the economy of the state or the national interest is the recipient of the benefits of this control effect, but this requires assumptions we are unwilling to make and for which evidence is not available. Our reservations flow from the fact that, so far as we know, there has never been any comprehensive judgment made as to the relative utility of various occupations to any clear definition of "the national interest" or "the economy of the state." Such actions as are taken in the name of these concepts are individualized and decided almost exclusively on military or defense production criteria with little evidence except an employer's argument. This seems to us at least a very short-range view and possibly an illusory or even a faulty one; Youth Corps or Job Corps work in Milwaukee, welfare work in rural areas, or any of a hundred other occupations or individuals might well be as valuable to the nation as some or even all engineers or toolmakers or farmers who receive consideration because their employers are alert and able to make use of the established criteria for deferment.

IV. DECISION-MAKING PATTERNS AND PROCESS

Because there is no supervision of any kind over appeal boards, the variations in their decision-making performance are even greater than among local boards. In both cases, the root cause is decentralized local autonomy, but local boards are normally subject to some modicum of constraint from their state headquarters or from public contact. Each appeal board is independent, however, and there are several forms of variability evidenced in their respective policy views.[24] Some appeal boards assign new classifications to cases almost two thirds of the time; others, such as in New York City, assign new classifications only 7 percent of the time. The appeal board in South Dakota assigned no new classifications in 1966. Where there is more than one appeal board within the same state, they may differ widely; in one case, an appeal board assigned more than twice as many new classifications as did another appeal board in the same state. Appeal boards also vary widely in the relationship between their decision on cases appealed from within the state and cases appealed from out-of-state local boards. Most of the latter claims are for occupational deferments and are presented by registrants who now live and work in the state where the appeal board is located but who are still registered with the local board of the state of their origins. One state's appeal board, with a record of reversing only 2 percent of cases from local boards within that state, assigned new classifications in out-of-state cases at the rate of 90 percent; conversely, some appeal boards assigned new classifications more often for instate cases than for out-of-state cases.

These variations appear to be idiosyncratic rather than patterned according to any identifiable characteristics of the claims presented or the actions of the local boards involved. Reversal rates vary regardless of

---

[24] *Ibid.,* Table 4.2, p. 112. All data in this and the subsequent paragraph draw on this source.

whether the bulk of claims are for occupational or for student deferment, and they vary between appeal boards regarding out-of-state cases, although almost all of these are occupational deferment claims. We can come closer to assessment of both the process and the product by more detailed inquiry into appellate operations in Wisconsin.

When the appeal is taken, the local board forwards the entire file in the case to the appeal board and awaits appeal board action. In Wisconsin, as in several other states, the files are forwarded via the state headquarters. This provides an opportunity for headquarters personnel to keep up with the actions of local boards and perhaps gain warning of idiosyncratic behavior, and effectively complements the reporting of local board clerks as to board policies. The file is also checked for obvious procedural or documentary omissions, and is returned to the local board for correction if it is not ready for appeal board action. In the case of one appeal board, the state headquarters also prepares a one-page brief of the facts of the case before forwarding the file to the appeal board clerk. After appeal board action, the file is routed through the headquarters en route back to the local board. In this way, the state headquarters keeps current not just on local board proclivities but also on the decision-making patterns of appeal boards, and is enabled to make its preferences known at several stages of the state System's activity.

The appeal boards normally meet once per month, but this varies according to the workload; the early 1960s saw only three or four meetings per year but there were two per month in 1966. Each appeal board develops its own style of decision-making, often a reflection of the chairman's personal approach. In both Wisconsin appeal boards each member classifies every case independently and at home, normally using the brief provided by either the state headquarters or the clerk. At the next meeting he reveals his vote, and discussion may follow in the event of a nonunanimous result. From this point, the procedure of the two appeal boards diverges, illustrating the individualization involved in the appellate process. One board operates on the basis of deferring to its member who is by occupation or knowledge closest to the subject of the registrant's claim; it considers the local board from which the case was appealed in terms of its known policies and standards; and it frankly views rural Wisconsin and out-of-state local boards as unaware of the needs of the Wisconsin economy. The other board tries deliberately to decide cases on an individual basis, without regard to the local board from which the appeal arose or the particular economic effects of the registrant's induction, and solely on the grounds of the rules embodied in national policy directives. In the analyses which follow, the former is Board B and the latter Board A; the sharp differences apparent in their performance accord with, but of course are not necessarily caused by, the nature of their decisional processes.

The decisional performance of these two appeal boards differs by year, by classification, and by the state of origin of appeals. Table 5.4 summarizes these patterns for the seven years of the 1960s, highlighting fiscal 1966, prominent classifications, and the difference in state of origin of appeals.

Board B is much more responsive to a claim for occupational deferment than is Board A. Not only does it assign more than two-and-a-half times as many new classifications in this category as does Board B, but it also is three times as likely to assign a new classification in an out-of-state appeal, probably in part also a reflection of the high proportions of II-A claims in those cases. This is a consistent difference extending back across each of the seven years, although the proportion of new classifications in Board B has dropped gradually as calls for induction rose and deferments were tightened. On the other hand, the two boards are quite similar in performance in student (II-S) and hardship/dependency (III-A) deferment appeals. Variation in the occupational deferment category entirely accounts for the substantial difference in overall performance between the two boards: 70 percent of Board B's new classifications were in the II-A category, as against 40 percent in Board A.

TABLE 5.4. APPEAL BOARD DECISION-MAKING, SELECTED CLASSIFICATIONS AND TOTALS, FISCAL 1960 THROUGH FISCAL 1966, WISCONSIN AND OUT-OF-STATE APPEALS

	APPEAL BOARD A		APPEAL BOARD B		TOTAL	
	NUMBER	NEW CLASSIFICATIONS	NUMBER	NEW CLASSIFICATIONS	NUMBER	NEW CLASSIFICATIONS
Classification						
II-A	257	20%	497	53%	754	42%
II-S	88	36	127	39	215	38
III-A	52	19	123	15	175	17
Total, all classes of Wisconsin appeals	633	26	1014	41	1647	35
Total for 1966 only	484	26	579	44	1063	36
Total, all classes of out-of-state appeals	49	27	102	83	151	64
Total for 1966 only	43	37	53	77	96	61

These two boards receive appeals from local boards within the same state System. Unless we make the unlikely assumption that local boards in one federal judicial district somehow develop different policies than those in the other, it seems evident that the two appeal boards are simply applying different standards. The evidence with respect to handling of out-of-state appeals, in which Board B assigned new classifications three times as often as Board A, leads strongly in this direction. So does the fact that the difference is consistent over time.

What are the effects upon the System, if, as appears, appeal boards even within the same state, vary so widely in their decisional performance and standards? Measurement is tenuous, because the local boards' areas differ and there are many forces at work to affect the boards' classification patterns. But, after eliminating all boards in heavily urban areas, we compared the remaining rural and small city boards in the jurisdictions of the two appeal boards as to the proportion of their eligible age group registrants who were in classification II-A during fiscal year 1966. Consistent with, though again not necessarily caused by, the different standards of the appeal boards, the local boards of appeal Board B ran about 7 percent above those of Board A in the proportions of registrants in classification II-A.[25]

Measurement of the impact of appellate decisions in other ways is even more difficult. Local board members pay close attention to the actions of the appeal board on their appealed cases, and in most cases they treat such actions as cues for their future guidance. But their resentment at being reversed would probably be only slightly greater if they should become aware (which they normally are not) of the differences in the standards being applied by the two appeal boards.

The most probable effect, but again one for which hard evidence is lacking, is that such variation will give rise to increased complaints against the System on the part of registrants or businesses whose activities or contacts cover the two areas. On a larger scale, given the mobility of students and other registrants, and the broad activities of businesses in various areas of the country, it seems likely that variation in the performance of appeal boards across the nation will become obvious and be a continuing source of criticism.

[25] This is not considered a very significant datum. For one thing, the proportion of eligible age registrants is very low, averaging 1.5% in the 80 boards of the state. The difference between the two groups of boards involved here was only .11% of the eligible age groups. The difference does, however, go in the direction one might expect if appeal board action were to have measurable impact.

The variation that has been noted between the two appeal boards of Wisconsin, and which is apparently repeated many times over on a national scale, should be seen in context. At least in these two boards, there were no differences except in II-A performance; for the rest of the appeal claims, their decision-making showed about the same proportions of new classifications. The impression created is one of individualized, case-by-case actions without patterned effects. This means that the appeal boards could serve as controls on flagrantly idiosyncratic local boards which take radical steps, provided that enough registrants appealed their cases. In the absence of appeal agents, it seems unlikely that large numbers of registrants will appeal classifications from the same local board at the same time. But the data show that policy departures by local boards do give rise to abnormal ratios of appeals, and even a small number of reversals by appeal boards might serve to blunt the individualism of the local board. In any event, it would alert the state headquarters and permit an opportunity for state officers to attempt to persuade the local board to revise its approach. In some instances, clerks have gone so far as to pencil a line under the printed notice of right to appeal as a hint to the registrant. The State Director always has as a last resort the power to take an appeal himself, if all efforts at persuasion have failed, but this seems to be much more of a symbolic or bargaining device than an operating weapon in the effort toward standardization. Despite the highly individualized and even arbitrary nature of their decision-making, the overlay of economic protectionism, and the wide variation among boards, appeal boards apparently *can* be an instrument for prevention of the grossest departures from general policy. This is the best that can be said for their contribution to uniformity of performance within the System, and, as we have seen, much can be said against them.

V. THE APPELLATE PROCESS: A SUMMARY EVALUATION

We have seen the appellate system as an independent organization within the larger Selective Service System, paralleling it with units at each level and acting through its autonomous and decentralized elements to create distinctive effects within the System. In our consideration of the inputs of appealed cases into the appellate system, we saw that the inactivity of the government appeal agents meant that some cases were generated by alert employers or by radical policy departures on the part of local boards, but that the remainder of the appellate workload was produced in haphazard fashion by (speculatively) the general propensities of registrants, as products of particular political cultures, to make use of legal recourses with varying frequency. This probably means that the appeal route is taken mostly by the better-educated registrant with the higher sense of political efficacy, and least by the poor or less-educated registrant.

The bases of membership on appeal boards, the activities of the state headquarters on behalf of local employers, and the greater reversal rate for occupational deferment claims all combined to make the appellate system (both in Wisconsin and nationally) into an instrument for the protection of the more vocal employers of the state. The other outputs of the appeal boards show only a random and individualized effect, although it was possible to identify instances where local board idiosyncrasies were limited.

For practical purposes, the actions of the appeal boards in Wisconsin were final. There are two possible ways in which further effects could be generated by or through the appellate system, but neither of these were employed with sufficient frequency or impact to take the primary influence away from the decentralized appeal boards. One possibility would be appeals from the state appeal boards to the National Board, but there were in 1966 only 32 appeals taken, 25 from Board A and 7 from Board B. The other would be the use of the courts as a final recourse after exhaustion of all internal remedies, but the few cases that developed in the 1960s concerned refusal to accept the civilian work program to which conscientious objectors were assigned rather than the workings or actions of the System itself. There were only three cases which raised issues concerning the procedures of the System or the substance of its policies. This is partly because Selective Service does not recommend, nor will the Department of Justice undertake, prosecution of a delinquent unless the facts of the case are demonstrable and the intent of the law clear. Even so, one of the decisions resulted in a requirement of additional procedural steps by local boards, and it was necessary to modify standard procedures of all boards in similar instances in the future. But these were peripheral sources of influence over the actions of the elements in the System, and we must look to the appeal boards themselves as the primary source of whatever effects the appellate system produces.

There is of course a clear divergence of perspective and function between appeal boards and local boards which helps to produce differing classification performance. Appeal board members are obliged to apply national deferment criteria in a context of a comparative view of the actions of many local boards, and with a concern for the economic implications of such deferments if instituted as general policies. Local boards, being products of specialized local environments, and perhaps having only one or a few men similarly situated, and faced with the obligation to deliver a specified number of bodies to the induction center at regular intervals, develop quite different priorities. For better or for worse, rural boards at least know more about the registrant than can the appeal board. Most local board members are confident that they are better able to evaluate the registrant's entitlement to deferment than the appeal board, and they may well resent what they see as a forced exception from their otherwise consistent and well-informed application of national policies.

These differences in function, perspective, and distance from factual sources are reflected in the President's Commission's finding regarding differences between appeal board members and local board members in attitudes toward classification difficulty and need for more specific guidance from national headquarters. Appeal boards see hardship/dependency classifications as creating the greatest problems for judgment, while local board members find that conscientious objectors create the most difficulty.[26] Appeal board members seem to be much more aware of conflicting interpretations of national policies, as might be expected, but to feel the need for clarification of directives much less than local board members. Twice as many local board members as appeal board members told the National Commission that directives concerning student and occupational deferment should be clarified.[27] Possibly the appeal boards feel better able to cope with ambiguity and less obligated to justify their actions.

The differing classification performance which results from these and other factors already noted means that the System has a continuing source of tension built into its regular operating relationships. We have seen that the autonomy of these appeal boards gives rise to individualistic interpretations of national deferment criteria which may vary within states as well as among them. The appeal boards are thus autonomous intermediaries within the System, acting on wholly variant standards, with no responsibility for the achievement of the major goals of the System, and injecting new variation into its performance.

Considerations such as the foregoing led the President's Commission to recommend substantial changes in the appellate system.[28] Three recommendations applicable to the System as it stands were that registrants be given 30 instead of 10 days within which to file their requests for appeal, that local boards record reasons for their decisions so appeal boards could

[26] *President's Commission Report*, Appendix, Sec. IV, Table 4.4, p. 116.
[27] *Ibid.*, Tables 4.6 and 4.7, pp. 116 and 117.
[28] *Ibid.*, p. 5.

have the benefit of a record and the registrant would be able to know the reasons for the decision, and that appeal agents should be readily available to assist registrants with appeals. As part of a general consolidation of local board, state headquarters, and appeal board offices intended to promote uniformity of performance within the system, the Commission further recommended that area offices (perhaps eight or ten) be established to maintain supervision over consolidated district offices (perhaps 300–500). Appeal boards would then have been reduced to eight or ten also, with special panels for the purpose of hearing conscientious objector claims. The latter provisions concerning fundamental reorganization and change in the basic orientation of the Selective Service System from decentralization toward automation and professionalism in classification were not advanced to the Congress by the President. Instead, he ordered further study of the feasibility of such changes. By Executive Order the President did extend the time in which an appeal might be taken.

Congressional action in June 1967 dealt with the appellate structure in only two ways:[29] persons were permitted to serve as government appeal agents or advisers to registrants even if they had reserve status, and the President was authorized (if he found it to be in the national interest) to *recommend* that criteria for classification be applied uniformly throughout the United States *whenever practicable*. In this way, the autonomy of the local boards and appeal boards was preserved, and apparently all thought of a consolidated System abandoned. For present purposes, evaluation of the appeals process must proceed on the basis of continuation of the experience described so far in this chapter.

How do these 115 irresponsible and independent intermediaries contribute to the operation of the Selective Service System? Let us compare performance with original goals, and then assess their consequences in more general terms.

We need not define "justice" in any comprehensive way, nor even specify the number of ways in which the System does not provide the level of "justice" required of other administrative agencies or processes by the courts, to argue that these procedures fall short of minimum standards. The inactivity of appeal agents, at least partly attributable to the social situation and the tasks with which they are faced; the denial of counsel,[30] and the absence of procedural and record-keeping requirements; the "curing" effects

---

[29] Public Law 90-40, 90th Cong., June 1967, amendments to Sections 6(h) (50 App. U.S.C. 456[h]) and 10(b) (3) (50 App. U.S.C. 460[b] [3]).

[30] In May 1968, the Senate soundly defeated a proposed amendment which would have authorized registrants to have counsel with them at personal appearances.

of appeal board action; and the limitations on the occasions and scope of review by the courts—any of these and probably many other features of the appellate system fall short of relatively uncontroversial minimum standards.

The real question is whether the needs of the government are so acute as to legitimate such inroads on minimum standards of justice. If the government's needs be defined exclusively as the securing of men for the army, it may be that they are; but that is an argument which might equally support even more drastic procedural omissions, and personal appearances or rights of appeal themselves might be considered expendable. We think that the government has a need for military manpower, but in a context of a need for public confidence in the fairness of the conscription system and of some degree of individual registrant satisfaction that he has been treated in a manner consistent with fairness and due process. We acknowledge that the goal of serving the government's needs, when defined in exclusively men-in-the-army terms, has indeed been served by this system, though we suspect at some cost.

The other dimension of the needs of the government which was built into the goals of this appellate system was protecting the national interest, defined in economic terms. The protectionism which we have seen is evidence that this has been accomplished at least in part. But there is little indication that the "national interest" which is invoked to provide deferments is a rational or carefully considered one, and we have suggested that it is both so heavily oriented toward scientific and defense production industries, and so particularized by the multitude of appeal board definitions, as to lose all claim to represent a long-range view of "the national interest."

So much for the accomplishment of the original purposes. What of the present consequences? We have shown that the variability of appeal boards injects new variation into the performance of the System; this is the more damaging because it is uncontrollable, insulated by decentralization and autonomy against even those techniques of standardization which can be brought to bear on local boards. If one goal to be sought within a conscription scheme is to treat all men similarly situated in the same way, the appeal boards are clearly obstacles to its accomplishment. Ranged against this dysfunctional consequence is the fact that the mere presence of an appellate process—*any* appeals system, apparently—contributes to registrants' perceptions of fairness in the System. Further consideration of the relative merits of this aspect of Selective Service must be deferred until Part II.

Chapter 6

THE IMPACT OF THE DRAFT

Our inquiry into the effects of conscription as it is implemented by the Selective Service System will follow two broad lines of analysis. First, we shall establish the nature of the impact of the draft upon identifiable—and differently affected—categories of registrants, who are proximate objects of the policies under analysis. In this initial stage, we shall be concerned with the descriptive side of impact analysis: who is affected, and in what ways, by the policies under examination? Second, we shall undertake to identify the causes of the different effects noted. Among cause-effect relationships, we shall seek to distinguish those consequences which are attributable to organizational characteristics from those which are inherent in the substance of deferment policy as enunciated by the Congress. In this stage, our purposes will be analytical, and the two questions guiding our inquiry will be: How precisely can we show what aspects of policy content create particular effects? Is it possible to show how much of the overall impact of conscription is due to the nature of deferment/induction policies externally set up for Selective Service to effectuate, and how much to the structure and operating characteristics of the System itself? As a corollary, and because the organization is shaped in part by the tasks it is assigned, we may gain some insight into the extent to which changes in deferment/induction policies might be related to change in organization structure, procedure, or effects.

The allocation of causal responsibility in a situation where a correlation has been established is a very tentative enterprise under any circumstances. We use the concept of "cause" here only to signify that a component of policy is in fact associated with an effect which has been identified, and the relationship appears close enough for us to reasonably infer that the latter is dependent upon the former. There is a further problem which inheres in

125

our effort to distinguish effects created by deferment/induction policies (the categories of deferment and availability established in Congressional enactments) from effects created by implementation policies (the structure and practices of the organization): the two are interacting causes of impact patterns, and their respective effects are not sharply distinctive. The weight of their relative responsibility for characteristics of impact varies from one area to another, at least, and we can allocate responsibility through description and inference even though we are not able to impose statistical controls. Later in this chapter we will attempt to separate the two causes of impact patterns, but only after those patterns have been clearly established.

If the substance of conscription policies had been our primary concern, we might have begun this study by analyzing the impact of the draft on various types of registrants. But we have confined our analysis to the policies represented by the structure and operating practices of the Selective Service System, and thus several chiefly organizational questions (and their implications) have concerned us so far. With regard to the output of the organization, our focus in this chapter, we have already shown that decentralization and local autonomy on the part of local boards have led to variability in performance, both *within* a single state, and *between* different states.[1] In the ensuing analysis of overall impact of deferment/induction policy as applied through the organization, we shall see that the effects of such system characteristics are overshadowed by a third form of variability: the varying effects produced by the substance of deferment policies themselves upon men of differing socioeconomic and other characteristics—variation which is particularly noticeable between local boards whose jurisdictions differ in socioeconomic character. The broad outlines of policy impact in the case of conscription are those of economic discrimination, produced by the nature of deferment/induction policy and the surplus of available manpower over military needs; organizational characteristics produce their secondary (but still significant) effects in complementing and supplementing fashion.

There has been little sophisticated analysis of the impact of conscription. Selective Service has not collected data which would permit ready assessment of its effects upon the society, so that we must employ some broad and occasionally crude means of measurement drawn chiefly from outside sources. Indeed, so few precise official data have been amassed that there developed in 1966–67 a considerable argument over such a basic

---

[1] See Chap. 4, esp. Figure 4.1, p. 83.

question as the incidence of military service on the part of college students.[2] Authoritative units of government reached quite different conclusions, some

[2] For example, General Hershey testified in 1966 before the House Armed Services Committee: "At the present time the best information we have is of the people we defer for college, about 56 percent of them get into the service, and only about 43 to 44 percent of those who do not go to college get into the service, and it is quite easily understandable, because we have over 2 million that have been rejected for educational reasons, and obviously they didn't go to college, and they didn't go into the service." (Testimony in *Hearings*, p. 9647. See also p. 9700.)

General Hershey's testimony, however, appeared to conflict with the testimony of Assistant Secretary of Defense (Manpower) Thomas Morris only a few days later: "Our analysis of Selective Service records of men reaching age 26 as of June 1964 revealed that only 40 percent of the college graduates had served, compared to 60 percent of the college dropouts, 57 percent of the high school graduates, and 50 percent of the non-high school graduates." (*Hearings*, p. 9930.)

This conflict in the testimony was apparently explained by the fact that Selective Service had used a weighted average of college graduates and college dropouts in arriving at their statement that 56 percent of college men had served in the armed forces.

Congressman Stratton (*Hearings*, p. 9932) detected the inconsistency and General Hershey commented that his figures were based only on men who had been in college, not necessarily on graduates. No Congressman commented on another important fact— that both General Hershey and Secretary Morris were looking only at the military service experience of college graduates and non-graduates. They were not addressing themselves specifically to the incidence of induction and service on active duty as draftees, as opposed to enlistment for active duty, enlistment in the Reserve or National Guard, and service as an officer.

The report of the Civilian Advisory Panel on Military Manpower Procurement to the Committee on Armed Services of the House of Representatives used unstated sources to arrive at this conclusion: "The deferment of students has not meant that they have been protected from the draft or received favored treatment compared to non-students. In recent years 60 percent of the college student group has served in the armed forces either as volunteers or inductees, whereas 57 percent of the non-college students were called to or entered military service." (Civilian Advisory Panel on Military Manpower Procurement, *Report to the Committee on Armed Services*, House of Representatives [90th Cong., 1st Sess., February 28, 1967], p. 11.)

The report of the National (President's) Advisory Commission on Selective Service reached a different conclusion: "For men with different educational backgrounds, there is a substantial degree of difference in their chances of entering military service. Men with less than an eighth-grade education and Negro high school dropouts are less likely to enter because more of them fail the written examination. On the other hand, graduate and professional students are much less likely to see active duty because many of them continue their student deferments until they are 26, fathers, or can receive an occupational deferment." (*President's Commission Report*, pp. 21–22.)

The disagreement between these two bodies is emphasized by their opposing recommendations. The Armed Services Committee Civilian Advisory Panel recommended: "Student deferments should be automatically granted by the local boards upon certification by the college or educational institution that the individual is a registered student, pursuing a full time course of instruction." (*Civilian Advisory Panel Report*, p. 12.) The President's Commission, in contrast, recommended (p. 7) that no further student deferments be granted.

based on generalized and out-of-date figures, and some on none at all.[3] The debate which erupted reveals clearly the extent to which a priori assumptions and/or preferences can structure judgments in the absence of comprehensive evidence. Nor was this the only area in which the impact of conscription was a controverted subject: the service rates of Negroes, the incidence and recipients of occupational deferments, and the role of Reserve and National Guard alternatives were also debated in a context of little reliable evidence.[4]

[3] In 1964 the Department of Defense commissioned a national survey of military service experience as part of an effort to ascertain whether adequate force levels could be maintained without the aid of conscription. One by-product of this inquiry was data showing the military service experience of men aged 27 through 34 by educational level. These data, shown in the table below, indicated that the lowest and highest educational levels (before entering service) experienced the least military service, with high school graduates, college dropouts, and college graduates seeing military service in roughly equal proportions. These data appear to suggest that liability for service is lower only for graduate students, and that college graduates serve in the same proportion as less educated men. The National Advisory Commission on Selective Service presented a chart showing these figures in its report and the *New York Times* used the chart as one of two

MILITARY SERVICE OF MEN AGED 27–34 IN 1964,
BY EDUCATIONAL LEVEL

Educational Level Before Service	Percentage Who Served
8th grade or less	41%
High school dropout	70
High school graduate	74
College dropout	68
College degree	70
Graduate school	27

Source: Albert D. Klassen, *Military Service in the United States: An Overview* (Chicago: National Opinion Research Center, 1966), p. 15.

illustrations in its precis of the report. Many of the arguments for the elimination of graduate student deferment and the retention of undergraduate deferment appear to rely on these data. They are, however, thoroughly dated and no longer applicable. Men aged 27 through 34 in 1964 were at prime military liability ages in the Korean War, and the comparatively small size of the manpower pool in relation to manpower requirements then resulted in a high proportion of eligible males seeing service. Data of recent applicability are presented in the text. This and the previous footnote are presented as an indication of some of the problems of data availability and usage encountered in the policymaking process.

[4] The *New York Times* (January 3, 1966) reported "Negroes are more likely than whites to be drafted into the Army, Defense Department statistics showed this week." Adding detail the article said: "In the 12 month period that ended last June, 16.3 percent of the men drafted into the Army were nonwhite. The percentage of the nation that is

For these reasons, we shall begin with a more thorough review of the nature of the impact of conscription as implemented by Selective Service than our principal concern with the effects of system characteristics would seem to mandate. In searching out the impact of the draft, we shall be asking not only who is drafted, but also who serves in the armed forces, and who does not and why. It would not be enough to examine the characteristics of inductees, for example, because so many enlistments are draft-induced; some local boards regularly find it necessary to order two or three times as many men for induction as are actually required, because they know that many men—presumably the better informed or more aggressive —will enlist in regular or reserve components of the services after passing their physical examinations or even after receiving their induction orders. It will become apparent shortly, we believe, that there is little evidential basis for doubting the existence of economic discrimination in deferment/ induction policies, and we shall then undertake the more detailed analysis requisite to defining the distinctive effects of system characteristics.

I. THE IMPACT OF CONSCRIPTION: WHO SERVES AND WHO DOES NOT?

In broad terms, the socioeconomic groups most valuable to the draft are rural, white, lower-income, non-college youths and physically and mentally acceptable Negroes. Three factors combine to establish these broad outlines

---

nonwhite is about 11, mostly Negro." The article also pointed out that Pentagon officials explained this circumstance by noting that whites were more likely to qualify for deferment than Negroes. Somewhat later (April 11, 1966) *Newsweek* wrote "But seldom has criticism [of the draft] been so vehement and so basic as at present. Most serious of the charges is that the boards have favored the affluent over the poor by granting student deferments to youths whose families can afford to send them to college. Thus, say critics, the U.S. Army has become the poor man's army, with a high preponderance of school dropouts, of the underprivileged and of Negroes." Bruce Chapman, however, in an article in the *Reporter* (June 16, 1966) took issue with the view that the poor and the Negro bore the brunt of military service. He argued, "If any social or economic group is discriminated against, it is probably neither the rich nor the poor but the lower middle-class high school graduates of merely average intelligence who are not in college. But since even within the high school graduate group only one out of two men actually serves in the military these days, the whole attempt to cite a pattern of discrimination on the basis of class or race becomes highly relative and slightly unreal." Similar examples could be cited at length. Congressman O'Konski from Wisconsin has said that the poor are drafted; Daniel Moynihan has said that the armed forces "have been systematically excluding the least educated, least mobile young men"; and the State Director of Selective Service in Tennessee has said that if any group is singled out "it's not the poor but the middle class."

of service liability: (1) a steadily increasing surplus of manpower over military needs, leading to more and more generous (and more permanent) allocations of deferments; (2) relatively high standards of mental aptitude, due in part to the surplus of manpower, resulting in high incidence of rejections among the poor, particularly the Negro poor; (3) manpower surplus-induced generosity in granting student and occupational deferments, combined with low priorities of call for married and older men, resulting in low incidence of service among the wealthier classes. We shall briefly review the evidence in each of these areas.

1. Manpower Surplus Leads to Liberal Extension of Deferments

Manpower surplus is the central fact of military manpower procurement problems in the late 1960s, and the steadily rising surplus will make these problems even more acute in the 1970s. By the early 1970s there will be nearly twice as many men turning 18 each year as there were during the years of the Korean War. But military force levels, even during the Vietnam War years 1966 and 1967, remained *below* Korean levels. Under such conditions, the incidence of military service among eligible age men must steadily decrease. Table 6.1 shows stages of these declining percentages

TABLE 6.1. MILITARY SERVICE EXPERIENCE OF 26-YEAR-OLD MEN

	Total 26-year-old Men*	Ever Entered Military Service	
		Number	Percent
Year			
Actual:			
1958 (Korean pd. men)	1,000,000	770,000	70%
1962	1,110,000	640,000	58
1964	1,190,000	610,000	52
1966	1,250,000	580,000	46
Projected:			
1974			
3,000,000 strength	1,870,000	790,000	42
2,700,000 strength	1,870,000	640,000	34

* Age 26 is used as the critical age for comparison because it is the practical upper age limit by which time service will have been experienced by all those who are likely to undergo military service at all (except doctors and dentists). The median age of induction dropped to below 20 years in 1966, so that there is considerable time lag before such experience will be reflected in such totals as are employed here.

Source: Defense Department estimates, reported in *Hearings,* p. 10005.

for men aged 26, by which time service will have been experienced by all those who are likely to undergo service at all (except doctors and dentists). These Defense Department projections were made prior to the 1966–67 buildup, and 1968 force levels will probably hold the service experience percentages at around 44 or 45 percent for 1973 and 1974. It is clear, however, that the steadily increasing numbers of men reaching eligible age will continue the downward trend of service experience. Only very large increases in military manpower needs can affect this trend; more than 2,100,000 men will reach their eighteenth birthday each year in the early 1970s, and the Defense Department estimates that (assuming pre-Vietnam force levels) only one out of every seven physically acceptable men will have to be drafted.[5]

The abundance of manpower creates serious problems in the choice of those who are to serve. Selective Service began to experience these problems in the late 1950s and early 1960s, because force levels were relatively low in those years—but the late 1960s and 1970s will make the question a permanent one even under relatively high force level conditions. The key question under such conditions is the combined ethical and practical issue of what standards should be employed in selecting the relatively few men who are to be inducted. Given its established tasks and policies, however, the only questions open to Selective Service in the 1950s and 1960s were of a lower order. Because of the practice of drafting the oldest eligible men first, low calls meant that the average age of inductees began to rise, creating several undesirable effects: the services received men of more advanced ages than they preferred, long periods of uncertainty developed for many men, and their jobs and careers were interrupted at later stages than before. The System's response was to make more and more liberal use of deferments, thus keeping the number of I-As smaller, increasing the pressure on such men to enlist, lowering the age of those actually inducted, and thereby increasing certainty and reducing career interruptions. In a sense, deferments were used instead of calls to drain men out of the I-A pool.

This use of deferment can be seen clearly by looking at the recent history of deferment practices. Strict criteria were applied during the years 1951–53 and then during the late 1950s and 1960s deferments were granted liberally. In 1965 tightening began again. During the Korean War student deferment standards were strictly applied but after the war this gave way to

[5] Assistant Secretary of Defense (Manpower) Morris, in testimony before the Senate Armed Services Committee, April 12, 1967. U.S. Senate, Committee on Armed Services, *Hearings on the Extension of the Selective Service Act* (90th Cong. 1st Sess., April 1967), p. 64.

TABLE 6.2. MILITARY SERVICE STATUS
OF 26-YEAR-OLD MEN

	1958	1962	1966
Status			
Entered service	70%	58%	46%
Not qualified	22	27	30
Dependency (including			
married non-fathers)	5	12	20
Other deferred and exempt			
groups	4	4	4

Source: Department of Defense estimates, 1966. See *Hearings*, p. 10006.

the assignment of a student deferment without regard to class standing or
Selective Service Qualification Test scores, and finally the test itself was
abandoned in 1963.[6] In 1956 fathers were placed in the last category in the
order of call, in effect removing them from liability. In 1963 they were put
in a deferred category (III-A) and married men without children were
granted the last place in the order of call, again for practical purposes
removing this class of men from availability. Later the latter move was
canceled, but fathers remain deferred.

The effect of these various changes can be clearly seen in Table 6.2,
which compares the proportions of 26-year-old men with service experience
and deferred status in 1958 (a year which reflects Korean service levels)
with 1962 and 1966. Lest it be assumed that the American male has
declined in physical and/or mental capacity since the Korean War, we
should note that the Defense Department too has modified its standards,
particularly mental standards, in the face of manpower surpluses, accepting
only those men who meet the higher standards: A separate classification
(I-Y) was established in 1961 for men whose qualifications were such that
they would be acceptable only in time of national emergency. In every
category of this table except military service, proportions have steadily
increased. It is not too much to say that those who actually see military
service under these conditions and practices are those who are left over after
all possible deferments have been extended. Deferments, originally intended
to maximize the efficient use of manpower resources, were applied in effect
across the board to reduce the pool of available men to manageable proportions. The chief consequence has been exaggeration of the liability of that

[6] For chronological summaries of changes in deferment practices and other relevant
policies and events, see the chronology sections of *Annual Report of the Director of
Selective Service* (Washington: Government Printing Office, 1951–1967).

TABLE 6.3. RESULTS OF PRE-INDUCTION
EXAMINATION OF DRAFTEES, 1965

	NUMBER	PERCENTAGE
Results of Exam		
Acceptable	688,631	56 %
Disqualified	540,345	44
Administrative reasons	15,516	1.3
Failed mental requirements		
only	227,809	18.6
Failed mental tests	(131,268)	(10.7)
Trainability limited	(96,541)	(7.9)
Mentally and medically		
disqualified	28,786	2.3
Medically disqualified only	268,234	21.8

Source: Table 9.3, p. 204, in *President's Commission Report.*

middle socioeconomic group which does fall within the upper and lower
exclusions wrought by deferment policies.

2. Mental Rejections Reduce Service among the Poor, Particularly the Non-white Poor

Well over a quarter of the young men potentially eligible for the armed
forces are rejected as physically, mentally, or morally unfit for service.
Standards of acceptability are set by the Defense Department and applied
through Armed Forces Examining Stations, at which registrants are given
physical examinations.

Table 6.3 shows that in 1965, when 1,228,976 men were examined, only
56 percent were found acceptable; the remainder were disqualified for a
variety of reasons that the table makes clear.[7] The most important single
reason for rejection was medical; over 21 percent of those examined could
not meet the physical standards of the military.[8] Very nearly as many could

[7] It should be clear that one reason for the low rate of acceptance is that a lot of
healthy and acceptable men have already gone into the army via enlistment, reserve
programs, and the officer corps and thus do not take pre-induction physicals. In a sense
the cream has been skimmed from the group taking pre-induction examinations. Then
too a lot of men who could pass the mental test have educational or occupational
deferments and never take pre-induction physicals.

[8] The most common reasons for medical rejection are: Bones and organs of
movement diseases and defects (15.4 percent of medical rejections); psychiatric disorders
(12.0); failure to meet anthropometric standards (11.7); and circulatory system diseases
(11). (*Hearings*, p. 10028.)

not meet the mental standards. Of these over 10 percent failed to meet minimum standards and were placed in class IV-F while about 9 percent were judged to be of "limited trainability" and were classed I-Y and thus made available for call in an emergency.[9] The Report of the President's Task Force on Manpower Conservation indicated in 1964 that of those men mentally unqualified for service almost a quarter could not read or do simple arithmetic.[10]

There are no clear connections between medical rejection and socioeconomic level. *Some* reasons for rejection may be found most frequently at lower socioeconomic levels, but other bases of rejection are unassociated with socioeconomic factors and still others may be related to high levels. But mental disqualification, which alone accounts for rejection of 18.6 percent of those examined, is clearly associated with poverty and low educational levels. This indeed is the main point made in *One Third of a Nation,* the report of the President's Task Force on Manpower Conservation. As part of its work the task force undertook a study of the men who failed the Armed Forces Qualification Test, and a sample of 2,500 men was interviewed. Four out of five of these men were high school dropouts; a quarter had not finished grade school. One fifth of the families had incomes of less than $2,000 a year in 1962 and 47 percent of the rejectees came from families with six or more children supported by a family income of less than $4,000. But one does not need *One Third of a Nation* to see a connection between mental rejection, poverty, and low education. One needs only to know that Negroes are twice as likely to be rejected as white registrants, a result of the fact that while their medical rejection rate is substantially lower than that of white males, their mental rejection rate is many times higher.[11] Census data show that twice as many Negro males aged 14 to 24 as white males are illiterate,[12] and the Negro registrant is much more likely than the white registrant to come from a poor family. In 1964 the median family income for white families was $6,858; for Negroes it was $3,839.[13]

This general relationship between low income and mental rejection

[9] Beginning in October 1966, men in Class I-Y began to be reclassified into I-A if they met specific lowered minimum standards for military service. This practice was known as "Project 100,000" and the Department of Defense announced the intention of taking in 100,000 men a year who would have been rejected under standards in effect until October 1966.

[10] *One Third of a Nation* (Report of the President's Task Force on Manpower Conservation, Washington: Government Printing Office, 1964).

[11] *President's Commission Report,* Table 9.1, p. 203, and *Hearings,* p. 10032.

[12] *Statistical Abstract of the United States, 1967,* Table 159, p. 116.

[13] *Ibid.,* Table 480, p. 340.

may be seen also in a comparison of mental rejections on a state-by-state basis. Table 6.4 shows that the registrants in the five states with the lowest

TABLE 6.4. PER CAPITA PERSONAL INCOME AND MENTAL REJECTION

RANK	STATE	INCOME	MENTAL REJECTION RATE (PERCENTAGE OF EXAMINED)
1	Connecticut	$3390	13.8%
2	Alaska	3375	9.4
3	Delaware	3335	16.3
4	Nevada	3289	12.8
5	Illinois	3245	15.2
46	Tennessee	1992	28.3
47	Alabama	1910	34.3
48	South Carolina	1838	45.7
49	Arkansas	1781	23.2
50	Mississippi	1566	34.1

Source: Personal income data from *Statistical Abstract*, Table 464, p. 330. Mental rejection rates from *President's Commission Report*, p. 206, Table 9.4.

personal incomes had rejection rates that were much higher than in the five states with the highest personal income levels. A possible explanation for this is not hard to find; the states with low personal income also spend less on schools than other states and have higher illiteracy rates. Mississippi ranked lowest among the fifty states (in 1965) in current expenditures per pupil in average daily attendance in public schools and the next four lowest were South Carolina, Alabama, Tennessee, and West Virginia.[14]

These gross data suggest that the employment of higher mental standards has the effect of reducing service among the poorer segments of the eligible age group. The initiation of Project 100,000 in October 1966, motivated at least in part by a greater need for men, means that some men who would not have met the higher standards will now see service.[15]

[14] *Ibid.*, Figure VII, p. 104.

[15] For discussion of Project 100,000 see among other sources the testimony of Assistant Secretary of Defense (Manpower) Morris in *Manpower Implications of Selective Service*, Hearings before the Subcommittee on Employment, Manpower and Poverty of the Committee on Labor and Public Welfare, United States Senate (90th Cong. 1st sess., March 1967), pp. 37 ff. It is of some interest to note that though Secretary Morris has justified Project 100,000 in terms of sharing the benefits of military service, a report of the Army Surgeon General explains the lowering of mental requirements in terms "of the increased demand for military manpower caused by the

3. Student and Occupational Deferments, Readily Available, Reduce Service among the Wealthy

Table 6.5 shows that the incidence of military service among 26-year-old men in 1964 was lower for college graduates than for men at any other educational level. Actually, the table overestimates the real service experi-

TABLE 6.5. MILITARY SERVICE OF 26-YEAR-OLD MEN IN 1964, BY EDUCATIONAL LEVEL

	Less Than High School	High School	Some College	College Degree	Total
Entered military service	50%	57%	60%	40%	52%
No military service (total)	50	43	40	60	48
Available for service (I–A)	1	1	1	3	1
Married (svc. unlikely)	—	—	—	2	—
Unmarried (svc. probable)	1	1	1	1	1
Not available for service					
Unacceptable (I–Y, IV–F)	25	12	14	12	18
Student deferments	—	—	2	6	1
Occupational deferments (II–A, II–C)	—	—	1	11	2
Dependency deferments	23	29	23	25	25
Other deferred and exempt groups	1	1	1	3	2

Source: Selective Service sample inventory of registrants, reported in *Hearings*, p. 10011. Figures may not add to 100% in all instances due to rounding.

intensified Vietnam conflict." Whatever the rationale, the lowered mental requirements resulted in the acceptance of many who had previously been rejected. Because of lowered mental requirements, only 12 percent of potential draftees failed mental requirements in 1966 as compared with almost 20 percent in 1965. (For these figures and the report of the Surgeon General see *New York Times,* June 6, 1967.) These figures make it obvious that Project 100,000 altered somewhat the impact of the draft, probably to the detriment of educationally deficient men.

ence of college men: Walter Oi's analysis shows that college men serve most often in the Reserves, while others perform their service on active duty. In the cohort of men born in 1938, he finds, "Over three-fourths of qualified high school graduates served in the active duty forces, while less than one-third of college graduates discharged their draft liabilities in this way."[16] Unpublished statistics from the Department of Defense support Oi's finding. In 1964, 15.7 percent of the non-prior-service accessions to the Army Reserve had completed 16 years of school while only 5.7 percent of the inductees had a college degree.[17] More recent data show that in the period December 1965 to February 1966 only 2.1 percent of the Army inductees had a college degree.

But this is not the only additional advantage the college man enjoys. As Table 6.5 shows, he is also in a better position to qualify for an occupational deferment. In July 1964, 11 percent of 26-year-old college graduates held occupational deferments while only one percent of all 26-year-old men held occupational deferments. And until February 1968 it went without saying that the college graduate was the only registrant who stood a chance of going on to graduate school and continuing his deferment. When these opportunities to avoid military service (or at least minimize it) are combined with generally available opportunities which are more likely to be exercised when men reach older age levels (fatherhood) there is small reason to wonder at the data in Table 6.5. It should be emphasized that the opportunities for going to college are not open to everyone equally: despite the availability of loans, scholarships, and jobs, men from upper income families are more likely to go to college than men from lower income families. According to the 1960 census, only 19 percent of persons aged 16 through 24 in families with income under $5,000 per year reported college attendance, while 33 percent of persons in the $5,000 to 7,500 per year range and 49 percent of those in the $7,500 to $10,000 range reported college attendance. In short, men from upper income families are more likely than other men to be able to qualify for one of several deferments. Even if they do not eventually succeed in avoiding service altogether, they are assured at least of the opportunity to control the time of their service—an advantage,

[16] Walter Oi, "Some Implications of an All-Volunteer Force," paper reproduced in full in Hearings before the Committee on Armed Services, U.S. Senate (90th Cong. 1st Sess.), on S. 1432, "Amending and Extending the Draft Law and Related Authorities," p. 455.

[17] From data supplied by Stuart Altman, Professor of Economics at Brown University and developed as part of the 1964 Department of Defense Draft Study.

not open to the non-college registrant, which may enable them to avoid service at times of greatest risk.

We stated earlier not only that college men were in a better position than anyone else to avoid military service, but also that Negro men who passed their physical and mental exams were very likely to be drafted. This statement is supported by the data in Table 6.6 below. Only a third of the white males who entered military service were inducted, while over half the Negro males who entered military service were inducted. The table also shows, as we might have expected, that 10 percent of white males discharge their military obligation in Reserve programs, while less than 2 percent of Negroes discharge their obligation this way. The National Advisory Commission on Civil Disorders reported that Negroes made up only 1.15 percent of the Army National Guard and only .6 percent of the Air National Guard.[18] Finally, it is worth noting that although Negroes have a high reenlistment rate in the armed forces, their initial enlistment rate is lower than that for white men as Table 6.6 shows.

The gross figures employed in each of the foregoing sections establish only the broad outlines of the impact of the draft. They suggest some causal relationships, but the aggregate nature of the data may conceal several perhaps countervailing factors which contribute to shaping the character of the overall impact. Within this general context of policy impact, a detailed analysis may facilitate specific identification of the important variables.

TABLE 6.6. FORM OF MILITARY SERVICE, BY RACE, OCTOBER 1964

	White		Nonwhite		Total	
Entered Military Service		66%		49%		64%
Inducted	22%		25%		22%	
Enlistments	30		22		29	
Officer programs	4		0.4		3	
Reserve programs	10		1.7		9	
Never Entered Service		34		51		36
Unfit for service	21		42		24	
Other deferred and exempt groups	13		8		12	
		100%		100%		100%

Source: *President's Commission Report*, Table 5.8, p. 158. Based on Census Bureau survey of civilian men aged 16–34 years and Defense Department surveys of active duty personnel, October 1964.

[18] *New York Times*, August 11, 1967.

II. THE IMPACT OF CONSCRIPTION: THE CASE OF WISCONSIN

Lack of individualized socioeconomic data for each registrant prevents conclusive characterization of the effects of all aspects of deferment/ induction policies, but more detailed analysis can bring us closer to specification of the effects of such variables as race, urban/rural residence, income, and enlistment patterns. For this purpose, we shall employ Selective Service classification data on a month-by-month, board-by-board basis for the 80 local boards of the state of Wisconsin, relating board performance to the socioeconomic characteristics of their jurisdictions as reported by the Census Bureau. We are still using admittedly imperfect aggregate data, but our appraisals are cautious and, in the light of their congruence with the general outlines of national data just established, such use as we make of these findings appears warranted.

Table 6.7 shows the state medians in proportions of eligible age (total

TABLE 6.7. PERCENTAGE OF ELIGIBLE AGE REGISTRANTS IN MAJOR SELECTIVE SERVICE CLASSIFICATIONS

		PERCENTAGE OF ELIGIBLE AGE GROUP IN EACH CLASSIFICATION: STATE MEDIANS OF EIGHTY BOARDS		RANGE OF VARIATION BETWEEN HIGHEST AND LOWEST BOARDS, 1966	
		FISCAL 1965	FISCAL 1966	LOWEST	HIGHEST
	CLASSIFICATION AND DESCRIPTION				
I–A	Available for service	9.2	5.8	4.4	8.3
I–C	Now in service	10.8	11.8	8.6	18.1
I–Y	Available in emergency	4.4	6.7	2.4	11.5
I–D	In Reserves	3.8	4.8	1.7	8.8
II–A	Occupationally deferred	1.3	1.5	.3	3.9
II–C	Agriculturally deferred	.9	1.0	—	5.7
II–S	Student deferment	6.6	9.2	1.9	19.7
III–A	Hardship and dependency deferment	17.4	18.8	12.5	25.2
IV–A	Completed service	18.5	17.1	12.3	23.7.
IV–F	Unfit for service	14.4	13.1	9.3	30.7
	(Enlistments)	(2.1)	(3.3)	—	—
	(Inductions)	(.7)	(2.0)	—	—

registrants less classification V-A, overage) registrants in each of the major classifications during 1965 and 1966, as well as the range between the highest and lowest local boards in 1966. The deferment categories with the most men are dependency/hardship (III-A), unfit for service (IV-F), and student deferment (II-S); the latter increased substantially (by 39 percent) between 1965 and 1966. The table shows that the highest board has ten times as many registrants in II-S and five times as many in I-D (Reserves) as the lowest board, and there are sharp differences as well in occupational deferment and unfit-for-service classifications. Clearly the distribution of deferments is not the same in every draft board jurisdiction. The table also indicates substantial differences among the boards in the proportions of men now in service and who have completed service. The highest board has more than twice as many men in service as the lowest board.

These differences among the draft boards are clearly related in some instances to the socioeconomic characteristics of the draft board area. Table 6.8 relates proportion of student deferments to the median family income in the board jurisdiction. Because many boards in Wisconsin cluster about the state median, we segregated them by the relatively narrow margin of one percent of the eligible age group above and below the median. The sharply contrasting distribution of boards in these two directions correlates closely with differences in income. This, of course, is what the census data already mentioned would have led us to expect. We can also relate student deferment and family income by means of the scatter diagram in Figure 6.1. We used proportions of families with income under $3,000 per year in the jurisdictions of the boards as the correlate of student deferment for purposes

TABLE 6.8. STUDENT DEFERMENTS BY MEDIAN INCOME
OF BOARD JURISDICTIONS

	MEDIAN INCOME OF FAMILIES	
	BOARDS IN LOW INCOME AREAS (BELOW $5,000)	BOARDS IN HIGH INCOME AREAS (ABOVE $5,000)
Fiscal 1966		
More than 1% above state median	11%	56%
Within 1% of state median	44	35
More than 1% below state median	45	9
	100%	100%
	(N = 46)	(N = 34)

FIGURE 6.1. ILS DEFERMENTS BY INCOME LEVELS

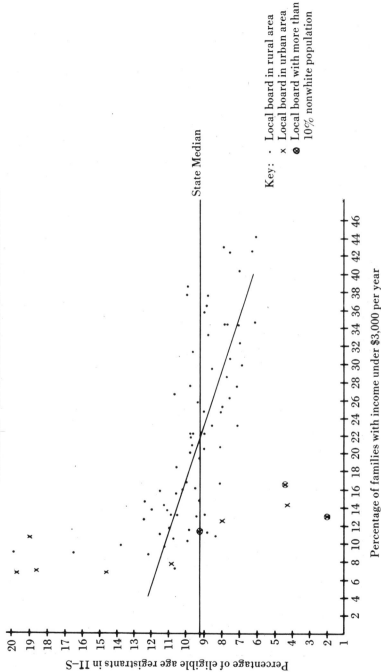

State Median

Percentage of eligible age registrants in II-S

Percentage of families with income under $3,000 per year

Key: · Local board in rural area
      × Local board in urban area
      ⊗ Local board with more than
         10% nonwhite population

of greater precision, and the general distribution is again deferment by income level. Some special features may lead to individualized variability, of course, such as the proximity of colleges and universities or the varying proportions of relatively wealthy persons in each board jurisdiction. We may note also that the greatest range in student deferment proportions, with relatively little range in income, is found in urban areas, suggesting the relevance of special factors in those areas such as nonwhite proportions within the population.

Not only are registrants from higher income areas more likely to have student deferments. They are also more likely to be eligible for occupational deferments (because they have been to college) and, most important, they are less likely to see military service than other registrants. Our analysis of Wisconsin local board data shows that registrants from higher income areas undergo military service at lower rates than registrants from lower income areas. Table 6.9 relates total military service experience (current service and completed service) proportions to the income levels of the board jurisdictions. The overall incidence of military service is lowest in the higher income areas, and highest in the lower income areas; the proportion of boards that are above the median decreases sharply as one moves from the lowest to the highest income areas, with only 11 percent of the boards in over-$6,000 income jurisdictions being more than 1 percent above the median. The overall lower service rate in higher income areas can be

TABLE 6.9. SERVICE IN ARMED FORCES
BY INCOME OF BOARD JURISDICTIONS[a]

	Median Family Income of Board Jurisdictions[b]		
	$3,000–$4,000	$4,000–$6,000	Over $6,000
More than 1% above state median	53%	36%	11%
Within 1% of state median	11	33	37
More than 1% below state median	37	31	53
	101%	100%	101%
	(N = 19)	(N = 42)	(N = 19)

[a] "Service in armed forces" includes classification I–C (in service) and IV–A (completed service).

[b] Median family income data based on U.S. Census, 1960. In the case of boards comprising less than an entire county (11 boards), census tracts were allocated geographically to construct socioeconomic profiles of each jurisdiction.

ascribed to a number of things in addition to occupational deferments. In the past it has been possible to continue a program of graduate training past the critical age of 26. And it is no longer unusual for graduate students to be married and have families, so that they have been eligible for the automatic fatherhood deferment.

To further explore the distribution of deferments and the incidence of military service we examined the records of 37 boards, all in rural areas in the state, where more than 20 percent of the families had incomes under $3,000 per year and less than 10 percent of families had incomes over $10,000 per year. The classification patterns of these boards were not surprising. As shown in Table 6.10, boards in low income areas are dramatically low in II-S deferments, distinctly high in unfitness, and high in hardship and dependency deferments. The combined effect of all these factors is a rate of service experience above the state median. We conclude that the unavailability of the student deferment has overcome countervailing factors and has exposed these registrants to a greater risk of military service.

To study the distribution of deferments and military service in a different way we compared the classification performance of two adjoining local boards in Milwaukee, one with high income, white residents and the other with a relatively low income, almost 50 percent Negro population.

TABLE 6.10. CLASSIFICATION AND ENLISTMENT CHARACTERISTICS OF LOW INCOME BOARDS*

	COMPLETED SERVICE & IN-SERVICE (I–C & IV–A)	STUDENT DEFER-MENTS (II–S)	HARDSHIP & DEPEND-ENCY DEFERMENTS (III–A)	MENTAL & PHYSICAL UNFITNESS (I–Y & IV–F)	ENLIST-MENTS
More than 1% above state median	43%	0%	51%	38%	5%
Within 1% of state median	27	49	38	46	92
More than 1% below state median	30	51	11	16	3
	100%	100%	100%	100%	100%
	(N = 37)	(N = 37)	(N = 37)	(N = 37)	(N = 37)

* "Low income" boards here include the 37 boards with jurisdictions in which more than 20 percent of families had incomes under $3,000 *and* less than 10 percent had incomes over $10,000.

FIGURE 6.2.   COMPARISON OF PROPORTIONS OF REGISTRANTS
IN SELECTED CLASSIFICATIONS, TWO BOARDS

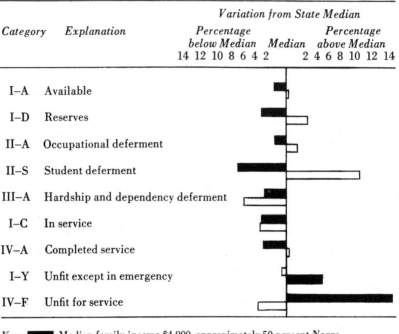

Category	Explanation	Variation from State Median		
		Percentage below Median	*Median*	*Percentage above Median*
		14 12 10 8 6 4 2		2 4 6 8 10 12 14
I–A	Available			
I–D	Reserves			
II–A	Occupational deferment			
II–S	Student deferment			
III–A	Hardship and dependency deferment			
I–C	In service			
IV–A	Completed service			
I–Y	Unfit except in emergency			
IV–F	Unfit for service			

Key: ■ Median family income $4,900, approximately 50 percent Negro.

☐ Median family income $8,500, approximately 1 percent Negro.

Figure 6.2 shows conspicuous differences between the two boards in the student deferment, occupational deferment, and Reserve deferment classifications. Since residents of the two areas have radically different opportunities to claim such deferments it is remarkable that service experience is so similar. With a much smaller pool of acceptable men, the low income board area provides nearly the same percentage of men to the armed forces, indicating that for those registrants in the area who are physically and mentally qualified, the chance of military service is high indeed.

The greater chance of lower income registrants going into service can be illustrated in yet another way. To test our hypothesis that the risk of military service for qualified men in low income areas was higher than the risk for qualified men in higher income areas we subtracted the "fit only in emergency" (I-Y) and "unfit" (IV-F) classifications from the totals of eligible age registrants in each board, and then computed the registrant's actual service liability by finding the ratio of the two service categories (I-C and IV-A) to the total. The resulting service liability ratios ranged from 1 to 3.2 in the wealthier urban boards in the state to 1 to 2.5 in the relatively low income, most heavily Negro board, and 1 to 2.3 in a very low income rural board. This means that actual military service was experienced by one in every 2.3 physically and mentally qualified men in the low income rural board, but by almost 50 percent less, or one in every 3.2 men, in the wealthier urban boards. In other words the income related bias in present deferment policies is sufficiently great to overcome the countervailing effects of higher proportions of unfitness in the lower income areas and to establish an income based pattern of military service.

Of course, it is possible that registrants from lower income areas have enlisted in disproportionate numbers, thus voluntarily creating the patterns we have discerned. In order to check this possibility we distinguished enlistments from inductions and compared both with the income levels of board jurisdictions. The results were not clear-cut, but the figures in Table 6.11 are instructive for their negation of the assumption that the poor enlist. The enlistment rate tends to fall in the lower income jurisdictions and rise

TABLE 6.11. ENLISTMENTS AND INDUCTIONS, BY INCOME LEVEL OF BOARD JURISDICTIONS, 1966

	Boards in Low Income Areas[a]	Boards in High Income Areas[b]
Enlistment Rate[c]		
Low	36%	22%
Medium	51	49
High	13	29
	100%	100%
	(N = 39)	(N = 41)
Induction Rate[d]		
Low	33%	49%
Medium	28	34
High	39	15
	100%	100%
	(N = 39)	(N = 41)

[a] "Low Income": More than 20 percent of families earning less than $3,000 per year.

[b] "High Income": Less than 20 percent of families earning less than $3,000 per year.

[c] Enlistment rate based on percent of eligible age group enlisting during fiscal 1966. (Low: less than 3 percent; Medium: 3 percent to 3.99 percent; High: over 4 percent.)

[d] Induction rate based on percent of eligible age group inducted during fiscal 1966. (Low: less than 2 percent; Medium: 2 percent to 2.49 percent; High: over 2.5 percent.)

relatively in the high income jurisdictions. Conversely, the induction rate is higher in the low income areas and lower in the high income areas. This suggests that the higher service experience of registrants in low income areas is not due to enlistments, but quite the opposite, to inductions.

We should emphasize that in our analyses of military service experience we have defined military service as active duty. Men in the Reserves who are classified I-D have in effect been defined as not having had military service. To be sure some of these men are prior-service personnel, but most are Reserve enlisted men who have had no prior service. Despite the liability of Reservists for active duty it appears to us to be an advantageous classification, certainly preferable to induction. Consistent with national data on the educational level of Reservists, in Wisconsin registrants in upper income, better educated areas are more likely to be in the Reserves. Among Wisconsin local boards, only the lowest income boards had less than 4 percent of their eligible age group in class I-D; the higher income boards were all above this figure. Moreover, the rise in Wisconsin Reserve proportions between 1965 and 1966 shown in Table 6.3 occurred chiefly in the higher income areas. The obvious point is that this deferment, like educational and occupational deferments, is not equally available to all registrants.

Our conclusion that military service is related to income can be supported by data quite different than those thus far presented. In an opinion survey of the Wisconsin adult population, respondents were asked, "How many of your close relatives and friends are now on active duty in the armed forces?" As Table 6.12 shows, the respondents least likely to have friends or relatives on active duty were in the bottom and top income levels. Respondents in the middle were much more likely to have friends or

TABLE 6.12. FRIENDS OR RELATIVES ON ACTIVE DUTY
RELATED TO FAMILY INCOME

	FAMILY INCOME			
	UNDER $4,000	$4,000– 9,999	OVER $10,000	NOT ASCERTAINED
NUMBER OF CLOSE FRIENDS OR RELATIVES ON ACTIVE DUTY				
None	51%	31.2%	47.5%	55%
One or more	48	68	53	45
Not ascertained	1	.9	0	0
	(N = 141)	(N = 323)	(N = 112)	(N = 31)

relatives in active military service. Similar findings were also apparent in data relating the respondent's occupation to his knowledge of friends and relatives on active duty and to his personal knowledge of men who were deferred. Professionals and farmers[19] were less likely than respondents in other occupations to have friends or relatives on active duty. And professionals were more likely than respondents in any other occupation to know men who were deferred from active duty. Seventy percent of them said they had personal knowledge of someone who was deferred. To be sure, these data from a public opinion survey would by themselves let us say little about the incidence of military service. But taken together with evidence that has already been presented they support the conclusion that incidence of military service is greater in the lower middle socioeconomic bracket.

III. DEFERMENT/INDUCTION POLICIES AND ORGANIZATION CHARACTERISTICS AS INTERACTING FACTORS IN IMPACT

Before we undertook our detailed analysis of local board performance in Wisconsin, there were two reasons to anticipate low variability among boards. One was the finding of the National Commission, reported in Chapter 4, that Wisconsin was a "low variability state"; the other was the emphasis on standardization and efforts expended in this direction by the state headquarters, described in Chapter 2. The evidence presented in the preceding section has confirmed that there is very little systematic variation among boards in Wisconsin except that associated with socioeconomic characteristics of jurisdictions. Many boards clustered about the state medians, and when they did vary from the medians the variance was related to one or more socioeconomic factors evident within their jurisdictions. The very substantial differences in proportions of men in various classifications so clearly evidenced in Table 6.7 above—in which some boards had few times as many men in a classification as did some other boards—appear to result from factors other than individual board preferences or idiosyncrasies. In other words, it is not the local boards of Wisconsin individually that create the patterns of differential service liability just documented: it is the inherent character of deferment/induction policies as they interact with the socioeconomic characteristics of registrants within the various boards' jurisdictions.

[19] Wisconsin had more men in classification II-C, agricultural deferment, than any other state in 1966—both in numbers and in proportions.

The Wisconsin analysis is therefore better suited for identifying the consequences of various aspects of national deferment/induction policies than for assessing the contribution of System characteristics to overall impact. But some effects of the System's structure and practices may still be seen in the performance of those boards, and we shall come to this subject shortly. First, however, let us be clear about what we have learned regarding the effects of particular components of deferment/induction policies.

The gross national data, refined by the Wisconsin analysis, permit us to attribute the distinctive socioeconomic impact patterns to the standards of acceptability and bases of deferment that are part of national deferment/induction policies. Mental rejections, reflected in both I-Y and IV-F classifications, closely follow income and education lines and operate to reduce service among the very poor and Negroes. Student deferments operate to insulate substantial proportions of the wealthier classes from service, overcoming the effects of medical and mental rejections in the poorer areas to establish 50 percent lower rates of service in some upper income jurisdictions than in some low income rural jurisdictions. Occupational deferments complement student deferments, further reducing service among the wealthier. Reserve and National Guard alternatives to active duty provide a route through which the upper classes may discharge their service obligations without major disruption of civilian careers. Present deferment/induction policies, it must be concluded, have the effect of focusing military service liability chiefly upon the lower and lower middle classes.

Some other characteristics of impact are also attributable to particular features of national deferment/induction policies. The especially high liability of mentally and physically acceptable Negroes, and the sharp contrasts between adjoining urban draft board jurisdictions, are due in part to the exclusions worked by mental rejections and student and occupational deferments interacting with the socioeconomic characteristics of the registrants. High service experience, we have seen, is chiefly attributable to inductions and not to enlistments. Indeed, enlistments appear to come from the middle and upper middle class registrants rather than the lower income and high unemployment areas; they rise and fall with the levels of calls for induction.

But national deferment/induction policies are not exclusively responsible for the character of impact: the structure and practices of the Selective Service System contribute in important ways to shaping these patterns. We may group the effects generated by the organization into three broad categories, reflecting the immediacy of their consequences and the extent to which they may be observed in the performance data of this chapter or inferred from organizational behavior and rhetoric.

First, there are two characteristics of System structure and practice which have contributed significantly to the overall impact described in the preceding sections. The organization's commitment to local boards with relatively small jurisdictions has the effect of emphasizing the economic biases inherent in deferment/induction policies and exaggerating the liability of the vulnerable classes. In the case of the two adjoining urban boards compared in Figure 6.2, for example, the relatively small size of the jurisdiction used as the unit for quotas and calls is partially responsible for the sharpness of the contrast. If the constituency for calls were the entire city of Milwaukee, the liability of physically and mentally acceptable Negroes would not be so great; it is the practice of following socioeconomic lines and defining areas of like socioeconomic character as the relevant jurisdiction that exacerbates the inherent economic effects of deferment/ induction policies. (There would still be lower service rates for the upper classes as long as the student deferment existed, of course, but the liability ratios would be more even throughout the city because the large exclusions worked by mental rejections within the Negro board would be diffused among larger numbers of acceptable men rather than focused on that board's remaining registrants.)

To take another illustration of the effect of the same System characteristic, consider the results which ensue from using many small rural jurisdictions as units for quotas and calls. Calls are assigned on the basis of where the available men are to be found, with every jurisdiction receiving calls for at least some men. The very fact that a draft board jurisdiction exists, then, obligates it to provide some men for each call; the existence of many rural jurisdictions, even though each may have relatively few men, means repeated calls upon that sparse total. Over time, this contributes to the high rate of liability in such areas. If the jurisdiction for calls were a statewide one, by contrast, liability would be more evenly distributed and less sharply focused. In every instance, of course, it is the provisions of national deferment/induction policies which make these men available, but it is the small size of jurisdictions employed by the System which forces repeated selections from particular bodies of available men. The effect is to render the economic effects of deferment policy most apparent in the jurisdictions with the smallest numbers of available men. Organizational structure, in other words, emphasizes the already established differentials of socioeconomic impact: the 50 percent greater liability of qualified men in the lower income rural boards must be attributed largely to this characteristic.

Another aspect of System practice visible in the evidence presented here is the varying stringency of application of deferment criteria. We have seen that deferments were more liberally extended as the manpower pool grew in the late 1950s and 1960s. Some deferments which are income-based, such as the student and occupational deferments, became permanent simply because there were more men than were needed. Raised mental standards, made possible by the same surplus of men over needs, reduced service among the lowest income categories. When there are too many men, the System must find ways of reducing the available pool; the use of deferments which relate to income differences has the effect of focusing liability more sharply upon those who have no physical, mental, or monetary means of avoidance. Reduction of the manpower pool—in order to facilitate selection by local boards and to focus pressure for the purpose of inducing enlistments—is not the only means of coping with manpower surplus, of course: the System could employ randomized selection processes, for example, which would eliminate the economic effects of generously extending deferments to all who can qualify and then inducting from those who are left over. Clearly, this would raise other problems and entail further consequences, and we mention the possibility at this point only for the purpose of noting that a non-inevitable System practice has indeed affected the overall impact of conscription.

Second, there are at least two types of System characteristics, evidenced in previous chapters, which affect overall performance in at least some states and probably in many individual instances in every state. We saw clear evidence in Chapter 4, Figure 4.1, of the extent of variability among boards with jurisdictions of similar socioeconomic character. This variability took two forms—variability among boards within the same state, and variability between boards of one state and boards of another state. Thus we have evidence of two overlapping kinds of variability imposed by characteristics of the organization upon the broad outlines of impact of national deferment/induction policies. The System's contribution to policy impact, we may then infer, is a wide range of different applications within the general framework set by the economic biases inherent in deferment/induction policies. Additionally, we saw in Chapters 4 and 5 that both local boards and appeal boards developed special rules and practices in their decision-making, the net result of which was extreme individuality in procedure and performance. These features of the organization make for extensive variability in national terms, and thus the wide disparities in treatment of similarly situated men which from time to time become apparent may be seen as products of System characteristics.

Finally, Selective Service has maintained certain practices and adhered to a consistent style of rhetoric in some areas, such that we may fairly infer (if speculatively) that some share of impact patterns is at least indirectly the product of the organization. Selective Service national headquarters has assiduously resisted collecting data on the character of board members, for example, or on the socioeconomic characteristics of registrants, enlistees, and inductees. If it had issued reports, or even collected the data, it seems probable that patterns of impact would have been recognized before this, and perhaps raised for public consideration questions as to alternative means of military manpower procurement. Selective Service has also rigidly defended its decentralized, locally autonomous form of organization, as well as the characteristics of deferment/induction policies, so it must bear some share of responsibility for the nature of the impact described, both in terms of policy effects and System effects. National headquarters has also consistently employed the rhetoric of manpower shortage, perhaps unconsciously or with the intent of promoting enlistments, with the effect that such attention as might have been forthcoming probably would be diverted from the fact of manpower surplus to the fallacy of manpower shortage.

It seems apparent, therefore, that Selective Service as an organization has contributed to the nature of the impact of the draft which we have outlined in this chapter. Organization structure and procedures have had an effect as independent variables upon overall impact. But characteristics of structure and procedure themselves represent policy choices, determined in part by the assumptions and goals of relevant policymakers and in part by the nature of the tasks assigned the organization. National deferment/ induction policies not only shape the impact of the draft: they also shape the character of the organization which administers them. The substantive choices reflected in the categories of deferment made available to registrants establish the types of men who are to be eligible to serve. How shall the choices be made?

The answer given by and through the Selective Service System has been choice by local boards. In the process, variability has been institutionalized and the economic biases inherent in deferment/induction policies exacerbated. The organization itself has become rigidly committed to the decentralized, local autonomy operation as a means of performing its task. Because of the resentments and tensions associated with the administration of conscription, it has also become defensive and unwilling to provide information about its operations. Because of the perceived need to retain the allegiance of local board members and state political structures, it has avoided attempts to control board members' characteristics *or* performance, thereby creating patterns of self-perpetuation, unrepresentativeness, and arbitrariness among board members as well as widely varying performance among the hundreds of local boards around the country. Had there been another answer to the question of who should choose among eligible men and how, the organization might have taken on a very different character. Any form of choice conducted from a national pool of eligible men by a single central source, for example, would be likely to foster a quite different organization.

IV. THE IMPACT OF CONSCRIPTION: SOME IMPLICATIONS

Most men do not undergo military service, but many of these men are nevertheless affected by the provisions of deferment policies and the operations of the System. Our analysis of impact should therefore include some consideration of who does what in order to avoid the draft as well as who serves. Some men are rejected because of circumstances beyond their control, such as physical or mental deficiencies, and we may hypothesize that they are unaffected by conscription, at least after they have received notice of the results of their examination. There may, to be sure, be some psychological effect in being told that one is unfit. Other men may deliberately alter their educational or career plans, however, in order to take advantage of deferment opportunities, in which case there is a further important dimension to the impact of the draft. Avoidance of the draft by taking advantage of options offered under the provisions of deferment policy may be contrasted with draft evasion in much the same way as income tax avoidance (buying municipal bonds, taking capital gains) is frequently contrasted with tax evasion.

As might be expected, there is little evidence about patterns of draft avoidance. We have already seen, of course, that men from wealthier families are better able to qualify for deferments permitting conscious avoidance, such as student and occupational deferments. We may infer that at least some of them actually do so, because we have seen evidence that the proportion of men in such classifications rises as induction calls rise—as from 1965 to 1966 in Wisconsin. National data on marriage rates showed a distinct rise in marriages, but only among the eligible age group, when married men were placed last in the order of call (thus effectively eliminated from service liability) in 1963. But it is difficult to find more specific evidence of modifications in educational or career plans in contemplation of the draft, at least after the beginning of college: in our sample of registrants who were students at the University of Wisconsin, for example, 88 percent indicated that they had done nothing in the way of altering their plan of study to keep their deferments, and 81 percent said that they had not altered their vocational or graduate study plans. These data may say no more than that only a small proportion are willing to acknowledge that they have altered their choice of courses or are now going to school full time instead of part time; but they may also suggest that draft-avoiding career plans are made early in life, as part of a culturally related middle and upper class career pattern which includes, among other opportunities, alternatives to active duty military service.

Although it is difficult to pinpoint extensive draft-avoidance activity, perceptions and images of draft avoidance abound among the general public. Table 6.13 indicates that substantial proportions of respondents among the Wisconsin adult population believed that they knew men who had taken various actions to avoid the draft. If these data were to be taken as indicative of actual patterns of behavior, we would conclude that more men had been "channeled" to the altar and the nursery than to deferrable jobs, and that the primary route to draft avoidance was enlistment. These respondents include a large share (nearly 30 percent) of persons over 65 years of age, and so estimates of the extent of draft avoidance are low. Among the respondents in the 21 to 25 age group, more than 40 percent know someone whom they think has gone to college to avoid the draft, over 50 percent say they know someone whom they believe to have married to

TABLE 6.13. PUBLIC PERCEPTIONS OF DRAFT AVOIDANCE,
WISCONSIN, 1966

"DO YOU PERSONALLY KNOW OF ANYONE WHO—WITHIN THE LAST FIVE YEARS—DID ANY OF THE THINGS I'LL MENTION MAINLY TO AVOID THE DRAFT?"

	Went to College or Graduate School	Got Married*	Had a Child	Took a Deferable Job	Enlisted
Yes	20.4%	32%	15.7%	10.4%	54.5%
Perhaps	3.8	4.9	4.1	2.0	3.0
No	75.3	62.6	79.4	87.1	42.2
N.A.	.5	.5	.8	.5	.3
	100.0%	100.0%	100.0%	100.0%	100.0%
	(N = 607)	(N = 607)	(N = 607)	(N = 607)	(N = 607)

* Marriage alone is now not a means of avoidance, but it was from September 1963 to August 1965. On August 26, 1965, President Johnson signed an executive order providing that registrants married after that date would no longer be placed on a lower order of call for induction.

avoid the draft, and over a quarter know someone whom they believe to have had a child to avoid the draft. While these figures may overestimate the extent of action to avoid the draft,[20] just as data on career plans may underestimate such activities, their implication is that some conscious avoidance occurs, and that the public believes that even more takes place. For purposes both of assessing impact and estimating reactions to such impact among the general public, these data carry significance.

These patterns of impact inevitably raise questions concerning the justifications and purposes behind various deferment provisions. One argument is that it would be an inefficient and wasteful use of manpower to draft without regard for civilian occupation, educational program, family situation, and so on. General Hershey has made this purpose of deferment clear: "A complementary function (to induction) is to insure, by deferment, that vital activities and scarce skills are protected and that the patterns of civilian life generally are disrupted no more than necessary by exercise of the duty and privilege of military service."[21] In addition to this protective function the System also points to another function of deferment—"channeling"—which General Hershey has also described:

> I do not believe that we are so rich in human resources that we can afford deliberately to ignore opportunities we have to channel people into training and the application of training. . . . There are enough factors over which we have no control which interfere with the development of the potential of our citizens, and with the best utilization of that potential when it is developed. By deferment we can influence people to train themselves and to use the skills they acquire in work critical to the nation, in civilian or military life.[22]

Other statements of the System have also emphasized the importance of channeling. For example, a press information bulletin distributed by Selective Service declares:

[20] The image of the draft as avoidable is no doubt built up by such stories as appeared in *Time* (June 3, 1966). "Still, draft ducking—or talking about draft ducking—has become a favorite extracurricular pursuit of the Class of '66. Potential inductees kick around notions of claiming to be afflicted with everything from chronic bedwetting to bad eyes, from homosexuality to bad backs—all exemptible ailments if the doctors believe in them. Men with allergies easily controlled by medication talk about not taking their pills for days before the induction physical. But it is mostly just talk. More comfortable is the notion of stretching a four year course into five. Or getting married and begetting children fast. Or taking a postgraduate job in such potentially deferrable fields as teaching, engineering, farming."

[21] Testimony of General Hershey, *Hearings*, pp. 9620, 9623.

[22] *Ibid.*

One of the major products of the Selective Service classification process is the channeling of manpower in to many endeavors, occupations, and activities that are in the national interest. This function is a counterpart and amplification of the System's responsibility to deliver manpower to the armed forces in such manner as to reduce to a minimum any adverse effect upon the national health, safety, interest, and progress. By identifying and applying this process intelligently, the System is able not only to minimize any adverse effect but to exert an effect beneficial on the national health, safety, and interest.[23]

There are several obstacles in the way of easily accepting these justifications for deferments. Although protection of the nation's manpower resources makes much intuitive sense, it is not at all clear that it is necessary under today's manpower conditions. In World War II, when deferments were part of the 1940 draft law, there was a great demand for military manpower, but there was also an obvious need for men in defense industries and essential civilian occupations. In that situation deferments were in all probability necessary and in any event they were minimal. But the conditions of World War II do not exist today and the nation's manpower supply is not under anything approaching the pressure that it was then. With a substantially larger population than in 1940 and a much smaller army than in 1945, one may well question perpetuation of the World War II rationale for deferments. Moreover, one can well challenge a deferment system (based on the need to protect manpower resources) which proffers deferments to large blocs of men as military needs decrease.

There is another difficulty with the protective purpose of deferments. They have in recent years been awarded with little or no regard for what is critical or what is in short supply. This is most obviously true with regard to student deferments. At a time when the supply of college students has never been greater, their protection has become virtually automatic, no matter what their field or quality of performance. But in other areas too the protective function of deferments is open to question. Before setting out to protect critical manpower it would seem necessary to identify with some precision the manpower that is critical and then to defer men accordingly. In fact, until February 1968 there was a critical skills list, but local boards did not consider themselves bound by it and often did not even refer to it.[24] The National Advisory Commission on Selective Service found as a conse-

---

[23] From a leaflet in a press information kit distributed by national headquarters.

[24] See Gary L. Wamsley, "Local Board Behavior," in Roger D. Little (ed.), *Selective Service and American Society* (New York: Russell Sage, forthcoming).

quence that half of the registrants given occupational deferments by local boards were in neither a critical occupation nor an essential industry as defined by the Department of Labor.[25]

The performance of the local boards in granting deferments is another major obstacle to acceptance of deferments as serving the protective function. Analysis of local board performance has made clear the amount of variability exhibited. Given the structure of the system there is no assurance that even if a carefully researched and detailed list of skills in short supply existed it would be followed by the local boards. This indeed is the difficulty with the provision in the 1967 law which says:

> The National Security Council shall periodically advise the Director of the Selective System and coordinate with him the work of such State and local volunteer advisory committees which the Director of Selective Service may establish, with respect to the identification, selection, and deferment of needed professional and scientific personnel and those engaged in, and preparing for, critical skills and occupations.[26]

Many of the same questions can be raised with regard to the channeling function. How can manpower be channeled rationally when it is not known where it ought to be channeled? Can the local boards reasonably be expected to channel men into critical industries that may not seem critical to them even if they know of them? Can a rural board reasonably be expected to channel men away from farming when a farm deferment is available and the registrant is a neighbor? More to the point, the surest deferment is fatherhood and though the System does not mention channeling men in this direction, it is fair to assume that at least some have been. And finally, although the System makes a point of channeling, it has never demonstrated the additions to particular occupations that could be accounted for by deferment practices.

Some may argue that, in a time when unemployment and lack of technical skills are evident among the lower classes, it makes some sense to draw such men into the armed forces. If this were the effect of present policies, of course, it would raise serious questions of value and propriety for many persons. But the issue does not arise in practice, because the men most closely fitting the description are *not* the men drafted; in short, there is no "fit" between those who are unemployable and those who are drafted. The least employable men are those rejected for mental unfitness with the

[25] *President's Commission Report,* p. 27.
[26] *Military Selective Service Act of 1967,* 50 App. U.S.C. 454(g).

greatest regularity, and inductees are drawn from the ranks of high school graduates who are employed.

With these challenges to the System's rationale in front of us, and given the large manpower pool and the apparently limited need for protecting it, it is easy to reach the conclusion that whatever real functions protection and channeling may have served in the past they may have today largely symbolic or formal purposes. Protection and channeling are positive or legitimate symbols that render acceptable the practice of allowing some men to stay home while requiring others to enter military service. Even though protection is no longer necessary the word provides a rationalization for what the organization is doing—taking some and leaving others.

If the protection and channeling purposes of deferment are mainly symbolic we must ask again what the purposes and effects of deferments are. One real function certainly has been to control the size of the pool of available manpower.[27] In addition, deferments may also aim at maintaining support for the draft and the Selective Service System. Although, of course, this is nowhere stated officially and explicitly, it seems a reasonable observation. The college deferments, the occupational deferments, the deferments for fathers—all these affect groups that might potentially threaten the System. Support or at least acquiescence may be obtained in part by the extension of deferments. (In the next chapter, we shall see that men who are safe from the draft are more likely to think the present system fair than are men not deferred.) To put the matter bluntly, deferments may have protected the draft and Selective Service more than they have protected the nation's manpower.

This "purpose" of deferments must be qualified in several ways. First, the support that is gained when a deferment is granted may be instantly lost if the deferment is taken away. The support or acquiescence that is gained when students are deferred may be quickly lost if student deferments are withdrawn. The problem is that a privilege comes to seem a right, and a deferment comes to seem an exemption. When the right or the exemption is withdrawn then opposition mounts. To avoid opposition and to maintain support, it cannot be withdrawn. What this means, of course, is that the deferment system is much more flexible in the direction of broadening than of tightening. Evidence for this view can be found in the history of the student deferment and the 1967 draft law. We have already mentioned that student deferments were tightly administered during the Korean War—when they were new. Then during the later 1950s and the early 1960s they

[27] James Gerhardt also makes this point in his "Military Manpower Procurement Policies: 1945–1967" (unpublished Ph.D. dissertation, Harvard University, 1967).

were relaxed and to get a student deferment it was enough to be a student. When the Vietnam buildup started, the Selective Service System tried to tighten up on students and specific criteria for the student deferment (rank in class and test score) were announced. But this time, unlike during the Korean War, there was much opposition. Student deferment had come to seem a matter of right.

The protective purpose of deferments must be qualified in another way. A deferment system designed to draw support may also draw opposition from those it leaves out. Groups or classes passed over may object to a deferment system that excludes them from the benefits—if they become aware of its operations and effects. If those left out have or gain visibility and power, then clearly a deferment system designed to protect may cease to, and instead draw fire. At the least, it will obtain support from only some (the beneficiaries) while being opposed by others (the burdened). And indeed the Selective Service System was in 1966 and 1967 under unprecedented attack from many quarters. The difficult position of Selective Service is clear: it cannot extend benefits (deferments) to everyone because it must induct some. Its problem then is to decide who to induct and who to defer while maintaining sufficient support. The solutions of the past appear to be increasingly unacceptable, and the problems which became visible to some in 1966 and 1967 seem likely to worsen. It may be that in the future any system of deferments will draw more opposition than support and the System may have to contemplate a procedure that inducts those needed but does not defer anyone. These are questions that the evidence of the next chapter seeks to resolve.

Chapter 7

PUBLIC ATTITUDES TOWARD SELECTIVE SERVICE

Although public opinion research has become a familiar part of the American scene, relatively little detailed attention has been directed at attitudes toward conscription or Selective Service as an organization. There have been in fact few inquiries into clientele or public attitudes toward the activities of any government organization.[1] The attention of academic social scientists has been taken up in large measure by studies of voting and

[1] No such studies are identified in one major inventory of the relevant literature: Wendell Bell, Richard J. Hill, and Charles R. Wright, *Public Leadership* (San Francisco: Chandler, 1961). Chapter 7, "Attitudes Toward Public Leaders," surveys research in this general area and concludes that this is one of several research gaps. Peter M. Blau and W. Richard Scott, in *Formal Organizations* (San Francisco: Chandler, 1962), characterize the state of the then-extant research by saying, "One serious shortcoming of most organizational research, including our own, is that there is no investigation of the publics related to the organization" (p. 74). There are some studies of attitudes toward specific policy areas, such as Gabriel Almond, *The American People and Foreign Policy* (New York: Harcourt, Brace, 1950) and Raymond A. Bauer, Ithiel de Sola Pool, and Lewis A. Dexter, *American Business and Public Policy* (New York: Atherton Press, 1963).

We should emphasize that study of public attitudes toward government agencies and their activities is needed in order to determine whether preferences, policies, and practices are congruent. Whether or not they are congruent is important if support for a democratic political system is to be maintained. David Easton has raised this issue in theoretical terms in his series of works developing a theory of the political system. See *A Systems Analysis of Political Life* (New York: John Wiley & Sons, 1965) and *A Framework for Political Analysis* (Englewood Cliffs: Prentice-Hall, 1966). The problem has been focused more sharply and explored empirically in such works as Morris Janowitz et al., *Public Administration and the Public* (Ann Arbor: Institute of Public Administration, University of Michigan, 1958) and Philip Selznick, *TVA and the Grass Roots* (Berkeley: University of California Press, 1949).

opinions associated with that act, and inquiry concerning attitudes toward government policy has been left almost entirely to commercial polling services. The American Institute of Public Opinion (Gallup), Roper, and Harris polls provide most of our knowledge about public attitudes toward particular government policies. From these we may draw some preliminary impressions about public response to conscription, but our primary focus in this chapter is on public attitudes toward the organization itself—and particularly to the local board concept.

I. PATTERNS OF NATIONAL ATTITUDES TOWARD CONSCRIPTION

We know that governmental policies, once enacted, tend to enjoy high levels of public approval. Two attitude patterns toward policy are well established:[2] in one, opinion is divided sharply until the government acts, and thereafter opinion shifts toward acquiescence to what has been done. In the other, opinion seems to "lead" government action, in that majorities approve of proposed policy well before the government acts. (Presumably, those who oppose are more effective in bringing their political influence to bear, in a kind of temporary delaying action.) But in both cases, action by government establishes a policy as part of the ongoing consensus, and future issues concern only means (or other details) of carrying it out.

Events and commitments by leading political figures, groups, or parties may contribute to the shaping of public opinion. Under most circumstances, only a small proportion of the population is aware and informed on any particular issue; but as circumstances evolve (such as in a public debate or a political campaign), one or another issue or policy may be brought to salience, and opinion is then structured by one or more of the opinion-shaping agents active on the national scene. In this way, substantial segments of the general public come to hold some very general, and frequently minimally informed—but nevertheless relevant—views on public policy issues.

Attitudes toward conscription (so far as national data permit characterization) illustrate several of these general principles. In 1938, before the

[2] These paragraphs draw on the general characterizations developed and supported at length in the standard works on public opinion: V. O. Key, Jr. *Public Opinion and American Democracy* (New York: Alfred A. Knopf, 1961), Chaps. 1–4; Bernard C. Hennessy, *Public Opinion* (Belmont, Calif.: Wadsworth Publishing Company, 1965), Chaps. 5–7, 21; Robert E. Lane and David O. Sears, *Public Opinion* (Englewood Cliffs: Prentice-Hall, 1964), Chap. 1.

prospect of another world war became decisively clear, two thirds of the public opposed a draft. But by mid-1940, opinion had shifted to exactly the opposite pattern. V. O. Key documents this change—a shift which, incidentally, suggests that acquiescence in conscription was well grounded before local boards (on which acquiescence is sometimes thought to depend) were established under the Selective Service Act enacted in September of that year:[3]

At the time of the intensive public debate over Universal Military Service (1948–51), perhaps because its latter stages coincided with the renewal of the draft in the midst of the Korean War, problems of conscription were highly salient. Universal Military Service was one of the three best known public issues in one study conducted in 1950.[4] It seems probable, however, that conscription receded from salience after the end of the Korean War. In some years of the late 1950s and early 1960s, draft calls totaled less than 100,000 men.[5] Extensions of the authority to induct were enacted by the Congress in 1955, 1959, and 1963 with only perfunctory consideration.

In August 1966, the Louis Harris organization asked a national sample, "As you know, young men 18 years old and over, if physically qualified, are subject to the military draft. In general, do you favor or oppose the draft as it now works?" Responses showed high approval. When the question was

AMERICAN INSTITUTE OF PUBLIC OPINION DRAFT QUERIES,
1938–1940

Date	Favoring	Opposing
December, 1938 (after Munich)	37%	63%
October, 1939 (after war began)	39	61
June 2, 1940 (after battle of Flanders)	50	50
June 23, 1940 (after French surrender)	64	36
July, 1940	67	33

Question: "Do you think that every able-bodied young man 20 years old should be made to serve in the army, navy, or air forces for one year?"

[3] Key, *op. cit.*, p. 277.
[4] Lane and Sears, *op. cit.*, p. 67.
[5] *Annual Report of the Director of Selective Service for Fiscal Year 1966* (Washington: Government Printing Office, 1967).

repeated in February 1967, only six months later, however, responses had shifted substantially:[6]

	August 1966	February 1967
Favor present draft system	79%	58%
Oppose present draft system	15	31
Not sure	6	11

The initial response probably reflected general approval of a well-established government policy amid circumstances of relatively low salience. The subsequent pattern may reflect increasing salience and perhaps higher levels of information. Given the normal conditions of low knowledge and dependence upon opinion-structuring agents (public officials or other reference groups such as political parties or voluntary associations), this appears to be a substantial change. No government action had occurred, draft calls had not risen—indeed they were higher in the summer—nor had any of the major political figures or institutions taken a clear stand in this period. Discussion had been limited to journalists' books and articles, not normally known as influential opinion-shaping factors among the general public, particularly within such a short period of time. Similar results were produced by Harris polls which sought to measure judgments as to the draft's "fairness": 1967 responses indicated that 40 percent thought the draft had worked fairly, as opposed to 43 percent saying "unfairly"; comparable figures in 1966 were 48 and 36 percent.[7]

These data, asking such broad questions and presenting responses only in aggregate terms, offer only limited insight into the nature of attitudes toward the draft. Their findings of substantial levels of disapprobation, however, are significant in that they are distinctly atypical: the general pattern is one of approval of established government policies, and particularly approval of conscription in wartime. They are remarkable also in the light of a more detailed opinion study conducted in 1964 which revealed notable unconcern about conscription except in the minds of those most immediately vulnerable to the draft. This study deserves more comprehensive reporting.

As part of the Department of Defense Draft Study of 1964, the National Opinion Research Center analyzed questionnaire responses from 102,000 servicemen, 6,500 civilian non-veterans, and 3,000 civilian veterans,

---

[6] *Washington Post*, February 20, 1967.
[7] Louis Harris poll, cited in *Newsweek*, July 10, 1967, p. 42.

all between the ages of 16 and 34.[8] The analysis revolved around the question, "In your opinion, is the present system of Selective Service (the draft)—very fair? reasonably fair? somewhat unfair? very unfair? have no opinion." In general, those with something to lose from being drafted were most likely to think the draft unfair, but all groups responded with at least majority support for the draft as fair. The tendency to view the draft as unfair increased with the extent of respondents' educational planning, so that the analysts coined the phrase "heavy investors" to describe most opponents of the draft. Men who planned little education beyond high school appeared unbothered by the draft, more than 80 percent of them indicating that they considered the draft fair.[9] Within both groups (both "high" and "low" investors in terms of plans for a civilian career), those who had experienced uncertainty in obtaining employment because of draft vulnerability were more likely to view the draft as unfair. Men among the "high investors" who considered the draft fair turned out to include high proportions who for reasons of dependency or occupation were least likely to be subject to the draft. The implication emerging from this study was that attitudes toward the draft were highly dependent upon personal vulnerability; few men considered conscription unfair unless they were personally threatened, and then only when they had made substantial investments in civilian education and careers.

This study was conducted under conditions of low induction calls and slight draft pressure. Presumably the intensification of draft pressure increases the number who are personally aware and likely to consider the draft unfair. But this finding—that the draft is an issue toward which a person is unlikely to feel adverse unless he has an individual stake which is being threatened—is an important clue for evaluating other opinion survey findings about attitudes toward conscription. It helps to explain the findings of several opinion polls during 1966 and 1967 to the effect that there was no agreement among the general public on any particular alternative to the present system.[10] It also underlines the significance of the increasing opposition to the present system that emerged during the latter stages of the debate in 1967: if it is true that one does not develop antipathies to the draft as a general policy—but only when he is personally threatened in terms of a civilian career—then the very close "fair" and "unfair" proportions may

[8] Karen Oppenheim, "Attitudes of Younger American Men toward Selective Service" (unpublished paper, National Opinion Research Center, University of Chicago, 1966), contains the data of most direct relevance and has been drawn on here with the kind consent of the author.

[9] *Ibid.*, p. 10.

[10] Louis Harris, cited in *Washington Post*, February 20, 1967.

indicate decisive disapproval among the relevant opinion-holding groups within the population.

These are fragmentary indications of what is in all probability a complex attitudinal structure. Nevertheless, they are as far as the available national data can take us. Perhaps the general public cannot be expected to hold clear views about conscription until the government has acted. Military manpower procurement is, after all, an intricate problem with many variables and few agreed facts to serve as guidelines. But some further insights into the bases of attitudes toward conscription are available through more detailed investigation in Wisconsin.

We are sensitive to the hazards of presenting survey data from a single state in a manner which permits the inference that similar attitudes exist across the nation. We make no claim that attitudes toward local boards which were found to exist in Wisconsin are representative of the nation. But we do have evidence that the attitudes toward conscription which are reported in the next section are paralleled in every major respect by national data: a detailed analysis of a Gallup Poll question—"Do you think the present draft system is fair, or not? Why do you feel this way?—asked of a national sample of 1,562 respondents on June 14, 1966, and kindly made available to us by William Chamberlain, a graduate student in social science and journalism at the University of Wisconsin, confirms that the social, attitudinal, and occupational correlates of attitudes in Wisconsin are indeed representative of the nation. With this encouragement, we have been emboldened to speculate that Wisconsin attitudes toward local boards may also be typical of the nation. In any event, we must investigate the nature of Wisconsin opinion toward conscription in order to lay the groundwork for analysis of attitudes toward local boards in that state.

II. ATTITUDES TOWARD THE FAIRNESS OF THE DRAFT IN WISCONSIN

In September 1966 a representative sample of 607 Wisconsin adults responded to a series of questions concerning the draft.[11] Once again, our primary interest lay in attitudes toward the organization, but we sought to identify characteristics of opinion about conscription itself as a factor of possible relevance to views about the Selective Service System. The key question for this purpose was, "First, with regard to your knowledge of the

[11] The survey was conducted by the Survey Research Laboratory of the University of Wisconsin, under the direction of Dr. Harry Sharp, whose cooperation is gratefully acknowledged. The sample was a clustered area probability sample and interviews were conducted by trained interviewers over a two-day period in mid-September.

draft here in Wisconsin, would you say it is working in a way that is fair to all, or not?" The state sample responded more favorably to the draft in this general question than it did when a subsequent probe was made of the reasons for taking such positions:

	GENERAL VIEW AS TO HOW THE DRAFT IS WORKING	SPECIFIC REASONS GIVEN IN DIRECTION INDICATED
Fair	41%	35%
Depends	7	—
Not fair	35	43
Don't know	17	21
Not ascertained	—	1
	100%	100%
	(N = 607)	(N = 607)

The proportions in the first column coincide with both Harris and Gallup findings from the summer of 1966; Wisconsin respondents do not appear to have held distinctive general views on the fairness of the draft. But the follow-up question ("Why do you feel this way? On what does it depend?") probably reaches closer to portrayal of more firmly based or second-thought opinion: respondents here were obliged to present the basis on which their general view rested, and in doing so they shifted toward the "not fair" category. There were blocs of 22 percent of all respondents who named inherent biases and escape provisions, and of 14 percent who specified the student deferment as the grounds for their disapproval of the draft; 11 percent specifically supported present deferments as a ground for approval, while 22 percent gave such general reasons as blanket liability, "taking them as they come," or equal eligibility. The pattern of reasons put forward in regard to fairness of the draft suggests that the "unfair" characterizers were able to offer more specific grounds for their views. Characterizations of "fair" were more often followed by vague or general reasons, particularly in the case of older respondents.

We have speculated that the absence of personal investment in problems of conscription contributes to general disinterest and inattention. There was ample opportunity for members of the general public to acquire information during the period prior to the survey, at least in terms of the number of newspaper articles on the subject. Factual reporting predominated, but there was regular attention also to statements critical of the draft and to proposals for its reform. In the four major newspapers of Wisconsin, we found considerable consistency in reporting factual matters concerning the draft: all reports concerning the state were drawn from state headquar-

FIGURE 7.1.   NEWSPAPER COVERAGE OF SELECTIVE SERVICE-
RELATED MATTERS, WISCONSIN, JANUARY–JUNE, 1966

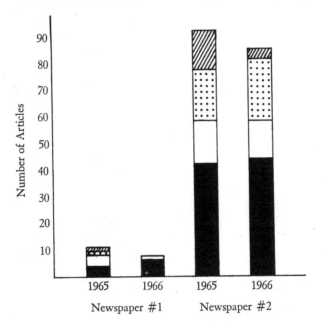

■ Factual reporting (draft calls, Hershey statements, non-protest events).

▢ Officials' reform proposals (plus editorial reaction and survey evaluations).

▦ Protest events (sit-ins by students, draft-card burnings, and action in
response to them).

▨ Other articles (humorous columns, letters to editor, cartoons, "question
of the day").

ters releases, and all others came from standardized wire service stories.
Figure 7.1 indicates the frequency and character of articles on and references to the draft which appeared in two of these papers over the first six
months of 1965 and 1966; the other two papers showed almost the same
pattern. All of these papers, and we may take them as constituting the chief
newspaper sources in the state,[12] carried articles on the average of twice a
week or more for the first six months of 1966; in most cases, the articles

[12] The newspapers were the *Milwaukee Sentinel*, the *Milwaukee Journal*, the
Madison Capital Times, and the *Wisconsin State Journal* (Madison).

were on page 1 or 2. There was ample background for a newspaper reader to become aware of and form judgments concerning the draft as a national policy during this period. Only an occasional article, however, mentioned the local board system.

Despite the availability of information, we found that there was neither much attention to, nor much structure behind attitudes toward, the fairness of the draft. In other words, the draft is an issue of government policy which normally elicits little public attention except from those who are intimately affected and who have much to lose from being diverted from civilian life; more important, it seems to be independent from the established opinion-structuring agents of American political life. Members of the general public receive few cues for attitudes toward the draft—not from their usual political sources, nor, in this time period, from major political figures or public officials. Instead, they develop views based on occasional and personalized experiences which they or persons with whom they are acquainted have with the draft. This is not to say that there are no differences between classes or groups of people with respect to the fairness of the draft, but only to indicate that these differences are relatively slight. Attitudes toward the draft depend much more on personal experience than they do on social experience, and thus they do not appear readily explainable from questions framed with more established patterns in mind. Let us examine the effects of some of the standard independent variables, and then move on to the more personalized ones.

Social Characteristics

One area of congruence between our findings and those of other studies of public opinion is in the effect of sex differences. Women are more likely to respond with "don't know" to questions which ask for a commitment based on knowledge. In this situation, they also were somewhat less likely to consider the draft fair than were men. Congruence was visible as well in regard to the basic finding of the NORC study of 1964: college people were, particularly in the vulnerable age brackets, less likely to call the draft "fair." The combined effects of age and education may be seen in Table 7.1. Within both age groups, support for the draft is highest among those with the lowest levels of education, and it declines as education level rises. But views of the draft as "fair" are generally higher in the middle-aged age group than they are in the younger. (The highest age group has not been included in the table because very few persons within it had either high school or college educations. Views of the draft as "fair" were distinctly lower among those with less than a high school education, however, and higher among the limited number of more educated persons. Granting the fact that these older persons seem to be less inclined to view the draft as fair [and, in this respect, to resemble the youngest age groups], very large proportions of respondents in this group say simply "don't know" when presented with this issue. All in all, our results with this upper age group are best treated as providing no grounds for relevant conclusions.)

Neither income, veteran status, nor place of residence (urban/rural) had much bearing on attitudes toward the fairness of the draft. The socioeconomic factor with the clearest association, however, was occupation. As Table 7.2 indicates, there are sharp differences between occupational groupings in regard to the view of fairness of the draft. These data should be taken cautiously because of the very small numbers of respondents in some categories. The pattern is plausible, however, in the light of our data on low levels of knowledge, lack of concern except in personalized instances, and the special fears of "high investors." Housewives once again show high "don't knows," and blue-collar workers lead in support among large groups. The sharp variations among professionals, managers-proprietors-officials, and farmers may indicate which groups consider themselves most vulnerable. We may speculate that the close association developed between managers and proprietors and the local boards (identified in Chapter 3) has some bearing on the very strong support for the fairness of the draft among this group. Some evidence in support of that speculation emerges from a comparison of the relative feeling of "fairness" expressed by each occupational grouping in urban as compared to rural surroundings. In

TABLE 7.1. FAIRNESS OF THE DRAFT, BY AGE AND EDUCATION, WISCONSIN, 1966

	Age 21–34			Age 35–49		
	Less Than H.S.	High School Graduate	College (Some or Graduate)	Less Than H.S.	High School Graduate	College (Some or Graduate)
Fair	47%	39%	34%	52%	45%	38%
Depends	6	7	10	5	8	3
Not fair	39	38	38	28	35	50
Don't know	8	16	18	15	12	9
	100%	100%	100%	100%	100%	100%
	(N = 36)	(N = 90)	(N = 50)	(N = 68)	(N = 75)	(N = 56)

TABLE 7.2. FAIRNESS OF THE DRAFT, BY OCCUPATION, WISCONSIN, 1966

	PROFES-SIONALS, TECH-NICAL, ETC.	MANA-GERS, PROPRIE-TORS, OFFICIALS	FARMERS	WHITE-COLLAR	BLUE-COLLAR	HOUSE-WIVES
Fair	34%	58%	31%	43%	45%	35%
Depends	6	0	3	12	2	12
Not fair	46	25	39	37	37	30
Don't know	14	15	28	8	15	23
	100%	100%	100%	100%	100%	100%
	(N = 50)	(N = 52)	(N = 36)	(N = 78)	(N = 203)	(N = 188)

general, each group showed much greater "fair" proportions in the area where it might be expected to be most numerous in the population: white-collar workers and professionals were much higher in the "fair" category in urban than in rural areas, and farmers were the reverse; managers, however, were strongly represented in the "fair" category in both locations.

Attitudinal Characteristics

In addition to one's position within the social structure, certain basic attitudinal stances often serve to shape opinion toward newly developing or otherwise secondary objects in the political world. These commitments include ideological positions, views toward the extent of the communist threat, political party associations, and, at least potentially in this instance, attitudes toward the Vietnam War. We found no correlations between respondents' party preferences or ideological positions (both measured by self-characterization, the latter in "liberal-conservative" terms) and their attitudes toward the fairness of the draft. Perception of threat from the communist countries was measured by asking respondents to indicate whether they thought such countries were a very great threat, a moderate threat, or just one of several problems that the United States faced. Although respondents divided into three roughly equal groups in reply, these perceptions did not carry over into correlations with attitudes toward the fairness of the draft. And those who responded affirmatively to the question, "Do you favor or oppose U.S. participation in the Vietnam War?" produced only slightly higher proportions of "fair" responses to the draft question.

TABLE 7.3. FAIRNESS OF THE DRAFT, BY EDUCATION
AND ATTITUDE TOWARD VIETNAM WAR, WISCONSIN, 1966*

	LESS THAN HIGH SCHOOL		HIGH SCHOOL GRADUATE		SOME COLLEGE OR MORE	
	PRO-WAR	ANTI-WAR	PRO-WAR	ANTI-WAR	PRO-WAR	ANTI-WAR
Fair	31%	24%	35%	18%	40%	6%
Not fair	20	26	28	18	42	12
	100%		100%		100%	
	(N = 151)		(N = 130)		(N = 93)	

* Attitude toward Vietnam War measured by question cited in text, and attitude toward draft by question cited previously. "Don't know" and "depends" responses to either question eliminated (total of 233 respondents).

Because attitudes toward the Vietnam War showed more correlation with attitudes toward the draft than other attitudinal characteristics, we sought to establish the distributions of such views in relation to other characteristics, if only as a means of setting a context for further exploration of attitudes toward aspects of Selective Service. Grouping respondents according to their educational levels and eliminating all "don't know" and "depends" responses, we emerge with the pattern of support for the war and the draft shown in Table 7.3. These data summarize much of what we have developed so far as to the distribution and sources of attitudes toward the fairness of the draft. Antiwar sentiment is strongest among the least educated groups, meaning the older and blue-collar respondents, but their margin of support for the draft as "fair" is greatest. Support for the War increases with education, but views of the draft as fair drop, and much more rapidly—probably because the college-educated respondents consider that they (or others like them) stand to suffer personally from forced diversion from civilian life. Together with the variations among occupational groupings, these represent the extent to which social factors appear to contribute to the shaping of attitudes toward the fairness of the draft.

Personal Characteristics

The individual life experiences and situations of members of the general public, randomly distributed among the population, operate to shape attitudes toward the fairness of the draft in more direct ways than do the broad social characteristics just analyzed. For example, contact with men who are potential draftees shows closer correlation with attitudes toward the draft than any of the social factors. Table 7.4 again eliminates

TABLE 7.4. FAIRNESS OF THE DRAFT BY CONTACT WITH
POTENTIAL DRAFTEES, WISCONSIN, 1966

| | KNOWLEDGE OF POTENTIAL DRAFTEES | | |
	NONE	ONE	TWO OR MORE
Fair	64%	50%	46%
Not fair	36	50	54
	100%	100%	100%
	(N = 180)	(N = 71)	(N = 205)

the "don't knows" and "depends" respondents (in this case, only 151) and compares attitudes according to extent of contact with potential draftees.

One set of attitudes which appears to arise in respondents without reference to their social situations is opinion regarding the deferment of undergraduate students. Disapproval of the student deferment seems strongest in the less educated groups, but there are many individuals who support it; conversely, college-educated respondents, perhaps for different reasons, provide a substantial proportion of the opponents of the student deferment. Whatever the origins of this disapproval, it carries a closer correlation with views as to the fairness of the draft than any other characteristic we were able to identify. Table 7.5 documents this assertion, drawing on responses to the question, "How important is it that undergraduate students be deferred from the draft?," asked as part of a series of similar questions with reference to all the major deferments in effect. It is clear that the student deferment represents one of the major structuring components of attitudes in respect to the draft. Those who gave reasons for their opposition to the draft in Wisconsin cited the student deferment more often than any other specific reason, and probably some of the 22 percent who felt that the draft contained biases should be added to this group. Part of the basis of this opposition to student deferment is probably the inability of some to qualify for it, along with the view that it permits some to avoid service that ought to be equally shared; the preferred alternative expressed by such opponents, both in Wisconsin and nationally, is some form of universal service.

Attitudes toward the fairness of the draft thus reflect respondents' personal situations to a considerable extent. We may speculate that positions regarding student deferment are related to contact with draft-age men, and that both are proximate correlates of views on fairness. Distributions of such personal experiences follow only very broad social lines, so that factors like age and education show only limited relationship with attitudes on the draft, and other factors reveal even less association. These speculations do

TABLE 7.5. FAIRNESS OF THE DRAFT,
BY ATTITUDE TOWARD STUDENT DEFERMENT,
WISCONSIN, 1966*

	How important to defer undergraduates?	
	Very Important/ Fairly Important	Should Not Be Deferred
Fair	66%	36%
Not fair	34	64
	100%	100%
	(N = 178)	(N = 163)

* "Don't knows" and "depends" responses to both questions eliminated (total of 266).

not account for the variations among occupations, but the reasons for these differences may become clearer as we examine attitudes toward the System itself, and particularly toward the local board as the instrument of administering the draft.

III. PUBLIC ATTITUDES TOWARD THE SYSTEM: THE LOCAL BOARD CONCEPT

In contrast to the amorphous and personalized structure of attitudes toward the fairness of the draft, public attitudes toward the local board system are sharply etched and follow clearly defined and politically familiar lines. The two sets of attitudes—the fairness of the draft and the practice of administering it through local boards—are not unrelated, of course; indeed, we can document associations between the two, and we might hypothesize that the local boards serve in a representative capacity, acting as a surrogate for reactions to conscription itself. In effect, the local boards may be the proximate political object against which members of the public can direct their disapproval of the draft. Views regarding the fairness of the draft itself may then be blurred or reduced in intensity, if only because the respondent considers local boards with which he is familiar to be atypically inept administrators of a conscription scheme which might not be itself unfair. This is not the only possible ingredient of attitudes toward local boards, however; to a considerable extent, our inquiry reveals dimensions of public attitudes toward government generally. Persons with confidence in their ability to affect government show high preference for the local board concept, while many persons not so endowed expect prejudiced behavior from the local board even more than they do from governmental bodies under normal circumstances.

Studies of attitudes toward decision-making institutions, the party system, and the roles of officeholders have recently begun to fill an important gap in empirical knowledge about the relationship of the people to governments.[13] A 1960 inventory of available survey-type materials which might contribute to such understanding found very few, and identified this as a major area for further research.[14] The nearly exclusive earlier emphasis on voting studies may be due to the periodic, focused, and apparently conclusive nature of elections. But attention to other forms of contact between people and government is long overdue: interaction between decision-makers, administrators, influentials, clientele, and general public goes on in a variety of forms on a continuing basis throughout the period between elections. It may well be more determinative of policy outcome and organizational priorities than the confused, multi-issue, personality-laden electoral process.

As yet, empirical inquiry has developed only scattered findings directly relevant to our interest in perceptions and evaluations of a governmental organization. In 1959 and 1960, a major cross-national study found that Americans were relatively high in expectations of equal treatment by both a governmental office (a tax question and a housing regulation were the problems hypothesized in the questions) and the police department (a traffic violation and a minor offense were the matters hypothesized).[15] Only respondents in the United Kingdom showed greater expectations of equal treatment, and then by the police; respondents in Germany, Italy, and Mexico showed distinctly lower confidence. When asked whether they anticipated serious consideration for their point of view, however, Americans fell behind both Britons and Germans in such expectations. The

---

[13] See Carl D. McMurray and Malcolm B. Parsons, "Public Attitudes Toward the Representational Role of Legislators and Judges," *Midwest Journal of Political Science,* IX (May 1965), 167–85; Roberta S. Sigel, "Image of the American Presidency," *Midwest Journal of Political Science,* X (February 1966), 123–37; Jack Dennis "Support for the Party System by the Mass Public," *American Political Science Review,* LX (September 1966), 600–15; David Easton and Jack Dennis, "The Child's Image of Government," in Roberta Sigel (ed.), *Political Socialization: Its Role in the Political Process, The Annals of the American Academy of Political and Social Science,* CCCLXI (September 1965), 40–57; Kenneth M. Dolbeare, "The Public Views the Supreme Court," in Herbert Jacob (ed.), *Law, Politics and the Federal Courts* (Boston: Little, Brown, 1967).

[14] Bell *et al., op. cit.,* Chap. 7.

[15] Gabriel A. Almond and Sidney Verba, *The Civic Culture* (Princeton: Princeton University Press, 1963), pp. 105–9.

authors speculated that Americans were high in expectation of equal treatment but then dropped to only about 50 percent in expectation of consideration because of some inherent ambivalence about political power and an incomplete assimilation of a subject relationship to administrative authority—in short, the familiar American impatience with bureaucratic "inefficiency" and "red tape."[16] Expectations of both equality of treatment and consideration for their point of view were low for the less educated groups in the United States and rose with levels of education.

Of more direct relevance to our inquiry are two sets of findings from attitude studies in Detroit in 1951 and 1955. In the first of these,[17] a sample of the city's population was asked to rate the city government and several of its services. Eighty-four percent of the respondents replied that city government was "very good" or "fairly good"; only 11 percent said "not good," and a minute 5 percent said "definitely bad." Lower socioeconomic levels were distinctly favorable to almost all units of government. Of four forms of governmental activity which were rated by the respondents, larger proportions of lower classes than upper classes rated government as "very good" in three.[18] Only the police department was more favorably received by the upper classes than by the lower classes. In each case, again with the exception of the police department, the upper classes were more likely to rate the performance of local government as "definitely bad"—although the absolute numbers of such ratings were so low as to indicate little antipathy to local governments.

General characteristics of attitudes toward local units of government are perhaps best described in Morris Janowitz and associates, *Public Administration and the Public—Perspectives Toward Government in a Metropolitan Community*.[19] This was a comprehensive study of various dimensions of attitudes toward agencies of federal, state, and local government, and included Selective Service as one of the three federal agencies. Knowledge about the functions and procedures of agencies was highest among the higher socioeconomic levels, but, again, the lower classes expected more from governmental services and approved them more. A high proportion of the sample (41 percent) believed that "political pull" played an "important part" in whether the government would help a private citizen with a problem, and another 28 percent felt that it played "some part." The

[16] *Ibid.*, p. 106.

[17] Arthur Kornhauser, *Detroit As the People See It* (Detroit: Wayne University Press, 1952).

[18] *Ibid.*, p. 214.

[19] Morris Janowitz, Deil Wright, and William Delany, *Public Administration and the Public: Perspectives Toward Government in a Metropolitan Community* (Ann Arbor: Institute of Public Administration of the University of Michigan, 1958).

authors interpreted this as a matter-of-fact assumption which only rarely was meant as an expression of outrage.[20] This was demonstrated in part by measuring self-perception of political self-confidence or efficacy: those who were low in this measure had correspondingly high expectations of political favoritism, while those with a high sense of political self-confidence or efficacy were lowest in assumptions of favoritism. Political party identification did not affect attitudes toward government and the authors concluded that—in contrast to the cleavages apparent in electoral studies—there existed a high degree of consensus regarding the propriety and effectiveness of administrative services.[21]

These findings suggest that perceptions and evaluation may reflect educational and class distinctions rather than partisan or ideological differences. Knowledge and sense of political efficacy, flowing partly from social experience and partly from personal attributes, appear to be vital potential determinants of attitudes. We may also anticipate ambivalent or even apparently contradictory attitudes juxtaposed within individual respondents. These are limited and somewhat unstructured beginnings from which to start, but when we have verified them in this context we shall be able to extend our analysis of attitudes toward Selective Service to explore further dimensions of public response to governmental activity generally.

Knowledge

Not all citizens have immediate personal reasons for knowledge about the characteristics or procedures of Selective Service. But the organization has existed and functioned with only a temporary interruption ever since 1940, and it might be expected that large numbers of people would have some kind of contact with it—as registrants, parents, relatives, wives, or simply as newspaper readers. Public knowledge about the System, however, is not great. We asked our Wisconsin sample, after a series of questions about the fairness of the draft, whether they knew who administered the draft in their local communities. Only 52 percent gave responses which we could accept as accurate, such as "the Selective Service boards," "the local draft board," and "the draft board." Other responses associated the draft with state, county, city, or local units of government, and a full 39 percent replied simply that they did not know. Table 7.6 compares various population groupings as to their knowledge about the draft as measured by this question.

[20] *Ibid.*, p. 49. The three questions used to construct the index of political self-confidence approximate those used in the study reported here, as noted in note 26, below.

[21] *Ibid.*, p. 107.

It is difficult to believe that men in the eligible age group could remain so uninformed about such a fundamental aspect of Selective Service. Nearly all of them physically entered their draft board office for the purpose of registration at age 18, at least some of them are still in contact with their boards, and yet the men in the 35–49 age group show more familiarity with the existence of local boards. Unless this question is taken to be defective for the purpose, these data appear to testify to the capacity of the public to carry generalized impressions without specific knowledge, even where they are themselves engaged with the organization. We see no reason to reject the question as a measurement of "knowledge" about the System. The professional and college-educated groups and the sex and class differences show familiar patterns of knowledge respecting governmental activities. The 48 percent who did not know that local boards were a part of the Selective Service scheme is made up chiefly of blue-collar, older, and less educated persons. The best conclusion appears to be that knowledge about the local

TABLE 7.6. KNOWLEDGE ABOUT THE EXISTENCE OF
LOCAL BOARDS, BY AGE, OCCUPATION,
AND EDUCATION, WISCONSIN, 1966

	Percentage with Knowledge	Total N on Which Percentage Is Based
Age and sex		
Age 21–34, male	62%	81
female	41	96
Age 35–49, male	74	99
female	53	100
Age 50–87, male	48	102
female	39	127
Occupation		
Professionals	78	50
Farmers	44	36
Managers	69	52
White-collar	63	78
Blue-collar	50	203
Housewives	36	188
Education		
Less than high school graduate	38	259
High school graduate	55	203
Some college or more	67	114

Question: "As far as you know, who decides which men are going to be drafted from this local community?"

board aspect of the draft is just lower than we—and the Selective Service System—might have anticipated.[22]

As part of our attempt to assess the "little groups of neighbors" interpretation of local boards, we asked those respondents who knew of the existence of local boards, "Can you give me the names of any of the local people who are responsible for drafting the local men?" Thirty people (10 percent of those who knew about local boards, but 5 percent of the total sample) gave a name; some of them were female names—possibly the clerk, rather than a board member—but no attempt was made to verify the accuracy of the names given. The low number and proportion are a sufficient suggestion that the "neighbors" assumption falls short of empirical verification in this respect as well as the ones previously discussed.

Evaluation

Low levels of knowledge do not prevent people from holding and expressing views about the draft or even about the local board concept. But we should be alerted to possible differences in viewpoint which might be associated with levels of knowledge, and the extent of knowledge will become one of the variables through which we seek to understand public attitudes toward the System. Let us look first at the general pattern of evaluation of the desirability of employing local boards for the purpose of administering the draft, and then at possible determinants of these attitudes.

At the conclusion of our inquiry into the extent of knowledge about the existence of local boards, those respondents who had been unaware were informed and then all were asked, "What do you think about having local people involved in drafting men? Is this a good idea, or not?" This question was followed by the open-ended inquiry, "Why do you feel this way?" The responses of the total sample to the key question were as follows:

Good idea	36%
Depends	7
Not good	47
Don't know	10
N.A.	1
	100%
	(N = 607)

[22] Janowitz and his associates found that 56 percent of their sample were aware of some form of appeals procedure within the Selective Service System. They do not indicate what standards of knowledge were required to fit that characterization, but it seems most likely that generalized responses were included; questions directed at registrants in our study elicited very little factual knowledge beyond what was probably an assumption that there was some right of appeal somewhere in the System.

We shall analyze the effects of knowledge on this evaluation shortly; for the moment it is more important to realize that these data show that the general public rejects the idea of drafting men through local boards by a clear plurality. Contrary to the System's assumptions and rhetoric, local boards apparently are not the key to public acquiescence in conscription.

That local boards *may* be the key to the acquiescence of certain (perhaps politically most significant) groups within the general public, however, remains a possibility in the light of the occupational breakdown of responses to this question. Table 7.7 presents this comparison. (This occupational breakdown represents the most precise measure of differences in attitudes toward local boards which we were able to develop. It is used in preference to indices of social class because of important differences between components of the same class levels with respect to the fairness of the draft and the desirability of local boards; professionals and farmers, but not managers or blue-collar workers, radically change their positions on the two questions, and combining them into their usual class groupings would present an erroneous impression of class consistency on the two questions.) The data indicate that there are sharp occupationally correlated differences between groups within the population with respect to the local board concept. The small numbers of respondents in some categories indicate that

TABLE 7.7. SUPPORT FOR THE LOCAL BOARD CONCEPT, BY OCCUPATION, WISCONSIN, 1966

	PROFESSIONALS	PROPRIETORS, MANAGERS, OFFICIALS	FARMERS	WHITE-COLLAR	BLUE-COLLAR	HOUSEWIVES
Response to Local Board Concept:						
Good	56%	50%	47%	42%	32%	26%
Depends	8	12	14	5	5	7
Not good	28	31	19	53	54	51
Don't know Not ascertained	8	7	20	0	9	16
	100%	100%	100%	100%	100%	100%
	(N = 50)	(N = 52)	(N = 36)	(N = 78)	(N = 203)	(N = 188)

Question: "What do you think about having local people involved in drafting men? Is this a good idea, or not?"

these findings should be treated with caution, but the general trend in the locus and extent of support for local boards seems clear.

Only the upper occupational levels—and farmers[23]—show decisive support for the local board concept, and the middle (white-collar) and lower (blue-collar) levels are almost as decisively opposed. Substantial margins of professionals and farmers, it will be recalled, felt that the draft itself was unfair, but both groups have reversed their stands with respect to local boards. Blue-collar workers, and to a lesser extent white-collar workers, have shifted in the opposite direction. Managers and proprietors have remained constant in their affirmative views on both questions. In short, where opinion of the fairness of the draft showed steady, moderate margins of "fairness" except for professionals and farmers, two small but apparently vulnerable groups, opinion toward local boards shows a strong negative feeling among the largest groups but support from those same professionals and farmers, together with another high status but small group, managers and proprietors. In the light of our previous findings concerning the groups from which local board members were drawn,[24] we cannot avoid acknowledging the possibility that this distinctive pattern of support for local boards has its base in the perceived self-interest of the respondents.

Some further understanding of the general nature of evaluations of the local board concept comes from an examination of the reasons volunteered in answer to our query as to why respondents held their views about the desirability of local boards. Table 7.8 presents an analysis of the major reasons, this time broken down by age and education. Once again, there is a caution to be entered because of small numbers, this time of college-educated persons in the three categories, but their responses conform consistently to each other and to the pattern established by the more adequate totals of less educated respondents. Support for the local board concept rises with education *and* with age: both factors are at work, but age is the stronger, particularly among the college-educated. Precisely the reverse effect is apparent in the negative categories. "Don't knows" are highest among the oldest and youngest age groups. The substance of the reasons

---

[23] The classification of farmers in dairying Wisconsin presents special problems. There are more dairy farms (and farm deferments) in Wisconsin than in any other state of the union, and the income of farmers is often commensurate with other occupations; farmers have been and are still in many areas dominant in both political and social institutions. Given all of these considerations, and the fact that farmers display the attitudes of upper status groups, we have classified them with upper status groups for the purposes of this analysis.

[24] See Chap. 3.

TABLE 7.8. REASONS FOR ATTITUDES TOWARD LOCAL BOARDS, BY AGE AND EDUCATION, WISCONSIN, 1966

	Age 21–34		Age 35–49		Age 50–87	
	H.S. Graduate or Less	College	H.S. Graduate or Less	College	H.S. Graduate or Less	College
"Good" Responses:						
Better knowledge of people and of community	15%	24%	20%	33%	28%	47%
Miscellaneous	9	12	10	11	3	6
Total "good idea" responses	25%	36%	30%	44%	31%	53%
"Not Good" Responses:						
Too much chance of favoritism	48%	47%	47%	42%	38%	25%
Pressure and hard feeling created	2	6	5	4	5	6
Total "not good" responses	50%	53%	52%	46%	43%	31%
Don't know, depends	25%	12%	19%	11%	26%	16%
Totals	100%	100%	100%	100%	100%	100%
	(N = 134)	(N = 51)	(N = 143)	(N = 53)	(N = 192)	(N = 32)

given is revealing also: of all age and educational categories, only in the oldest and college-educated group do more believe that board members have a better knowledge of the community than are concerned about the chances of favoritism in administration—and the number of respondents in this group is so small as to cast doubt on the validity of even this much support for the oft-heard argument for local boards. Expectations of favoritism dominate in the other groupings, sometimes by as much as a three to one margin. Nearly half of all respondents in the 21–34 age group—the real clientele group—believe that local boards are not a good idea because there is too much chance of favoritism.

These three independent variables—age, education, and occupation—show an association with evaluations of the desirability of local boards. No other socioeconomic or political correlates were found to have important relationships to attitudes toward the local board concept. It is in a context of the effects of these three major factors that we may search further for some more proximate and draft-related bases of opinion concerning local boards.

Evaluation and Knowledge about the Existence of Local Boards

Attitudes toward the desirability of local boards follow class lines first, with a lesser effect from knowledge: those who know about the existence of local boards are somewhat more likely to favor the idea, although they still disapprove by slight margins. Too few respondents in the upper age brackets were aware of local boards, and there were too few representatives of the key occupational groupings to permit detailed comparison by knowledge levels, so we have been obliged to compare our respondents only by educational levels and knowledge, as is done in Table 7.9. All "depends" and "don't know" answers have been eliminated from the table in an effort to clarify the structure behind opinions actually held.

The table indicates that knowledge about local boards does not lead to a favorable judgment in their behalf, except in the case of the college-educated respondents. Knowledge *does* moderate opposition in the case of the two lower-educated levels, but it does not result in a net favorable view. When those who are unaware of the existence of local boards are told about them, they uniformly disapprove of the idea, but the same educational level differences persist; the college-educated are least disapproving, while the less than high school respondents disapprove by the ratio of two to one. The implication from this and the previous table is that lower class (whether measured by education or by occupation) respondents disapprove of the

TABLE 7.9. EVALUATION OF THE LOCAL BOARD CONCEPT,
BY EDUCATION AND KNOWLEDGE ABOUT LOCAL BOARDS,
WISCONSIN, 1966

	Less than High School Graduate		High School Graduates		Some College or More	
	Know of Local Boards	Don't Know	Know of Local Boards	Don't Know	Know of Local Boards	Don't Know
*Evaluation**						
Good idea	20%	19%	27%	16%	42%	8%
Not good	23%	38%	31%	26%	36%	14%
	100%		100%		100%	
	(N = 204)		(N = 166)		(N = 118)	

* "Don't knows" and "depends" eliminated (total 119 respondents).

local aspect of the draft, and that these attitudes are only slightly moderated by knowledge about the local board system or by advanced age. The upper class (again measured by either educational or occupational indices) respondents are more decisively affected by such factors as age or knowledge, both of which contribute to increased approval of the local board idea.

Evaluation of the Local Board Concept, Knowledge about Local Boards, and Assumptions about Their Decision-making Processes

The Selective Service System maintains that the discretion possessed by local boards is vital to their success, as well as that the presence of local boards is critical to public acquiescence in conscription. The data have already indicated that the conclusion is erroneous, and additional data suggest that the premise is equally ill-founded. It would be remarkable if public approval of an agency of government were to be associated with assumptions about its possession of extensive discretion, and the issue would not be raised were it not for the System's argument in favor of local discretion as an element in popular acceptance of the draft. We asked those who knew of the existence of local boards whether they thought local boards decided for themselves which men should be drafted, or just followed orders from Washington.[25] Twice as many respondents replied that

[25] The question asked was, "Some people say that local draft boards decide for themselves which men should be drafted. Others say that the boards just follow instructions from Washington. Which of these two views do you think really is the way it happens?" (Asked only of those with knowledge of local boards.)

boards followed orders than said they decided for themselves. By itself, this datum would indicate that local discretion was not important to public approval.

Most important for our present purposes, however, is the opportunity these responses provided for an assessment of the relation between assumptions concerning the role of discretion on the part of local boards and respondents' views of the desirability of conducting the draft through such boards. It will be recalled that those who knew about the existence of local boards were more favorable toward the idea than those who did not know about them, although they still disapproved by a slight margin. Among respondents with knowledge, only 36 percent of those who believed that boards operated on the basis of their own discretion approved the local board concept, while 47 percent of those who believed that they followed orders approved the concept. The same pattern applies within any segment of the population: the assumption of board action along discretionary lines is associated with lower support for local administration, and assumptions about following orders from Washington is associated with higher support for local boards. This may reflect merely a limited support for local boards even among those who do believe them a good idea, or a general desire for uniformity in this particular function, but the finding is clear and consistent: local boards do not draw support on the basis of their discretionary power—they suffer for it.

Evaluation of the Local Board Concept and Political Efficacy

Studies of attitudes toward government as well as voting studies have repeatedly indicated that a sense of political self-confidence or efficacy leads to a more favorable evaluation of components within the political system.[26] Using an index constructed from three standard questions which are frequently used to measure this sense of political efficacy, we divided our respondents into the categories of low, medium, and high efficacy.[27] We

[26] See, as to the concept of political efficacy and voting, Angus Campbell et al., The American Voter (New York: John Wiley & Sons, 1960), pp. 103–5. Appendices A and B in Angus Campbell et al., The Voter Decides (Evanston: Row, Peterson, 1954) provide data on construction of such indices.

[27] The questions on which our index of efficacy was constructed are the following: "People like me don't have any say about what the government does," "Sometimes politics and government seem so complicated that a person like me can't really understand what's going on," and "Government officials don't care much about what people like me think." We wish to express our thanks to our colleague Jack Dennis for

184 Little Groups of Neighbors

found that those who scored high in efficacy were much more familiar with the existence of local boards and considerably more favorable toward the idea. Table 7.10 documents these findings.

High efficacy respondents did not differ from low efficacy people in their assumptions about discretionary or rule-oriented behavior on the part of local boards, but they did hold to the assumption that boards knew their local communities much more strongly than did low efficacy respondents. Our measure of "efficacy" is not simply a reflection of occupation or education, for approval of the local board concept rises with efficacy within every category of each. Although the small number of respondents in various categories prevents comparisons in depth, we may illustrate the extent of this relationship by combining the basic occupational categories as is done in Table 7.11. With occupation controlled, efficacy has a consistent

TABLE 7.10. EVALUATION OF THE DESIRABILITY OF LOCAL BOARDS
BY SENSE OF POLITICAL EFFICACY,
WISCONSIN, 1966*

| | | Efficacy | |
	Low	Medium	High
(1) Knowledge about local boards			
Know of local boards	28%	56%	75%
Did not know of local boards	72	44	25
	100%	100%	100%
	(N = 161)	(N = 344)	(N = 102)
(2) Evaluation of the local board concept			
Good idea	22%	38%	51%
Depends	5	8	8
Not good idea	53	47	38
Don't know, not ascertained	20	7	3
	100%	100%	100%
	(N = 161)	(N = 344)	(N = 102)

* For the question on which knowledge is based, see Table 7.6; for the question on which evaluation is based, see Table 7.7. Efficacy index is described in footnote 27 to the text.

use of these data. The index was based on a point-value scoring system which assigned 5 points for each "strongly agree" answer, 4 for each "agree" answer, 3 for each "both agree and disagree" answer, 2 for each "disagree" answer, and 1 for each "strongly disagree" answer. "High," "medium," and "low" characterizations used then discriminated among the 102 respondents scoring 13 points or more (high), the 161 who scored 8 or less points (low), and the 344 others (medium).

TABLE 7.11. EVALUATION OF THE DESIRABILITY OF LOCAL BOARDS BY OCCUPATION AND POLITICAL EFFICACY, WISCONSIN, 1966

| | Upper Status Occupations (professionals, managers, farmers, white-collar) | | | | Lower Status Occupations (blue-collar & housewives) | | | |
| | Efficacy | | | | Efficacy | | | |
	Low	Medium	High	Total	Low	Medium	High	Total
Evaluation of the local board concept:								
Good	37%	47%	59%	48%	17%	33%	44%	29%
Depends	5	11	5	9	6	6	11	6
Not good	42	36	31	36	56	53	45	53
Don't know, not ascertained	16	6	5	7	21	8	—	12
	100%	100%	100%	100%	100%	100%	100%	100%
	(N = 38)	(N = 124)	(N = 54)	(N = 216)	(N = 121)	(N = 218)	(N = 47)	(N = 386)

effect of only slightly lower magnitude than in Table 7.10. But the comparisons between the two levels of occupational status provided by the "totals" columns in each category remind us that occupation is still an important independent correlate of evaluation, and we conclude that both factors are operative.

Evaluation of Local Boards and Opinions as to the Fairness of the Draft

One final element in this complex attitudinal structure that remains to be explored is the relationship between attitudes toward the fairness of the draft and evaluation of the local board concept. There is a relationship, though not a close one, between the two attitudes: of those who believe the draft to be fair, 50 percent think the local board concept a good idea, and 50 percent think it not a good idea; of those who believe the draft is unfair, only 31 percent support the local board concept, while 69 percent oppose it. But we have no reason to think that attitudes toward the fairness of the draft are properly the independent variable here. Perhaps views of fairness are structured by evaluations of the desirability and effectiveness of local boards. If this were true, those who favored local boards would be more likely to view the draft as fair. Were we to state our findings in this form, we would report that two-thirds of those who favor the local board concept consider the draft fair, while slightly under half of those who oppose the local board concept believe the draft is fair. We have reviewed enough data thus far to indicate that any such facile associations are inadequate, and such an analysis would be as circular and vacuous as it sounds. Let us add some further factors and use this problem as an occasion for summarizing and interpreting our findings in this section.

We noted previously that occupational and personal factors, such as perceived draft vulnerability, particularly on the part of high investors, were associated with attitudes toward fairness of the draft—but that generally most groups considered the draft marginally fair. Quite different factors are operative in regard to attitudes toward local boards, however: some occupational groupings show much higher support for local boards than for the fairness of the draft, while others shifted in the opposite direction; political efficacy is highly relevant to attitudes toward local boards, but not to the fairness of the draft; views on the Vietnam War are related to views on the fairness of the draft, but not in any important way to evaluations of the local board concept; knowledge about local boards leads to greater approval of the concept, but the same knowledge correlates with lower images of the fairness of the draft. In general, then, we conclude that different sets of determinants are at work in the two areas. For attitudes toward fairness of the draft, high investment, vulnerability, and personal experience, together with some effects of views toward national foreign policy ventures, account for most of the variations; a general aura of acceptance of established government policy may add to the support found. For the local boards of the System, however, more familiar political factors—set in their usual social contexts—play the primary part in shaping attitudes: occupation, education, political efficacy, knowledge about the organization, and assumptions about its processes. Thus we find the determinants of attitude toward the function resting on one set of factors, while attitudes toward the organization which carries out the function rest on others. In neither case do attitudes appear to reflect partisan or ideological determinants.

This situation may be illustrated by comparing the proportions of various occupational groupings which take affirmative stands with respect to the two issues, as is done in Table 7.12. The level of approval of the draft remains constant, but attitudes toward local boards change with each step down the status ladder. And the lower totals in the final column demonstrate that important fractions of those who *support* the local board concept come from groups who do *not* believe the draft to be fair. In the case of professionals, managers, and farmers, for example, more than one-third of the support for the local board concept comes from persons who did not consider the draft fair, or, stated conversely, fewer than two-thirds of those who support the local board concept believe the draft to be fair. Different factors have shaped attitudes with respect to the two issues, and, in effect,

TABLE 7.12. ATTITUDES TOWARD FAIRNESS OF THE DRAFT AND DESIRABILITY OF LOCAL BOARDS, BY OCCUPATION, WISCONSIN, 1966*

	Believe Draft Is Fair	Think Local Boards Are a Good Idea	Are in the Affirmative in Both of These Categories
Occupation			
Professional, Managers, Farmer (N = 89)	57%	63%	40%
White-collar (N = 59)	54	44	34
Blue-collar (N = 148)	54	33	22
Housewives (N = 101)	55	35	22

* "Don't know" and "depends" responses eliminated (210 respondents).

separate constituencies have developed for each. Different people, as well as differently affected people, hold attitudes in these two areas.

This is not to say that the two matters are totally unrelated, of course. That would be proceeding too far in the other direction. There are visible ties between evaluations of local boards and views of fairness of the draft, particularly in the case of the better informed respondents. For example, among those who know that local boards do the drafting, only those who believe that boards are following orders from Washington believe the draft is fair—and those who think the boards are acting on the basis of their discretion believe the draft to be unfair. The importance of the basis of the board's decisions to these knowledgeable people is striking:

	Local Board "Decides for Themselves"	Local Board "Just Follows Instructions from Washington"
The draft is fair	39%	62%
The draft is not fair	61	38
	100%	100%
	(N = 67)	(N = 148)

There is no avoiding the fact that discretion is considered undesirable: in every occupational grouping, including those groups which most strongly support the local board concept, *those who believed boards operated on the basis of discretion thought the draft unfair, while those who believed boards followed orders thought the draft fair.* We do not know of a stronger case that could be made for standardization and uniformity in conscription, and perhaps for rule-orientation in administration generally. Such a commitment, and probably other similar factors for such informed persons, operate to tie the two subjects together. For most persons, however, the two apparently related matters seem to depend on different opinion-shaping forces, and the relationship between them is only general and perhaps frequently casual, given the low levels of knowledge that predominate in this area.

These findings suggest that the hypothesis stated at the outset of this section—that local boards might serve as surrogates for attitudes toward the fairness of the draft, perhaps acting as lightning rods and drawing off antipathies so that conscription itself remained unopposed—can be valid if at all only in limited ways. It could apply only in the sense that the local boards are tangible objects within the local political environment and therefore perceived and evaluated along with other governmental activities, and thus incurring no distinctive conscription-related character of their own. Conscription itself clearly floats beyond the immediate perceptions and reactions of the general public, and in part its remarkable detachment from its local administrators may be due to the attentive public's perception of their immersion in the labyrinths of local government.

Part II

THE IMPLICATIONS OF POLICY ANALYSIS

Policy analysis—the study of policy content, impact, and consequences—has not been a major subject of inquiry in political science in recent years. Most political scientists have concentrated their research efforts on describing and explaining aspects of the political process, from voting to political party and interest group activity to the decision-making of policymakers. When they *have* examined the content of public policy, it has been as the dependent variable and for the purpose of better understanding characteristics of the policymaking process which led to the production of that policy. One of our major purposes in this book, however, is to suggest that political scientists can make important contributions to policy analysis and, moreover, that they have much to gain in the understanding of politics from employing a policy focus (among other approaches) in the conduct of research and the conceptualizing of politics generally.

"Policy analysis" is a term that can have many meanings, of course. A broad usage might encompass research which identifies effects of present policy substance, interpretations of value priorities implicit in established policies and specification of criteria for evaluation which would permit identification of the "best" policies, theoretical projections which weigh alternative policies in various dimensions or in terms of resource allocations, stages of development, or environmental situation, and so forth. By contrast with what might be done in these directions, our experiment is decidedly limited. We use the phrase to denote analysis of the effects of component elements of public policy of a particular kind in a single subject area; using policy content as the independent variable, we attempt to define the consequences of policy components for the objects of those policies, and, to some extent at least, for the political system itself.

Central to the limited scope of our effort is the relatively narrow definition which we attach to the concept of "policy." Although the word is sometimes used to express broad societal goals, directions, values, priorities, or areas and forms of government, we employ it at three lower levels. We have sought to make each use of the term clear as to the level intended either through the context of usage or by sometimes repetitive distinguishing language. As a general definition, we use "policy" to refer to the substance of an accommodation or adjustment by participants to a problem or goal in their political context, expressed by action or conscious inaction by government. At one level, there is deferment/induction policy, the substantive provisions for deferment of some men and, by exclusion, the declaration of the availability of others. At a second and distinguishable level, there is policy in the sense of the nature of the implementing means by which deferment/induction policy is carried out; the structure and practices of the Selective Service System represent policy choices and imply consequences. Finally, policy may also be conceptualized as the patterns of impact created by the aggregate of decisions made by the implementor in the process of carrying out the provisions of deferment/induction policy. In the current experiment, we have confined our analysis to the consequences of policy content reflected in the structure and practices of the Selective Service System. The purposes we have in mind for policy analysis thus defined are illustrative rather than comprehensive, and, as we have suggested, distinctly modest.

The analysis of structure, impact, and reactions developed in the preceding chapters brings us to the point where we may be able to explore some of the potential payoffs inherent in a policy-oriented approach to the study of politics. In Chapter 8, our interests are most immediately practical. We make use of our identification of the relationships between components of policy and the nature of impact (Chapter 6), to project the probable consequences of current and alternative policies under conditions of the foreseeable future. By specifying who will be affected and in what ways by various policy options, and assessing both short- and long-range consequences of each, we may be able to so narrow the range of choice available that (at least in some instances) professionally responsible recommendations can be made. Because it is unlikely that value-priority questions can be eliminated from the process of policymaking, the act of recommendation raises important questions of propriety and capacity for the discipline of political science. We shall comment on these in the text and footnotes to this chapter where appropriate, but it seems clear at least that serious consideration should be given to the clarification of standards by which the professional quality of recommendatory efforts may be established. In a sense, Chapter 8 represents an attempt to highlight and perhaps to work out some of these problems by means of illustration. It also represents our best judgments as to what can be done to relieve some currently acute problems in the implementation of conscription.

In Chapter 9, our interests are more general; we focus on an important contemporary problem of government organization. We shall draw on the experience of Selective Service as a national government agency which has operated with the participation of citizen volunteers for many years, and on such other experience as is available, to develop some principles concerning citizen participation in government generally. Our data do not permit an exhaustive catalogue of propositions about citizen participation or participatory democracy, but there are key implications in the data which lead to some critical benchmarks that policymakers should take into account in any effort to attain citizen participation goals in the future. These benchmarks, we believe, constitute some of the first empirically supported principles yet developed concerning this problem (and opportunity) in governmental organization. They thus carry significance both for the political scientist, in the sense of increased understanding of political relationships, and for the policymaker, in the sense of guidelines applicable in decision-making in several subject areas of contemporary concern.

In Chapter 10, our interest is principally in the potential contribution of policy-centered analysis to a general theory of politics. The data developed concerning the output of the organization, its impact, and the reactions of special and general publics will be used to generate a sense of the processes by which feedback occurs, new demands arise, and both diffuse and specific supports are affected—leading ultimately to a clearer view of the forces impelling and impeding change in the organization's structure and practices. Political scientists appear to know much more about the ways in which demands give rise to new policy or modifications in established policy than they do about the consequences of policy for political systems, for adaptation and change by subsystems within it, or even for the generation of new demands. This is why we think there is something of theoretical consequence to be gained from a policy-focused analysis.

Chapter 8

ALTERNATIVE MEANS OF IMPLEMENTING CONSCRIPTION: PROBLEMS OF CHOICE AND RECOMMENDATION

Many challenges have been raised against the manner in which conscription has been implemented in the late 1960s. Some are rooted in fundamental dissent from dominant perceptions of international conditions and concomitant military necessities, or concern for the conflict between coercive military manpower procurement and democratic values, and find a target of opportunity in the actions of Selective Service. Others are directed primarily (and more narrowly) at alleged acts or omissions of the System as an organization. In each area, sharply variant value priorities and definitions of contemporary circumstances among political actors have led to substantial controversy. Our selection of the latter set of policies for purposes of our analysis has not circumvented the hard value choice problems involved in selecting among available alternative policies. The considerations of scope and manageability which led to our choice of the more limited policy focus, we hope it is clear, imply no judgments about the larger issues which we have not studied here. Even the closely associated issues involved in selection of alternative deferment/induction policies, for example, would require a different research focus, a larger body of data, and a wider approach than we have essayed.[1] Sufficient problems in assessing probable consequences of alternative policies and in policy recommendation remain in our still-broad

[1] For an indication of the nature of the issues involved, see the authors' "Selective Service and Military Manpower Procurement: Induction and Deferment Policies in the 1960s," in Austin Ranney (ed.), *Political Science and Public Policy* (Chicago: Markham Publishing Co., 1968).

set of policy problems—the structure and practices of the Selective Service System—to lend assurance that our experiment deals with a worthy subject. We shall apply our findings first to some proposals already extant and then move on to some further recommendations that seem indicated.

I. THREE CENTRAL FINDINGS

The implications of the data examined earlier may be drawn together into three central findings regarding the effects of the characteristics of Selective Service System structure and practices. We have seen that *first*, variability and nonuniformity (dissimilar treatment of similarly situated men) are salient features of System performance; *second*, local boards are not "little groups of neighbors" in any measurable sense of that term; and *third*, implementation of conscription by means of local boards cannot be a key to general acquiescence in the draft, because the local board principle is disapproved by majorities of the general public. Each of these central findings is made up of several components; together they suggest that nonuniformity is rooted in decentralization and local autonomy, and that there are no compensating virtues in the local board concept which counterbalance the undesirable effects of essentially arbitrary and unpredictable performance. Let us briefly review the evidence leading to this conclusion.

1. Variability and Nonuniformity Originate in Decentralization and Local Autonomy

The presence of citizen volunteers with legal autonomy in decision-making leads to tentative and deferential treatment by higher units within the System. Guidelines for policy applications are "advisory only," rather than precise and mandatory; no attempt at inspection or detailed supervision is made. Recruitment becomes self-perpetuating and boards become unrepresentative. Neither procedure nor performance can be standardized except by provoking potential conflict within the System. The result in terms of performance is variability among local boards within the same state, and also between the boards of one state and boards of another state. Similar autonomy on the part of volunteers in appeal boards introduces additional layers of variability within and between states and appeal board jurisdictions. Although some of the resultant variability among boards is attributable to the inherent differences in effects of deferment/induction policies upon registrants of differing socioeconomic characteristics (and is therefore not allocable to organizational structure and practice), these effects are exacerbated by the System's employment of large numbers of small and socioeconomically homogeneous jurisdictions.

Men with similar relevant characteristics are thus treated in widely different ways by various local boards across the nation. Nor is this result compensated for by other returns produced by the decentralization and local autonomy which have made nonuniformity a hallmark of the System. The next two findings are addressed to the two chief arguments made in defense of these System characteristics.

2. Local Boards Are Not "Little Groups of Neighbors"

We have seen evidence that board members are unrepresentative of the populations of their apparent constituencies, and even of that portion of the general public which is normally participant in public affairs. Instead, local boards are representative of local control structures, which proved to be very narrow segments of local populations. The "communities" to which they might be related proved hard to identify, because in many cases they were arbitrarily drawn districts within cities or collections of rural villages and towns with no social integrity. Perhaps because of the large number of registrants in many boards as well as the age and anonymity of board members and the reluctance of registrants to approach them, there was only infrequent contact between board members and registrants in most areas. Many registrants displayed little confidence in their boards' procedures or fairness, and their sense of disquiet appeared greater after contact with their boards. In many cases, registrants have moved out of the board's jurisdiction, so board members' knowledge of them or the needs of the "community" would be irrelevant; in such cases, according to the President's Commission, boards proved more likely to place the registrant in a I-A or other nondeferred classification.[2] Finally, we saw that when board members *did* possess personal information about registrants along the lines of the "little groups of neighbors" image, it was possible for such circumstances to result in undesigned use of draft board powers for purposes of social control.

3. Local Boards Are Not Generally Considered a Desirable Means of Conducting Conscription

Barely more than half of the general public was aware that local boards administered the draft. Of them, more disapproved of the idea than approved it; of those who had been unaware that the draft was conducted by

[2] *President's Commission Report,* p. 102.

local boards, two-thirds disapproved. These data alone seem to refute the popular-acquiescence assumption which has animated Selective Service since 1917. One vestige of that hypothesis was established: politically efficacious and influential persons, though a small proportion of the total population, were notably strong in their support for the local board principle, and we have speculated that this factor may have been instrumental in maintaining support for the System.

We take these data and findings to indicate that nonuniformity is caused by decentralization and local autonomy, and that there are no compensating returns realized in the way of "little groups of neighbors" effects or broad popular approval from these System characteristics. But is it clear that nonuniformity is an undesirable feature of the System? It is at least theoretically possible that nonuniform performance—dissimilar treatment of similarly situated men—could serve national or local needs. But this would require assumptions about the knowledge, decisional criteria, and procedures of local board members which are wholly at odds with the weight of the evidence we have examined. It also seems theoretically possible that nonuniform performance is a minor or unimportant characteristic of System performance. Aside from the evidence that awareness of nonuniformity appears to provoke complaint and contribute to reduction of support for the System, what empirical basis have we for concern about nonuniformity? Perhaps if the question is framed in that manner, its value component is most clearly exposed. We do not deny its existence, but we take similar treatment of similarly situated persons to be a lasting characteristic of legal aspiration if not performance throughout various areas of American public policy, from the equal protection clause of the Constitution to everyday public administration. It is hard to imagine this value as a controversial one where government policy is concerned. If the reader doubts this, let him imagine federal income taxes being determined not by nationwide criteria, but by thousands of local citizen boards throughout the country, with each man's tax varying with the whims of the board where he happened to reside. The point is that nonuniformity is extensive, that its causes carry no compensating returns, that it offends traditional and relevant values, that it provokes complaint and reduces support, *and that it is unnecessary.*

II. SOME ALTERNATIVES AND THEIR CONSEQUENCES

The National Advisory Commission on Selective Service declared unanimously in 1967 that there was "a critical need for policy uniformity" within the System. The proposals which that body made for reorganization of Selective Service are succinctly described and explained in a section of its Report:[3]

The Structure of the Proposed New System

The present Selective Service System is based on a rule of discretion, applied locally by more than 4,000 different groups following guidelines that are general in nature. Its lack of uniformity is a consequence of a deliberate policy of decentralization, which is considered one of its strengths.

This Commission sees the overriding need to be precisely the opposite: To achieve the greatest possible degree of equity demands, in the Commission view, a system based on impartial standards uniformly applied throughout the nation. The Commission proposes, in short, to introduce a new controlling concept into the Selective Service System: the rule of law, to replace the rule of discretion.

The Organization

To effect such a significant change in concept requires a modification of the system that administers it; for system and concept are woven too tightly together to permit a meaningful separation.

Administratively, the application of universal rules will remove the need for most of the routine decisionmaking which now is the chief function of the local boards.

Elimination of most deferments and the policy of selecting youngest men first for induction will make classification far more an impartial and standardization procedure than it presently is.

Moreover, the administration of uniform policy would be exceedingly difficult to effect through 4,000 decentralized agencies.

The Commission sees the need to restructure and consolidate the Selective Service System itself to enforce the uniform and consistent application of impartial standards on a nationwide basis. Its thorough investigation into the System as it operates today and into the inequities that are generated under current circumstances persuades the commission to this belief: Fairness, uniformity, and equal treatment for all can best be achieved through a system administered without regard for any geographical boundaries. Such a system should be administered in much the same way that other solely federal programs are operated which affect the lives and welfare of the nation's citizens, and distribute obligations among them.

The structure the Commission recommends includes:

The national office which now exists.

[3] *Ibid.*, pp. 31–36.

A series of regional offices—perhaps eight, aligned for national security purposes with the eight regions of the Office of Emergency Planning.

A distribution of from 300 to 500 area offices situated in a relationship to the population (but with at least one in every state).

Local boards would operate contiguous to—but not as part of —the area offices, and appeal boards would be similarly related to the regional offices.

Clear and binding policy regarding classifications, exemptions, and deferments would be established at the national level. These would be transmitted uniformly to the area offices through the regional offices, which would supervise the administration of the program at the area office level.

The area offices would be the registration and classification centers. A civil service staff, applying the regulations established by national headquarters, would classify the registrants within their respective areas of service and jurisdiction in a uniform and impartial manner. Such staffs might well be drawn from the cadre of able clerks, familiar with selective service machinery, who now serve the local boards around the country.

The use of automatic data processing equipment, to handle the great amounts of information that would be involved in cataloguing the information, would facilitate the routine operation of the system nationally. With the control available through the use of this modern information-transmitting equipment, registrants who change their permanent residence would under appropriate regulations, change their registration from one area office to another.

At the area office level, much of the registration and classification work could be handled by mail. Every registrant would be fully advised of his rights and of the operation of the Selective Service System by means of a pamphlet which would detail all his rights and all the means of review open to him, as well as set forth all sources of information and assistance available to him. This would be mailed to him with each classification.

It seems clear to the Commission that such a system would promote efficiency. But efficiency is only a by-product of the greater result the Commission seeks, which is equity.

Fairness can often be achieved only when there is a way in which an individual's relationship with a system can be personalized. The system the Commission proposes would provide avenues for such personalization. Young men confused or intimidated by the process, even in its simplified form, could visit their area offices for a personal handling of their registration and classification. An adviser to registrants would be available to give information and assistance.

And no matter how uniform the application of rules, there will always be dissatisfaction with classifications. A man might claim excessive hardship, or a conscientious objection, which the classification agents at the area office did not honor.

This is where the local board fits into the new System's pattern. Although the "neighborly" character of local boards seems to exist more in theory than in fact, the prospect of a man's being able to take his case to a group of citizens divorced from the federal system has great strength and merit. A local board composed, as are those today, of volunteer citizens, and conveniently located in the area office but independent of it, is the body to which registrants who wish to challenge their classifications could do so—within 30 days rather than the 10 days which are now allowed. Those boards would become in effect the registrant's court of first appeal. They would have the authority to sustain or overturn classifications made in the area offices.

The local boards under this new system although greatly reduced in numbers, will still have important responsibility. The Commission has certain recommendations to make concerning their organization:

> The Commission believes the composition of local boards should more realistically represent all elements, including ethnic, of the population of the country.
>
> The Commission recommends a maximum term of service of 5 years on local boards, with those terms of service staggered.
>
> It believes that a maximum age of retirement should be established for the future.
>
> The Commission believes the President should not be limited by law in the appointment of local board members to those whom the Governor of a state nominates. So far as the Commission knows, the selective service statute is the only one which so limits the President's power, and the Commission believes that in a matter of such importance the President should have the broadest possible options.
>
> Whatever the reasons which restricted local board service to men, they surely are not valid today. The Commission recommends that women be permitted to serve on local boards.

It seems clear to the Commission that the combination of firm rules universally applied—along with the recommendations contained in the next chapter—will substantially reduce the number of appeals that are made. But some will remain. And the fairness of any system must be gauged in part by the consideration given to those who believe themselves to be improperly or inadequately treated.

If the local boards deny the registrant's request for reclassification, he would be able, if he wishes, to take his case to the regional appeal board. An appeals agent would be available to the area office to advise him of the procedure open to him.*

The local boards would be required to make their decisions and reasons therefore known in writing, so the appeal board and the registrant would have the complete record available.

Appeal boards would be guided by the same criteria which the area offices use in their classifications. Whenever the application of this criteria justifies overturning an area office classification, however, those appeal board decisions should be transmitted around the System as expeditiously as possible—to other appeal boards, and to the national headquarters. This communication would have two important results: it would assist the national office in the refinement of its directives, and it would help insure uniform application of those directives by all appeal boards.

Appeal policies for conscientious objectors also need modification. The present policy is for the Department of Justice to conduct hearings for conscientious objectors. But the Justice Department also uses the FBI to investigate the man claiming conscientious objection and is the prosecuting agency for those who refuse to serve when they are denied conscientious objector status. The Commission has no wish to eliminate the FBI investigation or Justice's prosecuting function. But it believes the hearings could more fairly and effectively be conducted by special panels. It recommends that an adequate number of special panels be established above the local board level for the specific purpose of hearing conscientious objectors' cases.

The Commission found, in its study of the Selective Service System, that there is widespread public ignorance and confusion concerning the System's operations. In the new System it is proposing, it believes that—in addition to the efforts to familiarize registrants themselves with their rights and obligations—public information procedures should be made more effective at the national headquarters.

The Commission is aware that the restructured Selective Service System it recommends may involve some increase in cost. But it believes the cost will be justified by the assurance of fair treatment which a system governed by rule of law will bring, and by the efficiency its administration will make possible.

Summary of Recommendations

1. The Selective Service System should be consolidated and operated under a more centralized administration, with its control-

---

* At present both the appeals agent and the adviser to registrants (see page 32) are unpaid volunteers. The study of specifics which would precede the actual construction of the system the Commission is recommending might indicate that both functions could better be performed by salaried employees. Study might well suggest, further, that both functions should be performed by the same person.

ling concept the rule of law, to assure equal treatment for those in like circumstances. The System the Commission recommends would be organized as follows:

A. National headquarters should formulate and issue clear and binding policies concerning classifications, exemptions and deferments to be applied uniformly throughout the country.

B. A structure of eight regional offices (aligned for national security purposes with the eight regions of the Office of Emergency Planning) should be established to administer the policy and monitor its uniform application.

C. An additional structure of area offices should be established on a population basis with at least one in each state. At these offices men would be registered and classified in accordance with the policy directives disseminated from national headquarters. These area offices would be distributed on a population basis, with at least one in each state. (The Commission sees the possibility of 300–500 of these offices being able to answer the national need.)

(1) The use of modern data handling equipment, as well as the application of uniform rules, would facilitate processing, registration and classification.

(2) Under appropriate regulations, registrants would change their registration from one area office to another as they changed their permanent residence.

D. Local boards, composed of volunteer citizens, would operate at the area office level as the registrants' court of first appeal.

2. These changes should be made in the organization of local boards:

A. Their composition should represent all elements of the public they serve.

B. The maximum term of service should be 5 years.

C. A maximum retirement age should be established.

D. The President's power to appoint members should not be limited to those nominated by the Governors of the state.

E. Women should be eligible to serve.

3. The entire appeals process should be strengthened in the following ways:

A. The registrant should be able to appeal his classification to his local board within 30 days instead of the 10 days presently stipulated.

B. Local boards should put their decisions in writing so appeal boards will have the benefit of the record in making their decisions, and the registrant will be able to know the facts of his case.

C. Appeal boards should be co-located with the eight regional offices, although operate independently of them. The National Selective Service (Presidential) Appeal Board would remain as presently constituted.

D. Appeal agents should be readily available at the area offices to assist registrants in making appeals.

E. Appeal boards, guided by the same criteria which area offices follow in making their classifications, would communicate their decisions throughout the System to insure uniformity.

F. An adequate number of panels should be established, above the local board level, for the specific purpose of hearing conscientious objector cases.

4. Both the registrant and the general public should be made fully acquainted with the workings of the improved System and the registrant's rights and obligations under it, in these ways:

A. Easily understandable information should be prepared in written form and made available to all registrants each time they are classified.

B. An adviser to registrants should be readily available at the area office to inform and counsel registrants who need assistance with registration and classification problems.

C. Public information procedures regarding the entire System should be made more effective by national headquarters.

In associated recommendations, the Commission proposed changes in deferment/induction policies which would affect the organization's structure and practices. We have noted previously the close relationship between the System's tasks and the character of its structure and practices, and we shall comment on the implications of change in deferment/induction policy for organizational structure in the next section. For the moment, we may concentrate exclusively upon the Commission proposals for organizational change. The essential thrust of the Commission recommendations is removal of the System from state and local control, with all that implies for substitution of professionalized administration for discretion and variability. The state headquarters are eliminated, as is the use of state and local jurisdictions as units for quotas and calls. Standards are imposed for persons who are to serve on local boards, and the President is empowered to appoint members from nominations other than those made by the Governors. There is no indication of how such board member candidates are to be selected for nomination to the President, though consistently with general Commission intent we may assume that they would no longer be so largely self-perpetuating. Neither does the Commission indicate whether appeal boards would continue to be made up of volunteer citizens, but their association with the Regional Offices suggests that they would be more professionalized. The general image of the proposed System is similar to that of Social Security, Internal Revenue, or the Veterans' Administration, all of which operate with regional and area offices.

A second set of proposals for change in the structure and practices of the Selective Service System was made in 1967 by the Civilian Advisory Panel on Military Manpower Procurement.[4] Again, recommendations were made regarding certain aspects of deferment/induction policies, and proposals for organizational change must be understood in this context. The principal difference between the Civilian Advisory Panel (the Clark Panel, appointed by the House Armed Services Committee) and the National Commission (the Marshall Commission, appointed by the President) with regard to deferment/induction policies lay in the latter's recommendation to eliminate student deferments and shift to randomized selection processes to draw inductions out of the available manpower pool; the Clark Panel strongly opposed both actions, recommending instead that student deferments be guaranteed and random selection prohibited. From these commitments, the Clark Panel went on to recommend with regard to the System's structure and practices as follows:

1. That local boards be provided with clearer criteria for determining entitlement to occupational deferment and conscientious objector status.

2. That the tenure of local board members be limited to 10 years.

3. That there be no changes in the formula currently applied to establish state quotas for induction.

4. That a data processing system centralized in Washington not be adopted as an administrative device.

5. That care be exercised to insure that any effort to establish greater uniformity in local board actions avoids diminishing the discretionary authority of local draft boards.

It is clear that the two recommending bodies diverged sharply as to the appropriate organizational philosophy for Selective Service. The Clark Panel retained all the essential characteristics of state and local control, particularly emphasizing the need to protect local discretionary authority; state and local jurisdictions were to remain as the applicable units for computing quotas and calls, and the present character of organizational hierarchical relationships to be continued. Some recognition of a need for,

[4] Civilian Advisory Panel on Military Manpower Procurement, *Report to the Armed Services Committee of the U.S. House of Representatives* (Washington: Government Printing Office, 1967).

or at least of the desirability of, greater uniformity was indicated, but in a context of strong endorsement of local power to employ discretion in particular cases. The recommendation concerning board members' terms was a response to a felt need to promote wider service and allay public criticism of unrepresentativeness.

Do our findings and interpretations permit us to make reasonable projections concerning the probable consequences of these two sets of alternative policies for implementing conscription? In the case of the Clark Panel recommendations, which are limited in scope, it seems clear that they do. To a great extent, we need simply project as consequences more of the present characteristics of output and impact which we have outlined at length in prior chapters and summarized again in the first section of this chapter. Because manpower surpluses are rising, we may add that the variability and nonuniformity caused by present organizational features can only be expected to increase. The only Clark Panel recommendation which raises any prospect of reducing variability is the proposal for establishing clearer criteria for occupational deferment and objector status. The uses made of such criteria would probably be marginal, however, in the absence of a basis for and inclination to supervise local boards more closely, and we would not expect to find identifiable changes in effects from this source.

We also have a basis for estimating probable consequences of at least some of the President's Commission proposals. Several of the apparent causes of nonuniformity would be eliminated and replaced by structures and practices which seem likely to be operable either without such effects or with much lower incidence of such effects. The more than 4,000 local jurisdictions currently used as the basis of assigning calls would be replaced by 300 to 500 units, which would probably operate to equalize liability instead of focusing impact upon the special group of men rendered available by operation of the economic factors inherent in deferment/induction policy in the currently more limited jurisdictions. (A randomized machine-operated selection system centralized in one source would eliminate *all* effects from special socioeconomic characteristics of jurisdictions; the Commission proposed such a modification in deferment/induction policy and, if enacted, this cause of variability would be eliminated entirely.)

The elimination of the states as units of administration would remove any tendency toward self-protection or special features of policy guidance for local boards in classification within that state. Much variability, we have seen, arises among states as a result of differing instructions or practices generated within individual state systems, and presumably such effects would be reduced to potential variability among regional offices. The development of a general ethos of standardization within the organization, enhanced by the replacement of part-time local volunteers with full-time professional personnel operating in a context of careful instruction, inspection, and oversight, raises strong prospects of greater uniformity in performance. There appears to be no reason to doubt at least that strides could be taken in the direction of uniformity in much the same way as they have been in other similar federal instrumentalities. Centralization of appeal boards, with closer supervision of fewer and more professional boards as well as more formal reporting of their decisions, would add to the prospects of greater uniformity.

The forgoing analysis suggests that the performance of the System would in all probability be rendered more uniform and consistent across the country under the Commission's proposals. Other dimensions of probable consequences, however, remain to be considered. What effects, for example, may be projected with regard to public acquiescence and support? The data are less comprehensive and the problem is more complex in the case of public perceptions and cognitions, but we think the probabilities are that public acquiescence would at least be no lower, though it might rest on different bases. There would be fewer but more representative local boards, a factor which might lead some of the upper socioeconomic levels, particularly those with the highest sense of political efficacy in regard to local government, to have lower confidence in the System. There is no assurance that compensatory support would develop in other segments of the population, although the prospect seems likely. The use of professional classifiers instead of local notables might remove some of the image of bias and prejudice which many persons appear to hold concerning their local boards, and randomized selection processes might do the same. We see no reason to think that either professional classifiers *or* random selection methods would reduce *general* public acquiescence in either conscription or the implementing organization, though we acknowledge the possibility that the politically efficacious might be less supportive. The institution of fairer and more consistent procedures both at the area office level and in the appellate process could contribute to greater approval of the draft by all segments of the population. We do not think that our evidence suggests the prospect of new antipathies from shifting control to a federalized, Washington-directed System—particularly in view of the expressed greater regard for the System by those of our respondents who already believed it was Washington-run. Neither Social Security, Internal Revenue, nor the Veterans' Administration appear to suffer public disaffection because of their organizational character, although there is no clear evidence bearing on this point; the form of organization which those and other federal agencies represent is sufficiently familiar by now, however, to suggest that the development of special antipathies to the implementation of conscription in a similar manner is no longer likely, if it ever was.

We see no reason to anticipate greater difficulty in selecting or processing men for induction under the Commission's proposals than under current practices. Indeed, we would expect data processing techniques to expedite handling of records, and registration and other communication by mail would seem likely to be as acceptable as present forms of communication, much if not all of which (after registration) is by mail in any event. We are not cognizant of any consequences not intended by the Commission which would be indicated by our data.

III. THE RELATIONSHIP OF CHANGE IN DEFERMENT/INDUCTION POLICIES TO CHANGE IN ORGANIZATION STRUCTURE AND PRACTICES

In many respects it has been difficult if not impossible to separate organizational structure and practices from the tasks assigned the organization to carry out; indeed, the policies that the organization has been asked to execute, as we saw in Chapter 6, may both shape its character and determine its procedures. As a practical matter, it seems quite unlikely that change would be undertaken in either policy area without associated changes in the other. There are therefore theoretical, evidential, and practical reasons for squarely facing the question: what implications for organizational structure and practice are there in possible changes in deferment/induction policies?

Of all the allegations made concerning the management of conscription, two were found to be most compelling by the President's Commission, and the same two stand out starkly in our data: variability of performance throughout the System, and inherent economic inequities in deferment/induction policies. The structure and practices of the organization and the substance of its policies combine to establish these leading characteristics. They can be finally eliminated, if such is desired, only through changes in *both* sets of policies. Two basic principles express the relationship between the two sets of policies in these areas:

1. Nonuniformity of performance may be eliminated or greatly reduced through change in organizational structure and practice, but this

kind of change alone would not reach variability among boards which is caused by socioeconomic differences in registrants. Stated another way, changes in the System might succeed in reducing arbitrariness and dissimilar treatment of men who have identical socioeconomic characteristics, but only change in the character of deferment classifications will modify the differing impact of the draft on men of differing socioeconomic levels. No matter how consistently the draft is administered across the country, for example, as long as there is a student deferment followed by occupational deferments, under conditions of manpower surplus, there will be lower rates of service for the upper income levels of the society.

2. The use of subnational units for the allocation of quotas and calls has the effect of focusing whatever economic biases may be inherent in deferment/induction policies more sharply than would be the case if a national manpower pool were the unit from which selections are made. The smaller the unit, the more the effects of such economic biases will be felt; we saw that the results in Wisconsin were that qualified men in rural low income areas had a 50 percent higher rate of military service than similar men in high income areas. The use of states, or even regions, as units for allocating calls will have the same effect wherever there are draft-relevant differences in characteristics of the populations. If calls were made from a national pool, all men similarly situated (after granting of whatever deferments are allowed) would have an equal liability for call. In that event, the method by which the call is made becomes critical: use of random selection devices (whether lottery or birth date) makes it possible to maintain equal liability right up to the point where there *must* be differentiation and inequality—some men are to be inducted and some are not. But use of random selection devices *except* with a national manpower pool as the unit would succeed only in equalizing liability within the unit actually employed. And, of course, use of any selection method *other than* random selection in some form vitiates the entire effort, preserving all the variability described as well as exacerbating the economic biases of deferment/induction policies inherent in the use of small jurisdictions.

With these principles of the interrelationship of the two sets of policies in mind, we may briefly review deferment/induction policy alternatives, and assess their potential impact on the organization's structure and practices as well as the overall impact of the organization's activities. The President's Commission recommended the elimination of student deferments, random selection from a national pool of eligible men, induction (if at all) during the year a man is age 19, and limits on enlistment in the Reserves and National Guard by men being processed for induction. Each of these recommendations was intended to reduce inequities in the sense of differential impact on men of different socioeconomic levels. The Clark Panel's proposals, which ultimately were largely embodied in the Congressional action of June 1967, called for the firm guarantee of student deferments to all students of bona fide institutions of higher learning until graduation or until age 24, whichever came earlier. No deferments were to be extended beyond that time, but qualifying language reduces this limitation to exclusion of fatherhood deferments only, inasmuch as further deferment is still possible if conceived to be essential to national health, safety, or interest. The Clark Panel, and the Congress, also provided for tightening standards for granting of conscientious objector status and expanded opportunities for enlistment in Reserves and National Guard units right up to the point of induction. Random selection was prohibited without further legislation, but a "youngest first" call was endorsed. The Clark Panel acknowledged no inequities in current deferment/induction policies, and was animated chiefly by the desire to tighten "loopholes" in existing law.

The recommendations made by the President's Commission, taken as a package, would probably reduce inequity sharply, if not eliminate it entirely except for the ultimate inequity that some men must go while others stay. The elimination of the student deferment is less drastic than might at first appear, when it is noted that current and future conditions of manpower surplus suggest that not more than one out of every four or five male students who might otherwise have gone to college would be in military service, and that this situation would last for two years only or until such men emerged from service and began their schooling again. Random selection from a young age group would provide certainty for registrants not later than age 20 and assure equal liability for all while endangering the supply of skilled manpower only marginally. The recommendations of the Clark Panel and the subsequent actions of the Congress, on the other hand, will probably have the effect of continuing the present impact pattern of the draft. In addition, the prohibition of random selection methods of deciding who shall be inducted appears likely to result in local board discretionary selections which will emphasize the same economic distinctions as appear in the substance of deferment/induction policy. *Some* method of selecting the one man in seven who must be drafted will have to be found: barring random selection methods only requires each local board to develop its own criteria and rationale, or to freely extend those deferments which are available and which create the economic bases of military liability now evident.

The Commission's recommendations are consistent with its proposals for change in organization structure and practice. If there are to be only a few deferments, and random selection methods are to be employed, there is far less function for local boards. Conversely, there must be data processing capacity, and the professionalism in its use that accompanies full-time centralized operation. The recommendations are separable to the extent that it would be possible to institute changes in organization structure and practices while retaining present deferment/induction policies, but the reverse would not appear practicable. That is, the present local board system would be severely affected by instituting random selection among the young age group with no deferments; there would be almost no decisions to be made by the local board, and volunteers would probably lose their sense of function promptly. Further, if the purpose of revising deferment/induction policies were to eliminate inequities, it would be inconsistent to preserve the many small jurisdictions which exacerbate those inequities. The case for instituting the Commission's proposals for change in structure and practices is very persuasive, if it is assumed that the proposals for change in deferment/induction policies are acceptable.

Regarding the continuation of present deferment/induction policies, which is provided for by the Clark Panel recommendations and Congressional actions, the issue is more exclusively one of a choice of structure and practices. There are many functions—deferment judgments, selection decisions—of great consequence to be performed somewhere within the System; if data processing is prohibited along with random selection, as both were in June 1967, it would be difficult to reduce the role of local boards. The institution of either would permit consideration of a more centralized system—which may of course be one reason for the System's continued opposition to both. The effects of this nexus, of course, are to preserve the multidimensional variability which has been documented.

IV. POLICY RECOMMENDATION:
THE PROBLEM OF SELECTING
AMONG ALTERNATIVES

Let us be clear on the route chosen by the Congress in June 1967, when changes in the draft were considered. In general, the Clark Panel recommendations formed the basis for such legislative changes as were made before authority to induct was extended for four years. In regard to deferment/induction policies, for example, student deferments were guaranteed on a nondiscretionary basis until age 24 or graduation and random selection was prohibited without further legislation. In regard to structure and practices of the organization, the Congress reaffirmed its commitment to the decentralized, local autonomy principle. In the passage which comes closest to addressing the problem of balancing uniformity against local discretion, the revised statute provides:[5]

> The President may . . . recommend criteria for the classification of persons subject to induction under this title, and to the extent that such action is determined by the President to be consistent with the national interest, recommend that such criteria be administered uniformly throughout the United States whenever practicable; except that no local board, appeal board, or other agency of appeal . . . shall be required to postpone or defer any person by reason of his activity in study, research . . . or other endeavors found to be necessary to the maintenance of the national health, safety or interest solely on the basis of any test, examination, . . . or any other means.

The insulation of local board discretion is complete: the President may only *recommend* criteria for deferments, *recommend* their uniform application (but only *whenever it is practicable* to apply them), and *no national standards* are to be developed to intrude upon local discretion in selection. The closest that the Congress came to accepting any of the President's Commission proposals was in provisions regarding tenure of local board members. It will be recalled that the Commission had suggested 5-year terms and a maximum age limit, while the Clark Panel had recommended 10-year terms; the new law provides for 25-year terms and mandatory retirement at age 75.[6]

We cite the actions of the Congress in support of the point that no particular solutions can be predicted, nor are policy determinations immanent in data, in an area where value preferences are involved—as they clearly are here. Many explanations may be tendered, such as the possible existence of misconceptions about the consequences of various actions or about the extent of popular attachment to the local board principle, and/or merely inaccurate or insufficient data on which to base actions. We have not even mentioned such other highly relevant factors as the internal power structure of the Congress, the real extent of Presidential commitment to

---

[5] Section 6(h) (50 App. U.S.C. 456[h]).

[6] This is not to suggest that the new provisions were without effect. The *New York Times* reported on November 30, 1967, that four members of the Appeal Board of the State of Maine (aged 93, 81, 78, and 77 respectively) had been forced to relinquish their positions because of this change.

change in Selective Service as compared to other Presidential goals, the context of other issues before the Congress and nation at the time, or the potentially very real political costs of making changes in the draft during the Vietnam War.

Despite its fascination, we make no effort to explain the action of the Congress beyond those implications noted in Chapter 10. We are concerned here with the task of the political scientist in extracting prescriptive implications from policy research, and we have come now to the point where we must decide whether we can, as professionals, select between the two sets of recommendations for organizational change already described, and/or whether we can generate recommendations on our own. The choices made in 1967 between the two sets of recommendations indicate that the problem is not as easily resolved as might appear from the data and findings as we have stated them. We do not mean to make a problem where there is none; what may seem obvious to some is clearly not so obvious to others, and *professional* recommendation should rest on bases other than value judgments.

Our analysis of the probable consequences of alternative policies has clarified the implications of each, and perhaps it has (at least for practical purposes) simplified the problem of choice.[7] But it does not, and probably it cannot under most circumstances, fully solve the problem of choice. The critical question therefore is: can we, acting as professional political scientists, recommend one alternative over others? There is no doubt that we could do so in our capacity as citizens, of course, but do the training, expertise, and other professionals skills which we or others may possess as *political scientists* enable us to make recommendations? We believe that the answer depends upon the state of knowledge in the particular policy area, the character of the analysis conducted, and the objectivity with which data and interpretations are presented. Not all subject areas will admit of professionally responsible recommendation, but some aspects of some areas will; in other words, the issue of professionalism hinges not upon the *fact* of recommendation, but upon the manner and circumstances in which the recommendations are made.

In one sense, the content of public policy reflects the distribution of power resources and relative skills in wielding such resources among actors in the political process. But it also reflects a balance struck among assumptions accepted, conditions perceived, goals established, value priorities as-

---

[7] The next six paragraphs are drawn from the authors' article cited in note 1 above, and reproduced here with the kind permission of the sponsors and publishers.

serted, means available, and effects and by-products considered tolerable. Policies undeniably have, as one of several elements, a value component. But this need not in and of itself prevent the political scientist from making recommendations. The pressing character of public problems and the exigencies of governmental needs mandate employment of the social scientist's research skills and concepts, and those who develop superior knowledge will be asked to recommend solutions. In any given case, and whether or not the data and circumstances are sufficient to enable the researcher to act within the bounds of his professional expertise, it may be necessary for him to recommend measures to cope with public problems. In such cases, the social scientist will—and should—do the best he can with the data he may have at his disposal. But in some other situations, data and interpretations may be sufficient to enable him to make his recommendations within the limits of his professional expertise. In three of the six elements just defined as ingredients of the substance of policy, research may produce knowledge which will support recommendation as a professional act. These are the areas of relevant conditions, means available, and effects and by-products produced. Herein lies the strength of the social scientist: through sophisticated use of the current techniques of empirical research, he may be able to identify causes and effects with sufficient precision to be able to advise and recommend. The less we know, the more remains for mere speculation, and the more we fall back on value preferences; conversely, the more we know, the more it is at least theoretically possible to reduce speculation and both shrink the number of and focus the issues for value choices.

For the social scientist faced with a request to employ his knowledge and respond to the existence of pressing public problems with recommendations for their solution, there are at least three general ways to choose among alternatives. First, he might frankly declare what values he considers to be appropriate, and seek to defend their propriety in some way. This might be through evidence of their widespread acceptance within the polity, or through evidence of their relevance in the past or under similar circumstances elsewhere, or through justification which sought to demonstrate their propriety by other criteria such as their harmony with ideals of justice or democracy. Second, he might assume various possible values alternatively, in effect leaving the final choice to others. Among the alternative values considered, the stated goals of the present policy structure could be posited and means prescribed for their fuller attainment. Third, he might so assiduously develop data and refine interpretations of causes and effects in the areas of his peculiar strength (conditions, means, by-products) that the range of value choices would be drastically narrowed and so sharply focused that recommendation would involve a minimum of value preference. These broad categories of alternative-selecting approaches are arbitrary constructs, of course; rather than being really separable or mutually exclusive, they overlap and any real situation will involve aspects of each. But situations will vary as to the proportions of each, with some problems of alternative-selection emphasizing one more than others. The element of value choice is inescapable. We cannot avoid it, and it is better that we recognize it and confront it fully than to consciously or unconsciously conceal value preferences in the design or presentation of our research. There are, however, varying proportions of value choices involved in different acts of recommendation, and those in which there is a narrow area for value assertion (because of a well-developed set of data and interpretations) are professionally distinguishable.

Recommendation in the area of means for military manpower procurement, we believe, partakes sufficiently of the third category above that we can choose an alternative as political scientists. Our data fill the requisites about conditions, means, and by-products, and structure the choice to be made. The parameters within which we operate may be recalled by means of the other three elements in the policy balance—assumptions, goals, and value priorities. Our assumptions are that the United States will continue to have at least the present level of international commitments for the next five to ten years, that the maintenance of an armed force will be necessary, and that this force will at least for the next five years be composed of more than 2,500,000 men. We understand the goals of present policy to be the staffing of the armed forces on a flexible basis with minimum dislocation to the society and economy, and with maintenance of a level of public support and acquiescence sufficient to permit the accomplishment of the primary task. The major values with which the present policies have been designed are efficiency in use of manpower resources and equity in liability for military service. For the moment, we take these two as givens, and return to our data and interpretations.

We have seen that the *condition* which is most significant for military manpower procurement purposes is the steadily increasing manpower surplus over armed forces' needs. Sharp increases in the incidence of college attendance have also occurred in the last two decades. The *means* now employed—decentralized local boards with decision-making power held by civilian volunteers—give rise to variability both within and between states. In part, this variability results from the differential impact of deferment policies on areas of different socioeconomic character, exacerbated by the allocation of quotas and calls to small jurisdictions, but an important share of it is traceable to the discretionary actions of boards themselves. The principal *by-products* identified were inefficiency in utilization of manpower resources, inequities in service liability following income and college attendance lines, and antipathies on the part of many to the local board concept. Close interrelationships exist among these factors: rising manpower surpluses create the need to grant deferments freely, which precludes equity and inhibits efficiency; the use of local boards precludes efficiency and promotes antipathies among many members of the general public.

We think the following conclusions have been established: present conscription policies have delivered the necessary numbers of men to the armed forces in a flexible manner, no small attainment. But the goals of minimum dislocation have not been met as well as the evidence suggests that they could be, and there is even the indication that public acquiescence in one aspect of conscription is weak. The values of efficiency and equity have not been served, except in symbolic or rhetorical terms; indeed, the inequities revealed by the evidence are a major indictment of present policies—if the stated values of the policies are taken at face value. We think that the evidence suggests that improvements can be made which will enable conscription policy to continue to provide men flexibly, but with fuller realization of some of its other stated goals and reduced dislocations and antipathies.

We have no doubt that the Commission proposals represent not just the better of the two sets of proposals for attaining these goals, but that they are close to the most appropriate recommendations that could be made in response to the total context of conditions and goals now extant. We think that our findings establish two primary requisites for any conscription-implementing apparatus to achieve the goals that we have acknowledged: substitution of centrally established criteria applied by supervised professionals for local volunteers' discretion, and elimination of the practice of making calls based on subnational units. The Commission proposals would fully accomplish the former, and, if random selection were instituted along with the more centralized system which is proposed, the second would also be resolved within the context of their recommendations. We do not think that our evidence supports the view that substantial uniformity could be accomplished within the present structure: it would not be sufficient to retain the local board system and merely admonish or insist upon greater uniformity in performance. Local boards of volunteers without discretion are almost a contradiction in terms, to say nothing of the fact that the effects of many small jurisdictions and the operations of state headquarters would remain.

Change at least as drastic as the Commission proposals seems to be the only way of creating a real prospect of attaining substantial uniformity. Change which instituted only some of these proposals while retaining other contemporary characteristics of the System would work only marginal improvement, possibly not noticeable amidst the worsening impact of increasing manpower surpluses.

The prospect of converting Selective Service into an organization composed entirely of full-time civil servants does not chill us. It need not be an excessively centralized bureaucracy. Social Security, Internal Revenue, the Veterans' Administration, the Weather Bureau, and the Post Office, among others, all involve decentralized offices in contact with and providing services with reasonable effectiveness to large numbers of citizens. Local boards of citizen volunteers are not requisite to general public acquiescence, nor do they contribute in other ways to the discharge of this federal function.

In some respects, we would make recommendations which go beyond those of the President's Commission. We see no necessity for Selective Service to be an independent agency at all, and several reasons exist for the transfer of these responsibilities to other hands. The workload of Selective Service is variable, and in times of low calls there might be little for professional staff to accomplish. The counseling and personnel skills needed by classifiers, and the capabilities for data processing and manpower management and forecasting which are needed at decision-making levels, are not lightly achieved and should be integrated with other manpower activities. These seem to us reasons for considering the integration of Selective Service with manpower and employment activities of the Department of Labor. Additional by-products of such a change might be realized in the form of more rapid adoption of modern data processing techniques; the present organization and its personnel are not likely to become enthusiastic about or highly skilled in the employment of techniques which they have spurned and ridiculed over a period of years. Further, we see no reason for the continued emphasis on employment of National Guard and Reserve officers in the national and regional (state) headquarters of the System. The skills requisite to manpower management are as likely to be developed in the civilian sector in today's world; the involvement of military officers in conscription seems more a matter of past experience than of present skills, and this too could be more promptly and effectively corrected by inclusion of the System within broader civilian functions. We do not mean to nominate the Department of Labor particularly for a potentially onerous and perhaps unpopular task; we suggest that any civilian agency with data processing and analysis experience and now performing tasks which engage it in decentralized citizen-contact functions would be appropriate—the Veterans' Administration might be an equally practical choice, and one with some additional logical associations.

This last set of reflections has taken us well outside the bounds of our research, of course, and we offer these speculations only for what they are. But our point remains: among the payoffs which may inhere in a policy-oriented approach to the study of politics are professionally responsible recommendations. We think recommendation was possible here, but we do not mean to suggest that it always would be; the areas for speculation were reducible in this case, and the evidence narrowed the range of value choices. Perhaps some will feel that these necessary conditions did not obtain even in this instance, or that, even if they did, political scientists would have no special qualifications to undertake recommendation. Would those political scientists who are so inclined have any special discipline-based expertise to bring to the general area of policy recommendation, or would their role be interchangeable with, say, competent economists or sociologists? We think that the training and scholarly interest of political science as a discipline create a strong though not exclusive entitlement and responsibility in this area. While the interests and methods of social science disciplines overlap substantially, each discipline also has its own distinctive questions, problems, and areas of expertise. If the policies may be undertaken in part or entirely by governmental institutions; if the impact of these policies must be assessed in comprehensive terms, including the political consequences; if alternative administrative feasibility is relevant; if the alternative values to be maximized must be justified in terms of their demonstrable and probable consequences (past, present, and future); and if an understanding of the contemporary political process, its strengths, weaknesses, and supports is requisite—then political scientists should be included in such endeavors.

In short, we see competent political scientists as synthesizing the research products of many disciplines in professional and objective ways, interpreting these findings in terms of target goals and probable consequences within the polity, and formulating recommendations which will serve the nation's needs effectively. Continuously guided by the developing research techniques and findings of the pure empiricist and employing open and assessable evaluative standards in a professionally competent manner, the interested political scientist can add important dimensions to policy recommendation. He is not only able to make such contribution, but he brings an additional and desirable increment of professional expertise to the task.

Recommendation, of course, is only one of the several possible payoffs from a policy-oriented approach to the study of politics. In a way, conclusions about the professional quality of particular recommendations are only marginally relevant. Regardless of the final resolution of this phase of the problem, one vital implication is clear: empirical techniques will increasingly be employed by increasingly sophisticated social scientists to enable decision-makers to understand more adequately the multitude of pressing public problems and to enable them to predict the consequences of various alternative solutions.

Chapter 9

CITIZEN PARTICIPATION IN GOVERNMENT: BENCHMARKS FOR POLICYMAKERS

Is citizen participation "the decisive issue of the 1970s" as Richard Goodwin[1] would have us believe? It may be in rhetoric, and perhaps increasingly in proposals,[2] but it is surely not yet the subject of understanding or even, as far as we have been able to ascertain, the subject of extensive research. In effect, advocacy has been spurred by hope, and nonachievement ascribed to the resistance inherent in the status quo. Without any attempt to denigrate the resilience and self-maintenance capacity of the status quo, the following analysis tries to sort out the implications of the Selective Service experience and apply them to the general problem (and opportunity) of citizen participation in government activities.

I. THE SYSTEM'S EXPERIENCE WITH CITIZEN PARTICIPATION

We have observed various effects resulting from the presence of civilian volunteers in decision-making capacities within the System. Some of these effects are attributable to the particular citizens who happen to take part in this organization, and some to the mere fact of citizen involvement itself. And these effects are felt in a variety of ways in the different areas of the

---

[1] Richard Goodwin, "The Shape of American Politics," *Commentary,* XLIII (June 1967), 36.

[2] See the Bundy Report, urging decentralization and community control of the New York City school system, reported in the *New York Times,* January 1968.

System's activities. A catalogue of the major effects will facilitate a broader assessment of the problems and purposes of the principle of citizen participation.

The Impact of Volunteers on the Character of the Organization

We have repeatedly noted that the presence of citizen volunteers as decision-makers structures relationships within the organization, reducing opportunities for direct control and creating problems of cohesion and cooperation. Responsible officials must tailor the demands and expectations which they impose on their local units in accordance with the values and preferences there dominant. Conflict is avoided where possible, and spontaneous support assiduously cultivated. The immediate result is superannuation and longevity on the part of board members, which together with self-perpetuating recruitment processes may lead to unrepresentativeness and resistance to change. A corollary characteristic is a low-cost, low-spend ethic which appears to develop as a result of the organization's effort to demonstrate to its volunteers that it does not take advantage of their sacrifices.

The Impact of Volunteers on the Participants Themselves

One result of service on local boards seems to be an increased feeling of integration with the larger society. Many local board members probably had a high sense of political efficacy even before they began serving on their draft boards, but it is still possible that some increment was gained through their service.

We asked Wisconsin local board members to indicate what their major satisfactions were from their local board service. Only about two-thirds of our respondents answered this question, but of those who did nearly 70 percent gave such responses as "serving my country" or "doing a patriotic duty" or "doing a job that has to be done." While the Selective Service System over the years has sought assiduously to foster just this sense of self-sacrifice in doing an important patriotic service, our interviewing convinced us that this was a genuine feeling on the part of board members. There can be no question that the esprit de corps of board members is high, and almost all of them say that they would undertake local board service again if asked, despite all the tensions and responsibilities which they acknowledged.

No other response to our question about satisfactions came close in frequency to the patriotic service dimension reported above. The next highest number of responses, totaling about 18 percent of respondents, indicated a feeling that fairness of the board was assured by the respondent's presence. The converse implication is curious—i.e. that if the respondent were not on the board, it might not be trustworthy. Almost no board members gave answers that indicated they drew satisfaction from working with the other board members as a social group; this may be attributable to the salience of patriotic service and the free-answer form of the question, but there are other indications from our interviews that board members reach beyond an image of a local cooperative group to find their fulfillment in a sense of being part of a national function.

The Impact of Volunteers on Public Reception of the Organization

Insofar as reaction to the organization was related to participation by citizen volunteers, it appeared to be related to the respondents' social status and the particular volunteers who participated. Local board members were shown to be locally situated, civically active entrepreneurs, and reaction in the form of approval and disapproval of the conduct of the draft by local men followed predictable lines: professional and managerial classes and farmers endorsed the idea, while blue-collar workers and housewives condemned it. The implication was that respondents were supporting or opposing the principle of local control on the basis of whether the board members were like themselves or not—or possibly on even broader grounds of a general feeling of efficacy with regard to local government generally. Very few respondents at any socioeconomic level endorsed the principle that local boards should have discretion to decide who should be drafted. Only a small—though probably politically quite significant—segment of the public endorsed the idea of discretionary power in the hands of local men.

The Impact of Volunteers on the Performance of the Organization

The evidence examined in Chapter 6 indicated that there were several kinds of variability in the performance of local boards. Efforts to standardize decision-making within a single state faced substantial obstacles in the idiosyncrasies and independence of board members, and required considerable tact and skill. Even when one state succeeded in standardizing performance, the effect could be to distinguish that state's boards from all others in the national System, because others would either be operating freely under their own discretionary powers or be standardized around a different set of state guidelines. From the perspective of the national Selective Service System, diversity in performance among the 4,100 local boards is not only inevitable but accepted as a hallmark; the placing of local discretion in the hands of hard-to manage local volunteers seems to assure that uniformity of performance cannot be attained. We think this effect may be raised to the level of a general principle: the possession of substantial decision-making power in the hands of citizen volunteers in local constituencies is incompatible with similar treatment of similarly situated men across the country. If citizen volunteers are granted real power, in other words, uniformity of performance seems out of the question.

The Relationship of Volunteers to the Goals of the Organization

The use of citizen volunteers in decision-making capacities within the Selective Service System has marginally facilitated the attainment of some organizational goals, and effectively precluded others. If we take the System's basic task to be the procurement of the requisite numbers of men for induction with minimum dislocation to the society and the economy, we may quickly calculate the contributions made by the citizen volunteers: low cost, reasonably efficient procurement, plus heightened confidence in local boards on the part of local elites. We do not know that these could not have been obtained in other ways, but we do have evidence that the presence of citizen volunteers produced some increment in the direction of organizational goals in these respects. At the same time, use of citizen volunteers in this manner precluded attainment of uniform performance and probably contributed to the antipathies felt by lower socioeconomic strata against the local boards.

In a sense, of course, this catalogue of attainments and disadvantages in the System's use of citizen volunteers is beside the point: at the time of its inception, its planners saw little choice, and the System merely sought what appeared to be the most expeditious and inexpensive means of discharging its basic task. We do not mean to suggest that the System carefully weighed the pros and cons of citizen participation, opted for it, and has been proved wrong. In the light of the World War I and Civil War experiences, and under the exigencies of 1940, no other means seemed feasible. We *are* asking from the perspective of nearly 30 years' experience, what impact the use of citizen volunteers has had on the organization's capacity to reach its goals. The kinds of impact which have been experienced by Selective Service are of importance to us here because we seek to draw implications and attach general significance to our findings—to employ the lessons of this 30 year, 30,000-citizen experiment in suggesting some principles for implementing citizen participation in the future.

II. THE PURPOSES AND GOALS OF CITIZEN PARTICIPATION

Up to this point, we have been considering the impact of an organizational characteristic, citizen participation, upon the nature and performance of a particular national government agency. That organization was conceived as possessing specific tasks and goals which were affected by the employment of this device; citizen participation was thus viewed as a means toward certain ends. We are shifting now to a consideration of the purposes and goals inherent in the device itself, or to an examination of citizen participation as an end. We shall consider these purposes and goals only within the context of national government agencies, for that is the only sphere to which our data are directly applicable; within these confines, however, our intent is to identify the various purposes which may at times animate the decision-making employment of volunteer citizens. Citizen participation, in other words, may be either a means or an end, depending on the perspective from which it is viewed. As we proceed from the latter point of view and examine actual uses of the principle, it will become clear that, in practice, in any organization citizen participation has some of the character of each. It may be *both* a device for facilitating the attainment of organizational goals *and,* if not a goal in itself, at least a means whereby a wholly different set of goals may be attained. Rigorous clarification of the balance struck is essential to the understanding of any particular organization's use of the principle.

Initially, let us identify the goals of citizen participation. Stated abstractly, and without reference to a particular organization's experience or indeed to any practical attempt to implement them, these goals may be classified in two broad categories: individual goals, relevant to participants or others who derive satisfactions individually from the fact of citizen involvement; and general or societal goals, pertaining either to the substance of the decisions or policy applications made by citizens or to the general improvements accomplished or satisfactions experienced through citizen involvement. Individual goals would include the self-realization felt by a citizen from taking part in government and helping to shape his own destiny, the development of the capacity of the citizen to make meaningful decisions regarding public matters, and both the fact and the realization of contributing to community activities. As the citizen takes part in significant public decision-making, he develops his own innate potential and derives satisfaction and feelings of integration from the experience. He becomes better able to cope both privately and through community action with the pressures arising out of changes in the social and ecological environment.

General or societal goals would include the making of substantively better decisions, either because the citizen participants know more about the details of a problem than others, or because they have to live with the results of the decisions and a policy application is "right" insofar as it solves their problems or meets their preferences. Also included in this category would be the societal benefits attained through the more effective integration of alienated or marginal groups, the development of the capacities and level of satisfactions felt by all segments of the society, and perhaps a more general increment to public confidence in the system from more visible, less centralized operation. Securing informed public consent to the actions of government and focusing public reactions on applicable units of government might both be counted as among the possible goals in this category.

In any actual case, of course, several of these goals are involved. The priorities assigned any particular one vary with circumstances and the problem or subject area, so that in each actual instance of citizen participation there evolves a distinctive hierarchy or priority ranking of the goals of citizen participation. This hierarchy of citizen participation goals is in any actual instance merged with the needs and goals of the organization to establish a particular form of citizen participation. The task of the organization, the circumstances in which it must work, and the exigencies of time and resources which it has available for the purpose of attaining its organizational goals—all of these factors shape the parameters within which the principle of citizen participation can be employed. Clearly, the two sets of goals may in any specific functional area be incompatible: for some organizations, primary (organizational) goals may not be attainable through the device of citizen participation, or they may require that citizen participation be employed if at all only in a way which precludes the realization of some of the goals of citizen participation itself. Conversely, if the goals of citizen participation are granted primacy, the level of expectations regarding organizational goal attainment may have to be adjusted accordingly. Policymakers' evaluations or determinations must proceed on the basis of a decision as to the relative weights to be assigned to each set of goals.

The accommodations reached between these potentially conflicting sets of goals amount to one of the facts of life of any organization which now or in the future employs volunteer citizens in any form of decision-making capacity. Two questions succinctly encompass the variety of possible accommodations and provide a means to analyze the experience of participatory organizations—whether Selective Service, the TVA, the Office of Price Administration, urban renewal, or the Community Action Councils of the Poverty Program. These are (1) who participates in the governmental activity? and (2) in what manner, i.e. do they enjoy policymaking powers and if so to what extent?

1. Who Participates?

Participation may be by the clientele which the organization is set up to serve, or by those who are beneficiaries of its services; it may be by some number of citizens, drawn from the general public, who are thought to be in one of several possible ways representative of that public; or it may be by established local elites, whether officially or unofficially, i.e. as a specially constituted body made up of local officials or their nominees, or simply drawn from the ranks of those who usually carry responsibility for management of community affairs.

2. In What Manner?

Participation may include little more than an opportunity to ratify decisions actually made elsewhere; or it may include opportunities to determine the details of application of policy already established in major outlines elsewhere; or it may involve broad discretion in shaping the policies themselves, both as to substance and as to applications in specific situations.

The key to the accommodation between the goals of the organization and the goals of citizen participation is to be found in the combination of these possibilities. For example, participation by clientele or beneficiaries accompanied by involvement in policymaking suggests high priority for the goals of citizen participation; accompanied only by opportunities to ratify decisions actually made by others, however, it would suggest priority for the organization's goals and imply that participation was principally to facilitate the securing or manipulating of consent from the participants and others similarly situated. Participation by a body of citizens who are representative of the general public in some way which is relevant to the activities of the organization would carry the same alternative implications, depending on the extent of policymaking powers. Participation by elites or unrepresentative groups of citizens suggests priority for organizational goals under any conditions: if there is little or no participation in policymaking, the implication is that the local elite is being used to gain consent or to more effectively implement the organization's goals; if there is policy involvement, it is likely to be on a quid pro quo basis, in which the organization confers authority on the local elites in order to get its tasks accomplished, avoids challenging them on the way in which they do the job, and in return secures support from them for the basic task. In neither of the latter instances is there any substantial accomplishment of citizen participation goals.

The inevitable tensions between the two sets of goals are complicated further by the fact that most organizations must adjust to specific constellations of forces and circumstances in their environments. Some accommodation with political reality must be made, or the organization will stand no chance of accomplishing its goals—and thus local elites may play a larger role than would ideally be designed by one who sought to emphasize citizen participation goals. Also, the particular balance struck between the two sets of goals may vary over time within any organization, as its own priorities change or its environment evolves. We may summarize this discussion and prepare for a comparative analysis of the experience of several participatory organizations by conceiving of the goals of citizen participation as related to the two primary variables along the lines suggested by Figure 9.1. The

FIGURE 9.1

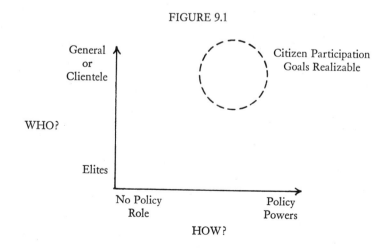

"who?" vector is a continuum of broadening participation, moving from the most narrow, elite participation to the widest, most representative or clientele participation. The "how?" vector is a continuum of increasing policy-making power, moving from none to high degrees of policy involvement. The goals of citizen participation posited in this section are more likely to be reached as the balance between the two variables approaches the upper right quadrant of the figure. A review of the experience of Selective Service and other participatory organizations will serve to test this prospect and generate some specific guidelines for the achievement of these goals under various conditions.

III. ORGANIZATION GOALS VERSUS CITIZEN PARTICIPATION GOALS: OCCASIONS OF CONVERGENCE

We have relatively little evidence directly applicable to the citizen participation characteristics and experience of the other national government agencies which have made use of the device in recent history. With the exception of Selznick's study of the TVA, no major study treats this problem in either of its important dimensions. Selznick himself dealt only with the organizational consequences of the use of citizen volunteers, and not with the general problem of involving citizens for their own improvement. His articulation of the dilemma of policy sharing is nevertheless useful as a starting point:

> Democracy in administration rests upon the idea of broadening participation. Let the citizen take a hand in the working of his government, give him a chance to help administer the programs of his positive state. . . . If analysis and appraisal is to be significant . . . it is necessary to inquire into the concrete meaning of such an unanalyzed abstraction as "participation." In doing so, we shall have to distinguish between substantive participation, involving an actual role in the determination of policy, and mere administrative involvement. . . . It is easy enough for administrative imperatives which call for decentralization to be given a halo; that becomes especially useful in countries which prize the symbols of democracy. But a critical analysis cannot overlook that pattern which simply transforms an unorganized citizenry into a reliable instrument for the achievement of administrative goals, and calls it "democracy."
> The tendency for participation to become equivalent to involvement has a strong rationale. In many cases, perhaps in most,

the initiation of local citizens' associations comes from the top, and is tied to the pressing problem of administering a program. The need for uniformity in structure; for a channel through which directives, information, and reports will be readily disseminated; for the stimulation of a normally apathetic clientele; and for the swift dispatch of accumulated tasks—these and other imperatives are met with reasonable adequacy when involvement alone has been achieved. Some additional impetus, not provided for in the usual responsibilities of the administrative agency is normally required if the process is to be pushed beyond the level of involvement. Indeed, it is doubtful that much can be achieved beyond that level. Such associations, voluntary or compulsory, are commonly established ad hoc, sponsored by some particular agency. That agency is charged with a set of program responsibilities. These cannot be readily changed, nor can they be effectively delegated. As an administrative organization, the agency cannot abandon the necessity for unity of command and continuity of policy—not only over time but down the hierarchy as well. What, therefore, can be the role of the coopted local association or committee? It cannot become an effective part of the major policy-determining structure of the agency. In practice only a limited sphere of decision is permitted, involving some adaptation of general directives to local conditions, and within that circumscribed sphere the responsible (usually paid) officials of the agency will play an effective part.[3]

This statement emphasizes one of the two critical factors which lie at the heart of the citizen participation problem. Some policy role for citizen participants is essential for their participation to be raised from mere involvement to a more meaningful status, and yet program goals of the organization may militate against its tolerance of such a role.

The example of the TVA indicates that one organization may, in different areas of its activity, provide illustrations of both poles of policy involvement on the part of participants. The "grass roots" of the TVA took two distinct forms. Its agricultural services and projects were funneled almost entirely through the existing and specially created facilities of the agricultural extensions of the area land-grant colleges. Extension employees carried out the local operations of the Authority, working with farmers' associations but retaining most of the decision-making authority over the projects. The participants in fact were the established agricultural entrepreneurs of the extension services, and their policymaking status grew to such proportions that the agency itself was ultimately subordinate to them in important ways. The electric power distribution functions of TVA, and

[3] Philip Selznick, *TVA and the Grass Roots* (Harper Torchbooks ed.; New York: Harper & Row, 1966), pp. 219–21.

some other experimental activities, were conducted through local cooperatives organized for the purpose. These were groups of local citizens who were users of the services, and their participation was minimal; TVA performed most functions directly, using the cooperatives as nonprofit "front" organizations. Thus, in the first area, the policy role of participants was great, and in the latter it was perfunctory.

Of equal importance for our concern with citizen participation as a principle is a second factor: the participants themselves. In the first area, participation was by the extension services, themselves little groups of elites; in the second, it was by clientele groups, but it was without policy involvement. When we combine the two dimensions of analysis, it is clear that the TVA did not approach realization of citizen participation goals in any comprehensive sense. Selznick's exclusive concentration on the organizational consequences of policy involvement runs the risk of glossing over this important conclusion.

Other available studies, however, do not go even this far in providing evidence of the results of citizen participation. We have seen that participation in the local price and rationing boards of the OPA was relatively broad, and that it broadened over time as national administrators required the inclusion of new groups.[4] But OPA found it desirable, as the war went on, to assert more and more control over the discretionary behavior of the local boards as a means of reducing variability. Rules grew more detailed, quotas were imposed in various ways, and repeated appeals to patriotic needs of wartime were made, all in an effort to gain control over policy applications made by the local boards. We may speculate that commensurate reductions in achievement of citizen participation goals occurred.

In the case of urban renewal, local administrators of projects are required by law to create and respond to citizens' advisory committees.[5] In practice, this has usually led to perfunctory participation and ratification of administrators' actions. Citizens' committee members are frequently the nominees of the administrators or of the local governing body where it is not itself the administrators, and/or the citizens' committees are citywide in a large city (rather than neighborhood-based) so their viewpoints are sympathetic to the administrators' interests.[6] But urban renewal

[4] This account relies on Emmett S. Redford, *Field Administration of Wartime Rationing* (Washington: Government Printing Office, 1947), pp. 10–13.

[5] The best source for relating statutory requirements to actual participation experience is "Note: Citizen Participation in Urban Renewal," *Columbia Law Review*, LXVI (March 1966), 485–607, a study based in part on 100 interviews in eight Eastern cities.

[6] Gerda Lewis, "Citizen Participation in Urban Renewal Surveyed," *Journal of Housing*, XVI (March 1959), 80–87.

has encountered—or inspired—an informal form of citizen participation on the part of residents of the affected areas. The neighborhood view of urban renewal is likely to be a reflection of its class composition, and in most cases this means that a negative reaction is indicated.[7] In some cases, neighborhood groups have been used as a means of gaining consent to programs devised by experts or others and felt to be in the city's interest, but even here there is occasionally some cost in policy terms.[8] More frequent is the case in which status quo groups take a stand against the project and seek its defeat or substantial modification. According to the most comprehensive study of this development, "the inclusion of neighborhood groups in renewal decision-making is becoming a political necessity."[9] At the same time, the author notes that such groups are usually undemocratic in that their leaders rarely permit members to vote on group stands, and their positions are in reality those of the leaders.[10] Their participation, which inevitably makes long-range planning more difficult, may thus be a means for leaders to gain acceptance of their preferences in return for delivering the consent of the affected.

The growing perception that effective urban renewal requires not only acquiescence, in the sense of non-opposition to programs, but also the rehabilitation of the neighborhood through willing cooperation by participating residents, has led to a search for other ways to promote participation. In a report based on 100 interviews in eight Eastern cities, a Columbia Law School group suggested new approaches to community organization which might have the effect of removing some of the barriers to direct participation.[11] So far, however, citizen participation in urban renewal seems to have been limited to middle class acquiescents on perfunctory statutory advisory committees, neighborhood interest group leaders, or lower class opponents of removal. Little continuing engagement of citizens in policy development or application within the organization has been accomplished; most citizen activity has been from the outside in opposition to the program. From its original commitment to citizen involvement as a means of securing consent

---

[7] The most politically sensitive analysis of this aspect of urban renewal is James Q. Wilson, "Planning and Politics: Citizen Participation in Urban Renewal," in James Q. Wilson (ed.), *Urban Renewal: The Record and the Controversy* (Cambridge: MIT Press, 1966), pp. 407–21.

[8] See Peter H. Rossi and Robert A. Dentler, *The Politics of Urban Renewal* (New York: The Free Press, 1961), pp. 283–88.

[9] J. Clarence Davies, III, *Neighborhood Groups and Urban Renewal* (New York: Columbia University Press, 1966), p. 206.

[10] *Ibid.*, p. 207.

[11] "Note: Citizen Participation," note 5 above, p. 599.

from a possibly unresponsive citizenry, urban renewal seems to be moving, out of necessity, toward efforts to grant a greater share of policymaking to the affected residents. The Community Action Councils of the poverty program offer another example. Although the Office of Economic Opportunity has sought to engage the poor in the direction of programs for their assistance, there have been few instances of success, and management remains for the most part in the hands of professional administrators or local governing bodies.[12] In some cases, such as Chicago, community action programs have been turned over to the city government; the poor may be participants through their political parties, but it seems probable that this form falls short of citizen participation in the sense that we have been using the term. Independent action agencies were set up in some cities, such as Syracuse, but eventually administration has come under the city governments and citizen participation has given way to professional management. In some cases, established groups have appeared to manage the consent of the indigenous poor. The poor themselves have not taken part in several cities where elections to Community Action Boards were held: a total of only 4 and 5 percent of those eligible actually voted in Cleveland and Kansas City respectively in 1966, and only 2,659 of 400,000 eligibles (0.6 percent) voted in a Los Angeles election in that same year.[13] This may be due to lack of interest or information, to an underdeveloped sense of political efficacy, or perhaps to a feeling that no purpose would be served by such involvement of the poor, either because of disbelief in real prospects of influence or because the project was seen as a sham.

In any case, it does not appear that real citizen participation has progressed very far as yet in poverty program activities. This experience almost reverses that of urban renewal. OEO began with a far stronger degree of concern for involvement of actual clientele groups, but found that intervening forces sought to take over or at least share in the management of its programs. Its recent adaptations seem reminiscent of those made by TVA, which came to terms with power centers in its environment in such a way as to tender a substantial degree of control over its policies to them.

---

[12] The best source for combined statutory and field analysis of participation in Community Action Councils is "Note: Participation of the Poor: Section 202 (a) (3) Organizations Under the Economic Opportunity Act of 1964," *Yale Law Journal*, LXXV (March 1966), 599–629. See also Jean and Edgar Cahn, "The War on Poverty: A Civilian Perspective," *Yale Law Journal*, LXXIII (1964), 1317.

[13] *Ibid.*, p. 618, citing the *New York Times* of February 27, 1966, February 20, 1966, and March 3, 1966, respectively.

The targets of OEO's efforts have in part shifted from clientele to leader-ship elements in the communities, with, we may surmise, corresponding costs to the attainment of citizen participation goals. Applying the same frame of reference to the experience of Selective Service, it quickly becomes clear that participation is by local elites and that their policymaking power amounts to an accommodation in which the organization confers such power in return for getting its job done and receiving the support of the elites. The task of Selective Service is sufficiently general that it can afford to tolerate policy power at the citizen level. It uses the citizen participants as a means of serving its ends, and citizen participation goals are irrelevant.

This brief analysis of the experience of various participatory organizations strongly suggests that citizen participation goals have not been realized. Indeed, the evidence suggests that they are realizable only under very special conditions of (1) organizational mission and (2) organizational circumstances and environment. Only when organizational goals and circumstances are such as to permit participation to meet our two criteria can we reasonably expect the two sets of goals to converge. Thus, the "occasions of convergence" are likely to be relatively few in number, and successful citizen participation in both senses at the same time requires both great care and fortuitous conditions.

IV. CITIZEN PARTICIPATION: CONDITIONS AND IMPLEMENTATION

In this section we seek to specify *when and how* organizational and citizen participation goals can *both* be attained under actual conditions of national government agency operations. Heretofore, we looked at the effects of citizen participation on an organization's capacity to do its job; at the purposes and goals of citizen participation itself; and at the accommodations reached by various organizations between the two possibly conflicting sets of goals. We saw that citizen participation could readily be employed as a device for securing consent or otherwise effectuating the organization's needs, but that such use had little to do with the real goals of citizen participation. It is the attainment of these latter goals *at the same time as* the organizational goals that presents the difficult problem. The intimations from the data so far reviewed are that either one or the other set of goals is likely to predominate, and that harmonious convergence in real situations is likely to be rare.

1. Conditions of Organizational Mission

In the organization's priority of goals, one of the chief goals must be the production of specific behavioral or attitudinal consequences in large segments of the public, which depend upon the development of self-generated motivations or affirmative dispositions on the part of individuals in that public. It is not enough that citizen participation be one convenient way of attaining the organization's ends, for this can lead too readily to dominance of organizational goals. The mission of the organization itself must have to do with the production of results attainable only by means of the citizens' shaping of policy, for only under such circumstances can the organization be expected to yield sufficient policy prerogatives to its participants to satisfy the goals of citizen participation. And unless it is prepared to yield, manipulation of consent is all that can be expected from citizen involvement.

If uniformity of performance across the nation is high on the organization's priority of goals, it is probably not appropriate for it to engage in any form of citizen participation which involves policy sharing, let alone the kind of policy sharing which is requisite to attainment of citizen participation goals. The more general and the more flexible the goals of the organization, the better it fits into the prospects of reaching citizen participation goals; if there are various ways in which the organization's mission may be performed and it therefore can acquiesce in diverse methods as determined by locally variant attitudes, it is better suited for citizen participation.

2. Conditions of Organizational Circumstances and Environment

The presence of substantial opposition greatly reduces the prospects for successful use of the principle of citizen participation. Any organization must come to terms with the political realities in its environment in order to accomplish its tasks, and it will be tempting for it to confer management of the local aspects of its functions upon opponents (or at least to permit them some veto or sharing role) rather than to adhere to true citizen participation standards. Similarly, a situation perceived as an emergency, in which there is heavy emphasis on the need to get the job done and on the speed with which it is to be accomplished, is an unpromising one in which to accomplish citizen participation goals. The tendency under such circumstances is to utilize ready-made vehicles of established authority, themselves unlikely to be open to the citizenry in general.

If the successful accomplishment of the organization's goals involves the probability of change in the status quo, the organization can expect that pressures toward penetration of the citizen participation apparatus will increase as it reaches closer to attainment of those status quo-changing goals. The needs of the organization for the maintenance of consent within the environment in which it is operating, of which this is only one example, may at any time have to take priority over the goals of broad-based citizen participation. Elite satisfaction and acquiescence, of course, may be attainable only at the cost of dissatisfaction on the part of others; this can be an insoluble dilemma for organizations in particular subject areas. The question is not so much *whether* there is to be an accommodation between elites and activists on the one hand and less active, nonparticipant strata on the other, but as to the *nature* of that accommodation; it cannot be sufficient for the organization to accept the product of the natural trend within the community, and it must be both willing and able to continuously work toward more inclusive participation.

The organization, it seems, must be able to admit normally nonparticipant groups into some form of policy sharing in such a way as not to unduly threaten the established elites which must be part of the operation. Somewhere within the organization, the inevitable tensions of stability versus change must be allowed to discharge themselves in activity which loses the support of neither element. This can only be done, by all the evidence assembled here, through impetus from the upper reaches of the hierarchy, and amidst occasionally severe conflict and probably one or more reverses. The problems for the upper echelons of authority within the organization are to correctly assess the nature of the tensions below so as to strengthen the hand of the weaker side (normally the nonparticipant groups being brought to a new or unusual level of involvement) just enough to gain real influence for them without forcing the established elites out of the program and incurring their political reprisal. Some degree of elite resentment is probably inevitable, perhaps even indicative of successful motion in the direction of attainment of citizen participation goals, and the national headquarters of the organization will no doubt be obliged to defend itself politically; the experience of OEO with the composition of the Community Action Councils is an example of this feature of the adjustment. The national headquarters will have to be prepared to persevere over long stretches of time in hewing to the line of maximum nonelite participation while retaining, however grudgingly, the cooperation of established elites.

A problem as delicate as it is vital is reached when it is sought to balance elite versus nonelite participation with the nature of policy sharing to be practiced. There is no permanent answer to be found in the apparently fortuitous mutually satisfactory arrangement developed within Selective Service, for the reason that few policy goals will admit of such flexibility in fulfillment, and the elite proprietorship of the local boards is under attack in any event. But perhaps there are some clues in the accommodation reached here: if the organization has several goals, and not just one or two, there will be a broader opportunity for compromise within it. Each element will probably hold to a slightly varying set of priorities as to what it seeks to extract from the activity of the organization, and its willingness to accept resolutions in each area will be promoted by the possibility that on another issue it will have more success. The presence of several issues on the bargaining table will permit a readier resolution of each one; each party can hold out the prospect of future agreement on a matter of lesser importance, or even trade to reach package adjustments, with resulting greater flexibility within the organization.

This suggests that a multifunctional organization might have lower potential for destructive conflict than unifunctional ones. It does not amount to an argument for using local governments or setting up a single multifunctional organization, because there is still the goal of maximum participation to be served, and this will require several participatory organizations. Besides, local governments would be too much the property of local elites. It would permit, however, using the same geographical unit for several multifunctional organizations, in the interests of integration of services, planning, and economy as well as to maximize chances for the development of a distinctive sense of community and acceptable patterns of representation. The same district, for example, might be used as the jurisdiction for various participatory organizations, such as housing and urban renewal, poverty and employment services, conscription and volunteer social services, etc. The more numerous the participatory organizations, the less will established elites be able to staff each in their own image, and the task of the national leadership will be facilitated.

These are still general considerations, though they approach closer to a specification of organizations within which citizen participation has its best chance for success. We have said that the organizations which may be able to permit convergence of organizational and citizen participation goals are those whose missions are general in character, admitting of local variations, and which further involve public behavioral consequences inspirable through participation. Even under such initially favorable conditions, other environmental factors and developments may preclude effective realization of both sets of goals together. Let us try to specify as precisely as possible what these considerations mean in concrete situations, using as illustration national government functions as they are now established.

Implementation: Which National Government Functions Are Appropriate for Citizen Participation?

Where do the goals of national policy have a general character, most likely to be effectively served when tailored to fit local situations? Where do they at the same time require the engagement of individuals in a manner such as to develop particular motivations within those individuals? Urban renewal appears to be one such area, because the general goal of rehabilitation of the cities can be served well by specific and locally diverse applications—with particular projects arranged to suit a given city's special problems, history, and characteristics. Nor is urban rehabilitation exclusively physical. It requires commitments toward community consciousness and group action on the part of individual residents, and for this reason participation seems an essential route toward realization of the organizational goal. The community programs of the poverty agency, and perhaps other welfare activities as well, also appear to fit these criteria. The national policy goal of raising the productivity and standard of living of chronically poor persons requires specific tailoring to the diverse needs and conditions of such people, and the goal includes the development of new motivations on their part and ultimately a new sense of integration into the society. In both of these areas there is a probability of a community interest, in that there is an identifiable social unit which shares certain characteristics, is similarly affected by external factors, and is conscious of its interdependence and sharing of conditions.

Some national government functions do not meet these criteria. Either their policy goals are particularized, or they require national uniformity, or they do not have anything to do with the generation of particular motivations among target groups of citizens, or they require a high degree of professionalization in applications of policy—or they display several of these characteristics. The collection of internal revenue, for example, is ill suited for citizen participation: its extractive nature requires consistency and uniformity in application to all individuals; policies are precisely formulated and the exercise of discretion in administration is confined within stated limits; rules must be (consistent with the nature of economic transactions) complex, and professionals and specialists are best able to interpret them;

and the motivation required is a willingness to prepare and submit a report —a motivation which, while impressive in its fulfillment, does not appear to depend upon framing or administering the policies themselves. There is a distinction between the constituencies with which revenue collection, on the one hand, and urban renewal and poverty programs, on the other hand, have to deal: the former is a very numerous body of individuals throughout the nation, having in common only the fact that they have earned income in the previous year, while the latter are more likely to be social groupings, defined originally by geographic or other boundaries, with shared but distinct conditions and a consciousness of their particular status. There is a distinction also in the nature of the policies sought to be carried out: revenue collection is extractive, and hence procedural fairness—uniformity and technical due process—are appropriate in application to individuals. Urban renewal and poverty programs are ameliorative and hence responsive to particularized needs and conditions, requiring flexibility and adaptability in applications whose impact is peculiarly localized.

This analysis suggests that Selective Service is not an organization in which the goals of citizen participation are likely to be realized. It has much in common with Internal Revenue, and could readily have been substituted for it in the preceding paragraph. In part, this conclusion emerges from our conviction that conscription should be applied with national uniformity—a judgment which the present System does not share.[14] But there is much more about the nature of Selective Service —its extractive nature, its broad relevance to numbers of individuals across the nation, its proliferation of rules and criteria, its lack of involvement with participant motivation—which suggests that Selective Service is an inappropriate function for citizen participation. (This is not to say, of course, that it is necessarily wrong to employ citizen participation, even in the elite form developed by the Selective Service System, but simply to note that the principle should not be employed with any expectation of realizing goals of citizen participation as such. Citizen participation in some form might still be entirely reasonable, but it should be recognized that it would then be exclusively for the purpose of attaining organizational goals. In such an event, evaluation of its use would proceed simply on the basis of the net returns to the organization from the particular use actually made. Our view of the net returns to Selective Service, based on the data of this study,

---

[14] It may be that this position is maintained by the System's spokesmen because the local board concept is taken as a given. If for some reason the national headquarters were to accept the idea that some other form of operation were possible, it might revise its position on this point also.

is that the local board principle as it is presently applied by the System fails to contribute as much to the attainment of organizational goals as it costs in loss of support and dissatisfaction.)

Implementation: The Problem of Who Participates

We have suggested participation be employed in those areas where the community has a group interest which may be articulated. Consistently, the problem then becomes one of representing that community in some comprehensive way, and assuring that participation (which must of necessity be by individuals) becomes participation by individuals *as part of* the community. The size and character of the "communities" or units to be employed is a critical part of this problem. For each function, and for each occasion when that function is to be carried out with citizen participation, it will be necessary to define the units of participation along lines reflecting the natural boundaries of affected people. The basis of definition may be geographic or social, depending on the specific function and conditions. The size of the "community" also will depend on the specific circumstances, but it should be small enough to maintain a consciousness of shared concerns which can be embodied in the actual participants.

A second aspect of the problem relates to the particular citizens who are engaged in participation. There is no assurance that broadly representative participation can be secured either from clientele or from the general public through elections. Although this route is ordinarily to be preferred to outside selection, however benevolent, it still does not reach around the self-selection factors underlying electoral candidacies to engage the dormant or apathetic citizens whose participation may be most vital. In all probability, special pains will have to be taken to design and implement mixed systems of elections within defined areas and from defined constituencies in order to maximize the prospects of inclusiveness.

Implementation: The Problem of Policy Sharing

The prospects of conflict between organizational mission and citizen participation goals are greatest in this area, and we have seen that the dilemma created may at times be insoluble. In general, we envision the organization as operating in a context where its mission is a general one, and where its fundamental policy goals are accepted by participants. These basic goals, then, would not be subject to participant redefinition. On all other matters of specific policy formulation and application, the organization must be ready to yield to participant determination. The problem arises as to how to tell basic goals from specific applications in any concrete instance. To oversimplify the alternatives somewhat, we may suggest a scale of the intimacy of impact: in policy matters which have limited and localized impact, the agency would be expected to yield as a matter of course; in those policy matters which have impact beyond the local community, and which raise issues of fundamental incompatibility with the basic tasks of the organization, the policymaking powers of participants would not be conclusive. At some point on such a continuum of local vs. national impact, limits to the policy role of participants would be acknowledged, and a residuum of authority would remain exclusively in the agency. The tendency of the organization is likely to be in the direction of setting those boundaries closer to the participatory units than the realization of citizen participation goals would suggest, and some definition of this line is probably incumbent upon policymakers outside the organization.

We know very little in empirical terms about the operation of citizen participation, but the experience of Selective Service and other participatory organizations permits us to begin to outline the nature of the problems involved. It is one thing to endorse the goals of citizen participation and hope for their realization, but quite another to identify the occasions and means whereby they may have a reasonable chance of realization. The device can easily be used for the management of consent, and probably its employment is most often undertaken at least partly for that reason. Though neither right nor wrong in itself, such action when undertaken by an organization for its own ends may lead to unfavorable reflections on the principle. That is why clarification of the purposes and goals of citizen participation, and the potential for harmonious convergence between them and the goals of any particular organization employing the device, are so important to the understanding of the principle and its effectuation.

Nothing in our evidence indicates that the principle is inherently unworkable, though we have seen much to suggest that it is very difficult to implement. We have sought to suggest empirically defensible ways in which the participatory principle might be realized more fully than it has been so far. It may be that it will ultimately prove to be unworkable, for some of the same reasons identified in the experience of the organizations on which we have drawn. But it has not yet really been tried under circumstances of careful design and continued attention. The values which are sought to be realized from it seem to be sufficiently important that the effort would be worthwhile.

Chapter 10

SELECTIVE SERVICE IN THE POLITICAL SYSTEM: OUTPUT, FEEDBACK, SUPPORT, AND CHANGE

The central concerns of empirical political theory are suggested by two disarmingly simple questions: Why do men do what they do in politics? What are the consequences of their actions? Building upon increasingly rigorous and systematic bodies of data, political scientists have sought to identify regularities in political behavior and to verify the nature of cause and effect relationships among important variables. Immediately, researchers with theoretical purposes concentrate on generating testable hypotheses and propositions which will serve to expand and refine the body of knowledge. Ultimately, of course, the goal of these efforts is the construction of general theories which will have both explanatory and predictive capacity concerning the phenomena of politics. Gabriel Almond has characterized the purposes of theory similarly:

> Modern political theory will consist in good part of a logic which will enable us to relate changes in the performance of political systems to changes in internal process and conversion patterns and to changes in recruitment and socialization patterns. Another part of it will consist of a logic which will enable us to move from empirical relationships to normative judgments.[1]

At this point, we make no effort in the normative direction. But we do see our findings as suggesting that substantial theoretical payoff is to be

[1] Gabriel A. Almond, "Political Theory and Political Science," *American Political Science Review*, LX (December 1966), 876–77.

found in analysis of the consequences of public policies. Specifically, we argue that analysis which takes the substance of policy as the independent variable and searches out the effects—both short and long range—of that policy *for the political system* can make important contributions to theories of politics.

Our focus is distinct from those employed by most contemporary political scientists. The chief thrust of modern research has been toward identifying the nature of conflicting interests, defining the substance and sources of political attitudes, describing the processes by which demands are asserted, and analyzing the decision-making characteristics of authoritative institutions and actors. These studies have greatly enlarged understanding of such features of politics as voting behavior, political party and interest group activity, and decision-making processes in such institutions as the Congress, the Supreme Court, and the executive branch. They have also made possible more comprehensive characterization of the nature of politics in subnational units such as cities or communities; recent extension of inquiry into comparative contexts has multiplied the insights available through focusing on these aspects of the political process. Much has been accomplished, and much more remains to be done, by work of this kind; such theoretical attainments as may be claimed by political science are due almost exclusively to process-oriented empirical research of the recent past.

Without in the least underestimating these achievements (indeed, perhaps only *because* of them), we argue that the quite different focus of public policy-oriented research can contribute an essential series of building blocks to theories of politics. The purpose of political science is not merely to explain why public policy has the form it has, nor is the making of policy the end of the political process: in an important sense, it is the beginning of a whole new process which has vital political relevance. Output begets impact, creates reactions, and leads to behavioral responses by the objects of policies. Different segments of the population are differently affected, and their responses take varying forms. New demands arise. Satisfactions and perceptions about government performance are altered. The very context of politics itself is changed. The demand pattern, the relative strength of support for public policies and the government itself, as well as the objective reality of the environment with which a political system must cope and to which it must adjust, are all affected if not structured by the consequences of public policies. To fully understand the nature and sources of demands and the processes of adaptation and change in politics, we must (among other strategies) set policy at the focus and trace its effects.

The full import of the distinctiveness in such an approach may not at first be apparent, because political scientists have been accustomed to refer to public policy in many ways, and the phrase itself holds no mystery. Courses are regularly taught in which public policy—in the sense of what government does in the way of programs for housing, education, or farm price supports—is the primary object of inquiry. For many, policy is the critical dependent variable through which the political process may best be understood. This is an eminently sensible view of politics, for it is by the output of a system rather than by its often complex decisional processes that its utility or desirability can best be measured, by the consumer of the product at least. For the average citizen, output has always been an important payoff. But we have in mind a use distinct from any of these for what we call policy analysis or policy-oriented research.[2] Some illustrations may serve to emphasize this point. In a deservedly well-known case study, *American Business and Public Policy—The Politics of Foreign Trade*,[3] Bauer, Dexter, and Pool documented the various factors which impinged upon the decision-making of the Congress in regard to trade legislation in 1962. Attitudes and activities of businessmen and trade associations were carefully related to the behavior of Congressmen to show in effect the extent to which members of Congress were free agents in such decisions. But suppose instead the authors had sought to measure the effects of the statute after it had been in operation for a span of years, asking who had gained and who had lost as a result of the new statute, what their responses had been, and what consequences had ultimately resulted for the structure and processes of the political system itself.

Or, in the case of Robert Dahl's *Who Governs?*,[4] suppose the analysis had focused not on the distribution of power that affected particular

[2] We do not mean to suggest, however indirectly, that no political scientists have sought to explore the impact of any form of public policy. Research in the area of public law and judicial politics alone, for example, has produced several "impact studies" in recent years: Frank Sorauf, "Zorach v. Clauson: The Impact of a Supreme Court Decision," *American Political Science Review*, LIII (Sept. 1959), 777–91; R. H. Birkby, "The Supreme Court and the Bible: Tennessee Reactions to the Schempp Decision," *Midwest Journal of Political Science*, X (August 1966), 304–19; Ellis Katz, "Patterns of Compliance with the Schempp Decision," *Journal of Public Law*, XIV (1965), 396ff.; D. R. Reich, "The Impact of Judicial Decision Making: The School Prayer Cases," paper presented at the 1967 annual meeting of the Midwest Conference of Political Scientists; R. M. Johnson, "Compliance and Supreme Court Decision Making," *Wisconsin Law Review*, 1967 (Winter 1967), 170–85. None of these works, however, reaches to the point of systematic examination of responses and ultimate effects on political structures and processes.

[3] Raymond A. Bauer, Lewis A. Dexter, and Ithiel DeSola Pool, *American Business and Public Policy—The Politics of Foreign Trade* (New York: Atherton Press, 1963).

[4] Robert A. Dahl, *Who Governs?* (New Haven: Yale University Press, 1961).

decisions in the urban renewal field, but on the impact of those decisions upon residents of the area, the generation of new opposition to the program, related public reactions, and consequent effects upon future official decision-making in the area. If these classic studies had taken such unlikely courses, they would have been roughly analogous to the approach we have set for ourselves. Or, to belabor the point, if the numerous studies of why school bond referenda win or lose, or under what circumstances fluoridation proposals are voted up or down, had sought instead to ascertain what difference it made (for the political system) that the school bonds were or were not approved, or the city's water was or was not fluoridated, then we would have more company. As it stands, focus on the content and consequences of public policies as a research strategy is uncommon.

It would be fascinating if frustrating to attempt to identify *all* the consequences—social, economic, cultural, technological, and so forth—of any given public policy. For purposes of a theory of politics, however, this is unnecessary. Although we must acknowledge some problems in establishing precisely what the limits of our interests are, we shall adhere closely to a *political* perspective, including as relevant only those factors which bear upon the bringing of claims upon governments and the tangible realities of problems which agencies of government encounter. The boundaries of relevance surrounding the public policy of conscription and its implementation are both permeable and flexible, for example, but they exclude enough that we can concentrate on a few important factors in reasonably efficient fashion.

Some recent developments in political science suggest that movement toward greater use of public policy as a focus for research and theory building is a natural progression from the current state of the discipline. Two leading political scientists, Don K. Price[5] and Vernon Van Dyke,[6] have recently published major works in the areas of government and science and the space program respectively, which draw attention to the capacities of the political scientist to contribute to an understanding of the potential implications of particular public policies. Although they dealt also with the politics of decision-making in these areas, and did not seek to develop data concerning consequences for theory-building purposes, they have widened the discipline's frame of reference merely by shifting their focus toward the substance and potential implications of policy content.

[5] Don K. Price, *The Scientific Estate* (Cambridge: The Belknap Press of Harvard University, 1965).

[6] Vernon Van Dyke, *Pride and Power: The Rationale of the Space Program* (Urbana: University of Illinois Press, 1964).

Perhaps more significant for our purposes, an important body of literature has been developed in the last few years which does employ policy for theoretical purposes. (Many of the varied implications of the growing interest in a public policy focus are surveyed in a recent publication sponsored by the Social Science Research Council.[7]) Beginning with impressionistic suggestions that political party competitiveness was related to levels of welfare produced by the state's political system,[8] research has proceeded more systematically to show that (at least under the techniques of measurement employed) there was little or no relation between political party variables and output characteristics.[9] In another round of inquiry, several different research efforts have shown that expenditures in the states and in several cities are essentially unrelated to political process factors and appear instead to depend on resources or other socioeconomic characteristics.[10] All of these studies, of course, employ policy content as the dependent variable. Policy content, in other words, is the vehicle through which new insight is to be gained into characteristics of the decision-making or other demand processes within the political system.

As an outgrowth of this development, however, attention has begun to be paid to the task of categorizing public policy content in order to make more precise use of it as a variable. It seems clear that the character of various policy outputs differs, for example, that some policies affect people and others things, that some affect officials and others masses, and that there is a difference in the consequences and processes surrounding expenditures from those that surround criminal punishments or rate regulation.[11] Most classificatory efforts are intended exclusively for the use of policy content as a dependent variable which might better explain process characteristics.

[7] Ranney (ed.), *Political Science and Public Policy.*

[8] V. O. Key, Jr., *Politics, Parties and Pressure Groups* (5th ed.; New York: Thomas Y. Crowell Co., 1964); Duane Lockard, *Politics in New England* (Princeton: Princeton University Press, 1959).

[9] Richard E. Dawson and James A. Robinson, "Inter-Party Competition, Economic Variables, and Welfare Policies in the American States," *Journal of Politics*, XXV (1963): 265–89; Richard I. Hofferbert, "Ecological Development and Policy Change in the American States," *Midwest Journal of Political Science*, X (Nov. 1966); ————, "The Relations Between Public Policy and Some Structural and Environmental Variables in the American States," *American Political Science Review*, LX (March 1966).

[10] Thomas R. Dye, *Politics, Economics, and the Public: Policy Outcomes in The American States* (Chicago: Rand McNally, 1966); Ira Sharkansky, *Spending in the American States* (forthcoming); the literature on cities is summarized in Lewis A. Froman, "An Analysis of Public Policies in Cities," *Journal of Politics*, XXIX (Feb. 1967): 94–108.

[11] Cf. the forthcoming summary by Herbert Jacob and Michael Lipsky in the *Journal of Politics* (Spring 1968).

Two merit our close attention because their classificatory approaches may be adaptable to use of policy content as the *independent* variable.

Theodore Lowi suggested a threefold categorization based, according to his description, on characteristics of impact: policies were seen as either "regulatory," distributive," or "redistributive."[12] Expanding on this beginning, Robert Salisbury has added the dimension of perceptions by political actors to that of prospective impact, and emerged with a fourth category—"self-regulative."[13] For our present purposes (because we have employed conscription-implementing policies only), definitions of these categories beyond the usual meanings of their titles is unnecessary; what is significant is the fact that these writers have sought to grapple with the early problems in the development and theoretical use of policy-oriented research. The purposes of the contemplated inquiry will naturally shape the categories developed, and if the understanding of impact, consequences, reactions, and new demands is central to the purposes of categorization, greater attention will have to be paid to such questions as: Who benefited? Who lost? What, in both cases, did they do about it? What were the effects upon the system? But this beginning will serve as one of our primary guidelines in this chapter.

The foci of political scientists who deal with general theories of politics are roughly similar to those of the main body of empirical researchers. The broad efforts toward integrative theory by Truman,[14] Herring,[15] Lasswell,[16] Deutsch,[17] Almond,[18] and others are primarily concerned with drawing together aspects of the input side of political activity—group interaction, or decision-making, or communication, or input functions are the chief integrative devices. One exception is David Easton,[19] whose systems approach makes him the only general theorist with a marked interest in the output

---

[12] Theodore J. Lowi, "American Business, Public Policy, Case-Studies, and Political Theory," *World Politics* (July 1964), pp. 677–715.

[13] Robert H. Salisbury, "The Analysis of Public Policy: A Search for Theories and Roles," in Ranney (ed.), *Political Science and Public Policy.*

[14] David B. Truman, *The Governmental Process* (New York: Knopf, 1951).

[15] Pendleton Herring, *The Politics of Democracy* (new ed.; New York: W. W. Norton, 1965).

[16] Harold D. Lasswell, *The Decision Process: Seven Categories of Functional Analysis* (College Park: University of Maryland Bureau of Governmental Research, 1956).

[17] Karl W. Deutsch, *The Nerves of Government* (New York: Free Press, 1963).

[18] Gabriel A. Almond, *The Politics of the Developing Areas* (Princeton: Princeton University Press, 1960).

[19] David Easton, *A Framework for Political Analysis* (Englewood Cliffs: Prentice-Hall, 1965) (hereafter *Framework*); David Easton, *A Systems Analysis of Political Life* (New York: John Wiley & Sons, 1965) (hereafter, *Systems Analysis*).

side of political activity. The emphasis that systems analysis places upon a moving equilibrium in which systems must adapt to changes in their environment apparently led him to develop constructs and speculative propositions for stages of the post-decision politics which we have been calling output, impact, reactions, and consequences for political structure and process. We shall employ in this chapter for descriptive purposes what Easton terms the stages of "the feedback loop." In the conceptual armory of systems analysis, major foci include the nature of a system's environment, its output or performance patterns, feedback (the responses from the members of the system which permit measurement of goal attainment and are the key to system adaptability), supports (the level of satisfactions of the members with the system and with the specific outputs in question), and output reaction (the changes in the system's output deliberately designed by the relevant authorities to bring performance into closer harmony with the purposive intents of the system and to maintain requisite supports).

These constructs were designed for use with regard to societal-level political systems, and not for what Easton calls "parapolitical" systems (the internal politics of groups or organizations).[20] The patterns of interactions surrounding the authoritative allocations of values in the subject area of conscription-implementation, however, appear to be sufficiently well established to permit treatment as a subsystem with many of the characteristics of a political system. Conscription-implementation is more than parapolitical, because it is society-wide in many respects; conceptually, it may be likened to the party (sub)system or to the judicial (sub)system of the national political system. With some adjustments and considerable simplification, we shall analogize from Easton's concepts to describe identifiable aspects of the output-feedback-supports-demands cycle. This framework will permit us insight into the special problems of change in the case of Selective Service, and in a final section we shall attempt to suggest some theoretical implications that emerge from the policy-output approach.

I. SELECTIVE SERVICE AND ITS ENVIRONMENT: OUTPUT AND INTERACTION

"Output" is a generic term which may include several distinct forms of organizational products. Easton uses the term to signify transactions moving from the system to its environment ("authoritative allocations of values

---

[20] *Framework*, p. 52.

or binding decisions and the actions implementing and related to them").[21] Not all outputs, of course, are functionally task-related. Some are relatively peripheral—mere by-products of basic organizational commitments—and others may even be dysfunctional. The concept of transactions is useful, however, because it suggests continuing exchanges with several publics, and it is inclusive enough to subsume various forms of output.

The analysis of patterns of impact of conscription in Chapter 6 provides a background of objective reality to the interactions of Selective Service with its environment. In this analysis of the direct output of the organization, we saw that impact was segmented according to the registrants' socioeconomic characteristics, so that definable populations bore heavy burdens of military liability and others (at least under conditions of manpower surplus) were relatively lightly encumbered by such obligations. These patterns are only the beginning of a characterization of the organization's relationship with its environment, albeit the central reality around which other interaction occurs. A varied set of perceptions and transactions completes the relationship of Selective Service and its immediate environment.

The component units of the Selective Service System operate in environments made up in part of the other elements within the organization and in part from the other actors and institutions of the political system. At each level of the organization, its units are related to a distinct set of external political forces and conditions. The environment of the national headquarters consists of such elements as the Defense Department, the White House, the Armed Services Committees of the two houses of Congress, the National Guard and Reserve Officers' Associations, representatives of the mass media, and ultimately attentive members of the national public. Interaction occurs regularly between the director and other representatives of national headquarters and the various elements of that environment; when Selective Service rises to national visibility, as it did in the debates of 1966–67, the nature of these interactions may be readily seen from the pages of Congressional hearings, national news media, and popular books. Scholarly inquiries frequently undertake to spell out the character of relationships between agencies and departments of the national government and other elements in the national political scene, permitting comparisons between various agencies, and between times of stress and more normal periods. These are important considerations to have in mind, but they are not our primary focus.

Our data and analyses have been directed at the state and local

[21] *Framework*, p. 126; *Systems Analysis*, p. 348.

activities of Selective Service, and it is the interaction between the organization and its publics at this operating level with which we are most concerned. This point of interchange between the agency and the people provides an infrequently used opportunity to assess the character of governmental performance, both in terms of the nature of the job actually done and the satisfactions or antipathies generated in the process.

The environments of the state and local units of the organization are in some respects separable, corresponding to the levels of the System, but we shall treat them jointly. The state headquarters, for example, is almost the only unit to have contact with representatives of the state's press and other media, and it is the primary focus of state interest groups who seek particular policy interpretations or guidance. But the local boards operate in the context of what those media say about Selective Service, and in response to what those interest groups have gained or sought—and our purposes are best served by taking them together. Our identification of the major elements in the organization's state and local environment, therefore, includes media and interest group representatives as well as major employers, veterans' groups, some local politicians, and several distinctive publics: local elites, registrants, attentive citizens, and a broader general public. Most of our attention will be directed at these distinctive publics, but we shall first summarize our findings with respect to the others.

Because it is not economical—or important enough, in most years—for news media to develop expertise among their reporters concerning Selective Service, state headquarters accurately perceives newsmen as ignorant and therefore threatening. The chances are good that an inadvertent phrase or a misplaced emphasis transmitted statewide may seriously embarrass the State Director with the public generally, with registrants or employers, or (more likely, and worse) with his local board members. A report that declares, on the strength of an interview with a state headquarters' spokesman, that the state's Selective Service System *"will do"* certain things is likely to raise tensions among volunteers, who understand no such command relationships to exist; this is particularly likely when, as is often the case, the news item concerns a change in procedure as to which no instructions have yet been received from national headquarters. The state headquarters has many risks and little to gain in its relationships with the press, and it is little wonder that a defensive posture is assumed. The self-fulfilling potential of such action is clear: reporters and public may come to believe that the System is secretive. For the most part, of course, the news media are content with wire service reports of national and state quotas and calls, and it is only in periods of relatively high inductions that problems arise.

In the absence of systematic data on the performance or local impact of the draft—information which the state headquarters does not have—interest groups and employers must base their actions on the sketchy reporting of the news media or on their personal experiences. Their grievances or arguments normally receive a sympathetic hearing from state headquarters officers, whose agreement with them may lead to guidance as to how to enable their members or employees to qualify for deferments, or, in some instances, to general policy statements for the guidance of local boards. There are few ways in which effective pressure can be brought to bear on the state headquarters, and employers' chief reliance must be placed on the officers' acknowledgment of the desirability of minimizing the economic impact of the draft on the state's important industries.

Neither officeholders nor other influential participants in partisan politics play an important part in the System's state and local environment (in Wisconsin, though perhaps they do in some states). This may be due to the tact with which the officers of the state headquarters deflect routine requests for information on behalf of constituents and handle other contacts with such political figures, but it is more likely the product of the peculiar insulation the System enjoys. In this state at least, public disclosure that a politician had obtained special consideration for a registrant would be disastrous to that politician's future and to the image of the System in the eyes of both general public and local board members. While the politician might want to serve an important constituent, he would probably be unwilling to risk public awareness of having done so—an unwillingness that the state headquarters can use to insulate itself against any such attempt. Contacts between the System and the partisan political world are thus frequent and friendly, but do not reach to the point where the actions of the organization are affected.

The several publics with which the System interacts include some intimately engaged and affected by it and some only marginally related to it; the nature of this interaction therefore varies sharply. The most intimately involved public is the semipermanent one made up of local board members. In important ways, of course, board members are members of the organization and communication with them takes place through internal mechanisms and processes; we have conceived of board members as the decision-making appendages of the organization throughout this study. But board members are also a public with which the organization interacts: they are board members in operating capacity only about three to six hours per month, and the rest of the time they are undergoing the experiences and reactions of other similarly situated citizens, albeit from a distinctive perspective. In other words, whatever information is conveyed about the System, whatever events occur and are interpreted, and whatever actions are taken by relevant figures—in the month between meetings—have their impact on board members too. The System must constantly be considering the impact that its actions may have on board members, both as part of the organization *and* as part of the general public. Their limited status as organization operatives, and their plenitude of individual interests and activities, give them this unique dual capacity of member and public.

That the organization does not succeed in converting board members into mere implements of its goals has been demonstrated from the data concerning board members' views on specific Selective Service policies: members, it will be recalled, showed substantial disagreement with organizational policies in the same areas as did the general public. At the same time, they were as a group attitudinally distinct from the other members of the general public in the direction of the organization's goals, so to them the organization's accomplishments were apparent. Considerable effort is expended by the System to maintain the self-image of sacrifice and dedication on the part of these board members, and it may be that much of what appears to be gratuitous or unfounded self-congratulation on the part of the System should be understood as being an effort to maintain good relations with board members. The more board members feel that they are appreciated, the more likely they are to cooperate willingly in carrying out the System's goals.

Overlapping with the local board members, and reached in part through them, is a second critical public: local elites. The recruitment processes employed by the System, as we have seen, draw local board members from the ranks of civically active middle-class entrepreneurs. Board members were shown to be part of a relatively small, circulating body of citizens who fill local public offices and engage in voluntary association activities. If board members are content with the practices of the System and display their satisfactions, these other local leadership elements will probably also consider the System to be working appropriately. In any event, they will have greater confidence in the System if they know those who are serving as board members and interact with them in the course of their daily lives. At stake therefore in the organization's relations with its board members is some portion of the System's acceptance and prospective support from locally significant middle-class elements.

Much more affected by the organization's actions, but much less of concern to it, are the registrants. Those who are even potentially vulnerable to induction have special reasons for attentiveness and concern for the

System's actions and statements. The System, however, takes little advantage of this. Very little information of any kind is made available to registrants, and the only direct communication which occurs takes place through the initiative of the registrant. The images of local boards which registrants hold are not favorable; perhaps they could not be under the circumstances, but it seems clear that little is done to moderate the organization's threatening posture.

Those registrants who are "heavy investors" particularly feel threatened by local boards and by the draft; registrants who have experienced some contact with their boards are even more likely to believe them influential in determining applications of conscription policy. Registrants are thus a very special subpublic, and it is not strange that their attitudinal posture should be distinctive. They are more likely to believe that local boards are determinative (make their own policies rather than follow orders) than the general public, and they are slightly more knowledgeable than others about the character and makeup of boards. Much of their information about the System, and hence much of their image of it, comes from nonorganization sources. Registrants reported that their chief source of information about the draft was the news media, and second came their friends and associates; local boards were only the third source of information, closely rivaled by the university itself. The interaction of the System and its primary policy objects is thus an indirect one. Communications are received by registrants from the media, and, perhaps much more important, in the social situation where the effects of friends and other factors may be felt. Board members too, it will be recalled, were found to be close readers of national news media regarding the draft, and probably the availability of this source also serves to detach them somewhat from the direct relationship with the System.

Completing the publics with which the organization maintains some form of contact are two others: that relatively small number of citizens who are attentive to conscription matters (politically conscious persons, parents of registrants, etc.) and the comparatively large number of people who are only marginally aware that there is an organization which carries out the tasks associated with conscription. The latter are probably prepared to accept the organization and its work along with all other governmental activities. Greater effort may be necessary with regard to attentive citizens, many of whom probably perceive the System in terms of a threat. These are the people for whom the symbolic reassurances may be intended, and in many instances at least they are the people whose employees or sons are eventually able to qualify for deferments. As we have seen, they view the draft as unfair somewhat more than persons in less attentive groups, probably due to their peculiar vulnerability, but they switch over to approval of the local board concept in very substantial proportions.

It is apparent that output patterns are indeed complicated: segmented impact on various subpopulations at different socioeconomic class levels is accompanied by varying perceptions and qualitatively different relationships between the organization and its several publics. These findings suggest the probability of several interdependent chains of subsequent response. The greater the manpower surplus, for example, the more the impact of the draft will be concentrated on lower middle class registrants, and the less the upper and upper middle classes will actually be threatened by the draft. Accordingly, both other interactions and subsequently generated demands, organizational characteristics, and public reactions may well follow different channels. In the development of theoretical implications from policy analysis, therefore, considerable attention will have to be paid to the interrelated and varied forms which output may take.

II. FEEDBACK

Feedback is information concerning the effects of system performance and responses to that performance. It is a vital element in the Eastonian construct because only feedback provides authorities with the information necessary to cope with stress, measure the nearness to attainment of system goals, and modify system behavior and performance to improve achievements and maintain support.[22] Specifically, Easton declares, authorities must know the conditions in the environment and in the system, the supportive state of mind of the members being voiced, and the effects which outputs have produced.[23]

Clearly, feedback is transactional in nature. It implies a state of mind on the part of the authorities within the system, and it imputes to them a certain purposefulness regarding goal attainment and adaptation. In some way, the system must seek to ascertain the nature of its impact and the character of conditions in the system and its environment. And the objects of its actions must develop reactions and be able to communicate them. Both the authorities and the members of the system have parts to play in the mutual accomplishment of the informing function.

As we have noted throughout this study, the authorities within the conscription-implementing subsystem have made almost no effort to ascer-

[22] *Systems Analysis*, pp. 364–69.
[23] *Framework*, pp. 128–29.

tain the effects of their performance. The national headquarters itself has foreclosed some forms of self-assessment by record-keeping omissions and procedures, and compounds this with an unwillingness to ask searching questions concerning performance. Nor have part-time authoritative elements in the subsystem (Congress, Defense Department, President) undertaken examinations of effects of performance, with the recent and partial exception of the President's Commission. When the authorities do not seek to learn, can the members bring information to their attention? Let us examine this question in some detail.

Conscription is one of many governmental policies, and Selective Service is one of many agencies of government administering specific functions. Both policy and agency thus compete for public attention (or seek to preserve inattention) in a context of many other governmental activities and world events, most of which have more specific and focused points of contact with the public. For many institutions, public officials, and other political objects, the political parties provide both cues for evaluation and a vehicle for expression of opinion on election day. Others, such as economic policy administration or church-state decisions of the Supreme Court, may be linked to established popular attitudes or values through ideological or religious commitments. No accepted source of similar guidance exists in the case of conscription and Selective Service, however, and perhaps in the case of some other government policies as well. The public thus receives communications from the media concerning Selective Service, and individual members of the public register, are drafted or deferred, or learn of similar events with respect to others, in a field free of basic structuring agents. Reception of such communications and other stimuli is variable and random, and no self-interest investment in the operation or improvement of the policy or its application develops for any sizable group of people.

In this low-saliency, unstructured context, we have found that different factors determine attitudes toward policy and organization, and that separate constituencies exist for each. To the national and state Headquarters of the Selective Service System, the validity of the organization's policy—indeed, the essential nature of the draft—depends on the existence of the local boards. Clearly, for the organization, there is an inherent merger of policy and organizational structure, but by the time these are perceived by the public they have become separated and nearly completely distinguished. Reaction to the draft is marginally favorable while reaction to the local board concept is negative.

Attitudes toward the local board aspect of the System showed sharp cleavages along class lines, with the upper classes strongly favoring and the lower classes as strongly disapproving administration of conscription through local men. Within both categories, those who felt more politically efficacious supported local boards more strongly. Although we cannot demonstrate that the connection is causal, we note that this segmentation of attitudes toward local boards parallels the patterns of impact of the draft that were identified: those who feel the weight of conscription most heavily disapprove of local boards most strongly.

The experience of Selective Service also suggests that the serene administrative consensus (high approval of all forms of government activity) which Janowitz and his associates found to exist at the local level[24] may have been particular to that place and time, or to specific functions. In our inquiry, the sharp cleavages found regarding local boards were at least as sharp as the cleavages usually associated with elections. Furthermore, the class pattern of approval and disapproval of government was reversed. In the Detroit study, lower classes expected more and sought more from government, and rated it more highly than did the upper classes; here, the lower classes rated local boards much lower than did upper classes.

Perhaps the Selective System is unique in its threatening character, and in this respect should be compared, if at all, only with the (lower-class-disapproved) police function in the other studies. More likely, we have another indication of the vital importance of distinguishing between types of policies for the purposes of conceptualizing impact and feedback patterns. Selective Service is an extractive rather than a service-providing agency, at least in the eyes of its potential inductees. Both conscription and law enforcement may be viewed as a service by one class level in the population, and as threatening and exploitative by other class levels. In the Lowi-Salisbury classification schemes, conscription at least is redistributive, and we may hypothesize that redistributive policies will be segmentally received and perceived by the members of the system.[25] The lines of differential reception might not always be class-based, of course, but those who benefit from the policy are likely to be more favorable than those who are burdened by the policy under most circumstances.

[24] Morris Janowitz, Deil Wright, and William Delaney, *Public Administration and the Public: Perspectives toward Government in a Metropolitan Community* (Ann Arbor: University of Michigan Institute of Public Administration, 1958).

[25] Even these early recognitions suggest the excessive simplicity of the categorization which Janowitz *et al.* offer as dimensions for assessing the people-government relationship: "(1) the extent of knowledge possessed about the unit of government, (2) the extent to which people believed that government helped them, (3) their moral evaluation of the principles on which government operated, and (4) their esteem for the bureaucracy and employment with it" (*ibid.*, pp. 4–6).

A further difficulty inheres in the process of feedback from members of the system: There are no available channels through which reactions can be effectively expressed. None of the established instruments of linkage between people and government took up questions concerning conscription implementation. There was no political party or electoral vehicle through which opinion could be felt, nor would it appear that the structure of opinion would make it profitable for a political party or candidate to seek to make conscription an issue—for the subject cuts across party lines and could lose more votes than it would gain.

Diffusion is thus complete. The policy area has very low visibility for most people, with a resulting small and shifting constituency made up for the most part of young men of relatively insignificant political weight. There is further diffusion created by the detachment in public perception between the general policy of conscription and its implementation by local boards, and by differing perceptions and evaluations of the desirability of the present form of local administration on the part of various socioeconomic levels within the population. Additionally, there are no vehicles by which these diffused perceptions and reactions could be communicated to any "authorities." We may add, speculatively, that the whole area is probably overlaid with symbolic attachments to serving one's country in patriotic terms, with fears of communism, and with the general willingness to do what appears necessary to support government commitments.

Under such conditions, there is little likelihood that the effects of system performance or the responses of members of the system will be made known. Given the disinterest of the authorities in ascertaining such matters, the failure of feedback seems complete. With only the occasional and readily dismissable allegations of journalists and popular writers as a source of feedback, it is understandable that both national headquarters and other responsible authorities could cling to rather badly misconstrued images of the efficacy and acceptability of Selective Service.[26] Or, to be somewhat less charitable, it may be that under such conditions the views of those who are the most visible and who carry the most political weight (in this case the middle class local activists who support local boards and enjoy deferments) are a sufficient source of support and the other factors are dispensable.

The problem of inadequate means of feedback from public to govern-

---

[26] This assumes, of course, that analysis is to take seriously the stated goals of the System. It could be that those goals and values (equity and efficiency, for example) are intended more for symbolic reassurance than for practical effectuation. See Murray Edelman, *The Symbolic Uses of Politics* (Urbana: University of Illinois Press, 1964). We shall consider such possibilities in the final section of this chapter.

ment has consequences which reach well beyond the specifics of Selective Service. The draft is probably only slightly more out of touch with popular views than some other governmental functions, if it is at all. The problem seems particularly well worth raising, however, because of the saliency which the draft appeared to have in 1966 and 1967: it is not often that a government function not in the partisan political arena rises to such visibility, and if a feedback problem exists under these conditions it must be endemic to the subject and perhaps to a broad area of the political system. And where there is a feedback problem, there may also be support problems: if popular preferences cannot effectively be expressed, if there is no way to focus desires on a major governmental function, then surely that function is threatened with a loss of support and, if it is important enough, the system itself may feel the defection.

III. SUPPORTS

The concept of supports serves to focus the question of the conformity of government action with popular preference, in itself a vital measuring standard of democratic government. If the system's output is inconsistent with popular preferences, presumably the ultimate effect would be withdrawal of consent. But ascertaining the nature of preferences, perceptions of output, and the processes of cognition and evaluation on the part of various publics, creates substantial problems. Easton generalizes in the same vein:

> To determine the consequences outputs have for support, we would have to know whose demands need to be satisfied to maintain a level of support sufficient to enable a system to persist, how frequently this would have to occur, how many of the demands, even of these significant members, would have to be met, and the like. . . . It would . . . be vital to trace out the consequences of these outputs as they affect the environment and the system itself and create the kinds of conditions that create or destroy supportive sentiments.[27]

It is clear that we intend a somewhat greater role for popular preferences generally than does Easton, whose concept is limited to that support, from whatever segment of the population, which is requisite to maintaining the system. Our assumptions proceed from a long-range view which hypothesizes that no system can long afford disapprobation on the part of substan-

---

[27] *Framework*, p. 127.

tial numbers of members, and that it must either gain their approval, reduce their disapproval to a neutralized state, or substitute other gratifications, if it is to maintain itself.

Easton distinguishes between diffuse support, by which he intends generalized acceptance of the regime or political good will, from specific support, which he sees as the immediate satisfactions from receipt of the benefits of the output of the system.[28] Diffuse support may be accorded to the government independent of its daily outputs in any particular area, and is generated out of one's political culture and experience. The two forms of support are linked in his theory, with the erosion of specific support ultimately leading to a weakening of diffuse support.[29]

This distinction is suggestive of the dichotomy we have empirically identified between the sources and structure of support for the local board concept and the more generalized support for the policy of conscription itself.[30] Because we are dealing with only a subsystem of a larger political system, however, we are reluctant to press the analogy. Included within the range of diffuse support here would be many other factors, such as general support for all acts and policies of government, for the institutions of the United States, and for patriotic attachment to the nation itself. All of these objects of diffuse support lend credence and a form of halo effect to the Selective Service System and other elements in the conscription-implementing system.

But our data have established a much clearer pattern of approval and disapproval of the local board concept, which bears a close resemblance to specific support. The data concerning perceptions of Selective Service provide a base for characterizing the present state of such support in some detail. First, it appears that the Selective Service System is perceived less as a federal instrumentality than as a unit of local government. At the state level, it is closely associated with the political processes and ethos of the state, and those who are active in such political activities are likely to encounter state headquarters officials regularly. At the local level, the System is personified by a locally resident local board clerk and five members of the locally dominant elements of the community. It therefore carries much of the same

---

[28] *Systems Analysis*, p. 273.

[29] *Framework*, p. 126.

[30] The concept of diffuse support in the Eastonian sense has elsewhere been applied to a subsystem within the political system, without (apparently) encountering intrusions from a halo effect from other revered political objects. See Jack Dennis, "Support for the Party System Among the Mass Public," *American Political Science Review*, LX (Sept. 1966), 600–15. The analysis measures diffuse support explicitly conferred upon the party system as such.

relationship as local elites do to their community, becoming in effect and in local perception an extension of the local elite management of local governmental functions. Patterns of public orientation—acceptance and rejection —toward Selective Service (in the sense of local boards) are the same as for local government generally, in that those who feel efficacious toward one feel the same toward the other. The only dimension of public attitudes which reflects the national character of the organization is the strong disapproval of the exercise of discretion on the local level. It will be recalled that those who believed that local boards followed orders from Washington rather than made their own choices were more likely to approve the local board concept. This seems to be an exception to the general thrust of our other findings to the effect that local boards are viewed as one of several units of local government, amounting to a minor element of ambivalence in otherwise consistent attitudinal structures.

There are both advantages and disadvantages accruing to the System from its association with local governing elements and mechanisms. Attitudes toward conscription as a national policy become detached from attitudes toward particular local boards or the local board concept generally. For some publics, this means satisfaction with local boards despite apprehension stemming from vulnerability and fears concerning conscription; for other (and larger) publics, it means disapproval and opposition to local boards despite acquiescence in conscription stemming from a lack of alternative career plans and perhaps a general fatalism about government policies. The System gains support from some, but loses support from others, by virtue of the manner in which the local boards are perceived by their relevant publics. It seems clear that, at least in the short run, the System has on balance benefited greatly from this attitudinal phenomenon: the very people who are most apprehensive, because they have the most to lose from conscription—and who are politically the most effective, both in their communities and in the nation—are brought to the side of the System through their integration with the local boards and local governing structures generally. The costs involved, in the form of disaffection of lower classes and the less efficacious from local boards, are not great—again, at least in the short run. These people appear to accept conscription more readily, though perhaps this is because they see no alternatives in the way of careers which are greatly preferred to it; their resentment of local board operation is not particularly significant because they are relatively powerless politically.

This pattern of perceptions and resultant supports suggests that the locus and strength of supports for the System were sufficient to enable it to continue unchanged, at least at the time of the survey in 1966. We doubt no less than Easton[31] that perceptions are the critical datum in regard to support, rather than actual patterns of output. But our concern for the long range implications of our findings and for the prospect of change in the System impels us to raise the obvious further question: what happens if perceptions fall more closely in line with the actual patterns of output? What changes in the levels of antipathies to the System might be forthcoming if those who bear the real burdens of military service become more cognizant of the actual patterns of output? And, given the association between support for local boards and support for the draft itself, empirically identified here as well as hypothesized in the diffuse-specific support linkage, might a reduction in support for conscription then follow? If so, of course, that would leave very low levels of support for the draft, for it does not enjoy high support from the upper classes even now. Such a line of speculation emphasizes the importance of a question raised earlier: to what extent do other sources of diffuse support (the national government, patriotism) lend a halo effect to the Selective Service System? To what extent, in other words, can symbolic diversions direct attention away from the realities of Selective Service performance, and for how long?

IV. THE PROSPECTS OF CHANGE ("OUTPUT REACTION")

The foregoing analysis of feedback and support characteristics is central to our conclusions concerning the insulation of the Selective Service System from change. In Eastonian terms, stress in supports or incomplete goal attainment, if recognized through feedback processes, leads to "output reaction,"[32] or change in performance. But neither half of the feedback transaction is operating, and there is at least one form of short-term support. The Selective Service System has developed (perhaps quite unconsciously) a special constituency of the politically relevant members of the public, including those persons who feel most threatened by conscription, by means of deferment and local board management policies; the very people most likely to seek change are thus rendered quiescent. Others who are less likely to, but might still seek change are so situated as to be either unconcerned, powerless, suspect, or a combination of all three: large numbers of persons have no personal contact with the draft and hence are unconcerned or

[31] *Systems Analysis*, p. 388.
[32] *Ibid.*, p. 430.

inattentive to it as an issue; persons from lower socioeconomic statuses do not perceive alternatives in life which are much better and frequently feel that their views would not matter anyhow; and registrants who criticize the draft on any grounds may well be suspected of an unpatriotic unwillingness to serve. Even if there were a significant body of persons seeking change in the System, there are no vehicles within the political system by which such opposition could be effectuated. The complexity of the alternatives and the structure of support for the present System make it unlikely that means of implementing conscription can become an issue between the two major political parties, and there are few imaginable ways in which expression of opposition to the local board concept, distinct from the draft itself, can be made. In all probability, the issue would have to be conscription itself, which rests on distinctive attitudinal bases and presents wholly different kinds of questions. But until that issue is reached, the present Selective Service System as an organization is likely to endure, with only such changes as it sees fit to make for its own purposes. What are the prospects that it will do so?

Some basis for prediction may be found in the past experience of the organization, which as we have seen has remained constant in structure, goals, procedures, and in leadership since 1940. The orientation toward change of the national headquarters, articulated by General Hershey before the House Armed Services Committee in June 1966, may be summarized in the following quotations:

> I wouldn't recommend any change of the draft law. I would recommend and keep on recommending, perhaps unsuccessfully, that we apply it to more and more people.

> At the same time, there is concern over "inequity." Equality of ability, equality of service do not exist. Selective Service, in issuing orders for induction, can approach equality only to the extent of the numbers that Armed Forces requisition.

> . . . those bold enough to suggest improvements eventually fall back on suggestions of a lottery. The idea that a lottery solves any of our problems is an illusion.

> Well, Mr. _____, I suppose part of it is the fact that I don't know what people are talking about when they talk about national standards. You always find them in paper, but when you start applying them, then—for instance, people would like to take everybody born in a certain month of a certain year on a call for a certain month and the first thing you know you get so much detail you don't get any men.

Now, this inequity is relative, and you get your balance sheet only from time to time, but I have never had faith that you could, from a central place, set up a detailed standard that would not handicap the local boards more than it would help them.

But I do have more confidence and I am willing to put up with the mistakes of the local board down there, who can look into all the facts, than I have in a computer.[33]

This stance is elaborated upon in written comments concerning some specific proposals which the national headquarters submitted to the Committee after the hearings:

We do not believe that more detailed mandatory criteria for local board classification guidance is desirable or would be beneficial to the registrant or the country.

It is believed that the Governors of the states have selected outstanding citizens for the President to appoint and that the System has been working remarkably well.

It has been our feeling through the years that procedures should be kept so simple that it would not be necessary to have legal counsel at a hearing.

It is not believed that it would be beneficial to the registrant or his counsel to have the right to appear before the appeal boards.

The fact that there are only ten days to permit an appeal induces the registrant, the dependents, or the employer to immediately appeal the classification if one of them thinks it is desirable. Extending the period of appeal in most cases would result in no benefit to any of those concerned and might result in those having the right to appeal to put it off until even the longer appeal period had expired.

If a local board of jurisdiction were changed when a registrant moved to a new area or a new state, there would be thousands of local board files continuously in transit. The Selective Service System would be unable to operate under such a procedure.

The present system of allocating calls from National Headquarters to State Headquarters immediately upon receipt from the Secretary of Defense and based on the percentages of those available in each state has worked fairly and effectively.

The decentralized, or local board, or grass roots operation of Selective Service began with the First World War and demonstrated that the Nation would much more willingly support com-

[33] See *Hearings;* General Hershey's testimony appears on pp. 9620–9727.

pulsory military service operated by their neighbors at home, than they would a program operated by a remote impersonal organization.[34]

In hearings held almost a year later the opposition to change was muted, no doubt because the President had announced his intention to make changes, but it was still clear that the Director was not enthusiastic about changing.[35] In one respect, to be sure, Selective Service has exhibited flexibility—it has responded to high calls and low calls, to manpower shortage and manpower surplus. But this is only the flexibility of the automobile manufacturer that makes more or fewer cars in response to demand. In goals and procedures, in end and means, it has not changed.

It is small comfort to learn from March and Simons' classic *Organizations,* "We would expect data in reports of operating statistics to trigger innovative effort when the data showed performance falling below present standards."[36] We have seen that Selective Service keeps no data, conducts no evaluations, has no standards, except those which relate to the single indicator of satisfactory performance—the delivery of the assigned number of men to the induction stations each month. Satisfaction with performance in those terms permits the screening out of criticism.[37] Longevity of service, not to mention self-perpetuating characteristics of local boards, serve to maintain established norms and reduce the prospect of innovation further.[38] Maintenance of the status quo has been facilitated also by the lack of any major increment of personnel[39] or of technological advances within the System. The effect of all these forms of resistance may be, of course, to make for drastic change when new leadership or personnel enter the

[34] *Ibid.,* pp. 9986–95.

[35] See "Amending and Extending the Draft Law and Related Authorities," Hearings before the Committee on Armed Services, U. S. Senate (90th Cong., 1st Sess., April 1967). General Hershey's testimony appears on pp. 610–57.

[36] James G. March and Herbert A. Simon, *Organizations* (New York: John Wiley & Sons, 1958), p. 183.

[37] The relation between satisfaction and low level of search for alternatives to the status quo is discussed in *ibid.,* pp. 182–83 and also in Anthony Downs, *Inside Bureaucracy* (Boston: Little, Brown, 1967), p. 171. March and Simon make a particularly interesting and relevant point. "The most important proposition is that, over time, the aspiration level tends to adjust to the level of achievement. That is to say, the level of satisfactory performance is likely to be very close to the actually achieved level of recent performance."

[38] Downs, *op. cit.,* pp. 98–99, 17.

[39] In 1955 the paid civilian employment of the Selective Service System was 7,123. In 1960 it was 6,230; 1962: 6,805; 1963: 6,916; 1964: 7,108; 1965: 7,587; and in 1966: 8,564. *Annual Report of the Director of the Selective Service System* (Washington: Government Printing Office, years indicated).

organization, or when outside forces mandate change. Anthony Downs offers a suggestion as to the probabilities of change in an established and operating organization: "It is easier to adjust actions than rules, easier to shift rules than to change structure, and easier to alter structures than adopt new purposes."[40]

Under present conditions, the organization seems unlikely to initiate the change (or output reaction) which might bring performance more nearly into harmony with stated goals or improve the level of supports from broad segments of the population. Nor do conditions within the larger political system appear likely to bring to bear forces sufficient to accomplish such change. This analysis has not even reached the question of the extent of support for the present System within the Congress, or on the part of applicable interest groups such as the National Guard or Reserve Officers Associations or the American Legion: the implications are that change is not likely to be produced through the familiar or hypothesized processes supposedly designed to produce such results.

V. CONCLUSIONS

A single study, particularly one at such an early stage of inquiry in an uncharted area, should not be expected to generate extensive theoretical applications. Nor is it necessary for us to attempt to do so: we seek only to demonstrate that some theory-building *potential* inheres in a policy-oriented approach to empirical research. For this, we need show no more than that such inquiry may serve eventually to develop or refine theoretical formulations concerning relationships between major variables whose interaction has important political relevance.

Although our study has been confined to the political processes surrounding a single policy area, we do have findings and interpretations, however sketchy, which suggest linkages between policy output, impact, reactions, and effects for political structures and processes. We shall employ these modest materials to support our argument that theory potential inheres in a policy orientation in two ways: first, by raising the possibility of generating some limited propositions and hypotheses out of the presently available data, and then by suggesting some possible implications of our findings for the more inclusive general theory which has informed our

[40] Downs, *op. cit.*, p. 173.

presentation in this chapter. We begin with some efforts in the former category.

We have seen that deferment/induction policies as they are applied by the Selective Service System create differing impact upon registrants of different socioeconomic levels. Some types of men experienced military service at much higher rates than others. These are the output-impact patterns which led us to characterize conscription as having a segmented impact, varying according to characteristics of the objects of the policies. Responses in the way of support for the local board followed similar lines, and we have referred to them also as segmented. These findings lead us to hazard a proposition to the effect that the more segmented the patterns of impact are, the more there will be a definable locus of strongly held specific support for the organization's actions. Further, the evidence leads us to hypothesize that the more a readily definable source of support is available for present performance and characteristics, the less the organization is likely to be concerned with the problems of adaptation and change. Indeed, if the support forthcoming is from usually influential political strata, the authorities may ignore the problems of adaptation and change entirely, at least until the coalition of opponents becomes very large.

These characteristics of the relationship between impact, supports, and system adaptation and change may be limited to those areas where the policy itself is redistributive. What distinguishes redistributive policies from other classifications is the fact that the benefits allocated to some are at the cost of burdens borne by others; in other words, the relationship among the objects of the policies is competitive, and one side's winnings are equivalent to the other side's losses. Our references to conscription as extractive or redistributive are intended to convey this aspect of these policies, and we think it possible that the impact and resultant support patterns which are apparent here may be peculiar to policies of such character. Regulatory policies, for example, which may be positive sum arrangements in which all parties end up somewhat better off than they were, might not give rise to the same sharp benefit-burden impact and the same clearly defined pro and con pattern of response as do redistributive policies.

This set of hypotheses suggests relationships between policy content, impact, support patterns, and change which reach across many intermediate possibilities for more precise theoretical development. For example, we could probably develop hypotheses concerning the relationship between feedback characteristics and change. In this case, we saw that there was a complete lack of feedback activity from either of the necessary parties to the transaction. But under some conditions of system inquiry, patterns of impact might be ascertained and performance modified accordingly; no doubt this is often the practice in areas of government action concerned with the economy, such as the balance of payments or inflation. And even in the absence of interest on the part of the authorities, in some cases feedback could be so insistently registered that it could not be ignored; cutbacks in some areas of government spending could be imagined as having such potential. Presumably, it would be possible after sufficient experience to specify the kinds of conditions in each sector of feedback activity which would combine to maximize the prospects of change. In similar fashion, the relationship between support distributions and change could probably be spelled out. Some degree of disapproval from some segment of the population may be anticipated with regard to most policy areas, but only certain levels from particularly influential elements of the society are likely to mount effective pressure toward change.

Much more could probably be done with the Selective Service System's special characteristics than our generalizing purposes have led us to attempt so far. In this case, for example, the implementation of conscription through local boards produced what must be an exceptional degree of unanticipated by-products of the basic policies. This was due to the nature of the System's task—the provision of a set number of men at the induction centers on specified days—which allowed the decision-making units to determine their own procedures and standards as long as they delivered the requisite number of men. Under these conditions, their discretionary and idiosyncratic behavior multiplied the by-products, which in turn probably created an unusual distribution and variation of intensity in support patterns. Also, Selective Service may be unusual in that it has asserted and steadily defended a fixed primary commitment—to the local board concept—and all other priorities are established in light of that constant; a more flexible approach to priorities and procedures might have altered several of the effects noted in the study.

These tentative hypotheses seem to us to raise the prospect that policy-oriented research might contribute to theories of the relationships between policy output characteristics, new demands, and effects upon ongoing political processes and structures. Our findings also suggest some implications regarding existing general theories, such as systems analysis, which already include sections dealing with output processes. In this regard, we mean to be highly tentative indeed, for we have examined only a subsystem within the political system, and then only at a single moment in time, and our use of systems analysis categories has been both crude and by analogy. Under these circumstances, we offer our reflections only for the purpose of indicating that research of this type may lead ultimately to theoretical refinements if and where appropriate.

Although our findings relate only to one subsystem policy area, they appear to raise some questions about the empirical validity of some basic systems analysis assumptions. Indeed, it would be surprising if one of the first empirical ventures in the area contained no possibilities of refinement in theories of which parts had to be constructed with little available instruction from current research. Acknowledging that the conscription-implementing subsystem may be distinctive, however, we still think that some question exists as to the propriety of placing goal attainment and adaptation to change at the center of the animating purposes of the output-feedback-supports phases of the system's activities. In this case, at least in the short run and perhaps in the long run (how long is "long?"), there was little purposiveness on the part of the authorities and no adaptability. Was there no stress in the proper sense, or was it the wrong kind of stress? Or does the spasmodic and scattered stress of 1966–67 presage change at some later time, perhaps when the System is under new management? There remains some residual doubt in our minds that there was evident in this subsystem the kind of purposefulness and concern for goal attainment and maintenance of supports that systems analysis appears to posit as the motive forces behind adjustments within the system. It may be coincidental that just the right group—those whose sons are deferred—are both politically influential and supportive of the Selective Service System. We have seen so little calculatedness in the authorities within this subsystem that we do not readily assume it here.

We concede that the apparent nonexistence of what is taken as a fundamental commitment on the part of a system's authorities may be due to the fact that we were studying only a subsystem. But it occurs to us that a societal-level political system has no real existence as such, but only as a group of semi-autonomous subsystems; these subsystems interact with each other to some extent, of course, and they draw upon each other for supports or other effects at times (e.g. the Selective Service System may count on extensive defenses against change arising out of the power distributions in the Congress). The "authorities" who are taken to be consciously seeking to adjust performance to improve goal attainment or maintain support must be located *within* such subsystems, however, at least in major part, unless we are to accept some severely challenged assumptions about the locus of power in American politics. In the conscription-implementing subsystem, such purposiveness was not found; perhaps it is because of unique features of this subsystem, but perhaps it suggests that other basic motivators animate the system, or indeed that not purposiveness but merely interests and powers dictate actions and responses in politics.

It is obvious that general theory must abstract from and oversimplify reality. We have moved swiftly from some sketchy data in a narrow field to enter tentative reservations to a single facet of a widely encompassing theory, not to challenge that theory so much as to demonstrate the relevance of a form of research to the elaboration and refinement of theory. Our case may rest if the potential of relevance seems within the bounds of reasonable expectation.

INDEX

Almond, Gabriel, 68n, 69n, 159n, 173n, 241, 246
Altman, Stuart, 16n, 25n, 137n
American Institute of Public Opinion (Gallup), 160, 161n, 165
Appeal advisers, 104
Appeal agents (government)
  compensation, 103
  function, 102–3
  non-functional character, 103–5
  occupation, 103
  recommendation for change, 202
  recruitment, 107
  relationship to appeal boards, 104
  veteran status, 103
Appeal boards
  decision-making process, 116–20
  jurisdiction, 102
  local autonomy, 106
  members, 102
    attitudes toward classification difficulty and national guidelines, 43
    compensation, 106
    selection process, 105
  number of, 100
  standardization, 120
  state headquarters, relationship to, 105
  variability, 116
    in new classifications, 116
    in reversal rates, 116–17
    in Wisconsin, 117–20
Appeal process
  alternatives to, 110
  and the level of induction call, 115
  function, 111, 115
  information problem, 104
  patterns of use, 111, 113–15

Appeal process (*Continued*)
  procedures, 101–2, 117
  public attitude toward fairness of steps in initiation of appeal, 111
  purposes
    justice for registrants, 100–01
    expedite delivery of men, 100–02
    protect national interest, 102
  recommendations for change, 202–3
  time requirement, 107
  transfer option, 102, 115
Appeals
  number of, 112
  ratio of to number of registrants, 113
  sources of, 112
  vs. level of call of induction, 115
  vs. state political and social culture, 113
  who appeals, 121
Appellate system
  Congressional changes in 1967, 123
  performance vs. goals, 123–24
  recommendations for change, 122–23
  Selective Service System, relationship to, 120
Alabama State Selective Service System, 84

Bauer, Raymond A., 159n, 243
Bell, Wendell, 159n, 173n
Bensman, Joseph, 72n
Birkly, R. H., 243n
Blau, Peter, 50n, 78, 159n
Bloomberg, Warner, Jr., 76n
Browning, Rufus P., 76n
Buchholz, Bernard, 113n

Cahn, Edgar, 232n
Cahn, Jean, 232n

355.223
D26

99601

DATE DUE
